1985

The Ethics of Intensity in American Fiction

The Ethics of Intensity
in American Fiction

BY ANTHONY CHANNELL HILFER

University of Texas Press, Austin and London

The Dan Danciger Publication Series

Library of Congress Cataloging in Publication Data
Hilfer, Anthony Channell.
    The ethics of intensity in American fiction.
    Includes bibliographical references and index.
    1. American literature—History and criticism. 2. English
fiction—19th century—History and criticism. 3. Ethics in
literature. 4. Self in literature. I. Title.
PS169.E83H5 810'.9 80-23484
ISBN 0-292-72029-7

Requests for permission to reproduce material from this
work should be sent to Permissions, University of Texas
Press, Box 7819, Austin, Texas 78712.

*To the memory of Gordon Mills,
philosopher of literature, connoisseur of science,
"the conscience of the English Department."*

Contents

Acknowledgments

A couple of ideas in this book go all the way back to Richard Hocks' oblique conversations when we were both graduate students at the University of North Carolina.

More recently, a grant from the University Research Institute of the University of Texas gave me the spring of 1977, time for research and writing without which I could not have completed this book.

Several colleagues read first-draft chapters and gave unfailingly good advice. I want to thank Jack Farrell, Walter Reed, and Ramón Saldívar for their help on my chapter on Victorian fiction. I owe an especial debt to the late Joe Doherty. An assistant professor, overloaded with work of his own, Joe Doherty wrote a three-page commentary on my Whitman chapter, many suggestions from which I incorporated into the final version. Warwick Wadlington's influence on the Dreiser chapter is self-evident. Of course, any mistakes and misapprehensions in these chapters are all my own and probably the result of "self."

Roger Abrahams, during his term as chairman of the English Department, was never sparing of intellectual and moral support. I have also benefited by trading ideas with William Scheick and Max Westbrook.

I have learned from my students as well as my colleagues and wish to give a blanket acknowledgment to the students in my seminar on Pragmatism and American Fiction, with a special mention of my Jamesian student, Karen Olander.

Thanks also to Joyce Coleman, my copy editor, for her improvement of my manuscript.

Finally, my greatest debt is to four readers who were subjected to my entire manuscript, in one form or another, and who were always exactly right in their judgment of its strengths and lacks: C. Hugh Holman, David Halliburton, Joel Porte, and the late Gordon Mills, to whom I have dedicated this book.

Preface

This book traces a major change in the way late nineteenth- and early twentieth-century American fiction represented character. I focus on seven works which highlight various aspects of the new mode: "Song of Myself," *A Modern Instance*, "The Beast in the Jungle," *The Wings of the Dove, Sister Carrie, An American Tragedy*, and "Melanctha." These works reveal a shift from the self defined primarily in terms of a preformulated ethical code and judged adversely if it departs from that code to the self defined in terms of its emotional intensity and judged adversely for any failure of nerve. In the first mode character is seen as the sum of an individual's ethical choices; in the second, character is seen as the process of an individual's longings. In the first mode, a character is almost always wrong to yield to desire; in the second, a character is frequently wrong not to. An ethics of restraint tends to give way to an ethics of intensity, ethos tends to be displaced by pathos. But the tendency cannot terminate in pure intensity or pure pathos for a fictional character, since the character must negotiate his passions with others and with his world. Nor are the writers free from ambivalence about the new and old moral paradigms. Whitman comes closest to such a dubious purity; he is included in this study because his radical affirmation of pathos defines one pole of my discourse. In my introduction I cite Irving Babbitt as the opposite pole, the voice of pure ethos. Between these poles the authors in this study find their energy.

In discussing the major figures in this study I examine how the tension of ethos and pathos forms part of the texture of their works. Lest texture overwhelm structure, however, I have divided each chapter into sections, the titles of which point the argument. The first section of the introduction defines the two major terms of this study's discourse: ethos and pathos. The second establishes a parallel between pragmatic philosophy and the literary works I will examine (and also gives my reasons for doubting they had a direct influence on each other). I intend to show, first, that both philosophy and fiction moved away from conceiving the self as substance and toward conceiving the self as process and, second, that self conceived in terms of process is more likely to be judged for the intensity and extensiveness of its emotions than for the rightness of its ethical choices.

So much has pathos *become* our paradigm of character that it is difficult to find effective defenders of the traditional concept of ethos. My intention is not to glorify the mode of pathos but to trace a dialectic of development from ethos to pathos, deriving a moral paradigm not from the one or
the other but from the gap of indeterminacy created by their opposition.[1]
This is why I have drawn on Babbitt's lively defense of classical ethos in my
introduction and why, in chapter 1, I am as interested in the strengths as in
the weaknesses of the Victorian ethical emphasis—which had, it is important
to note, its own form of process analysis: the disclosure of the rationalizing,
dishonest consciousness.

Still, my review of the ethos of the Victorian novel is necessarily one-
sided. It leaves out writers like the Brontës who operated more in the mode
of pathos and, admittedly, scants the passional element that in one form or
another can be found in all the Victorian greats. My purpose in chapter 1 is
only to demonstrate what the late nineteenth century felt was the Victorian
novel's imbalance toward ethos. To account adequately for the dialectical
tensions *within* the Victorian novel would require a book in itself—one I
would very much like to see written.

My second chapter analyzes Walt Whitman as a poet who is almost a defining example of the pathetic mode, while my third chapter extends the definition of ethos by examining William Dean Howells' *A Modern Instance*. This
novel bases its processual analysis on conventional ethical principles as thoroughly as any Victorian novel. The James, Dreiser, and Stein chapters show
pathos developing into an ethos—the ethics of intensity—while, in the process,
reclaiming some of the ethical ground of Victorian fiction.

This book, then, is a study of a turn, in the American novel, toward
pathos, process, and self-realization.[2] As such the study is a construction,
parallel to, or a rival of, such other constructions as the American Adam, the
Imperial Self, the Performing Self, the Protean Self, the Puritan-Originated
Self. My own study has been influenced by the critical-historical paradigms
developed in Tony Tanner's *The Reign of Wonder*, Richard Poirier's *A World
Elsewhere*, and, especially, Gordon O. Taylor's *Paths of Thought*. Taylor's
book concisely and convincingly relates changes in American prose style to
pragmatic, processual philosophy. Both our books are concerned with ethics,
character, and style, but while Taylor's emphasis is more on style, mine is
chiefly on ethics. I believe that my construction, which draws on all these
others, is true and illuminating—but it is neither definitive nor exclusive. The
intrinsic limit of critical discourse is that all criticism is a construction, and
that all constructions are partial—a viewpoint I base not on current continental criticism but on William James's radical empiricism and pluralism.

My view of character also finds support in James's philosophy. My approach presupposes that fictional characterization is mimetic, while at the
same time I examine writers who, to one degree or another, were deconstruct-
ing social and ethical identity into pathos and process. Thus I confront the
critical view that deconstructs pathos and process into verbal fictions. Characters are, *of course*, verbal constructions. But it is equally a matter of course

that no character in literature can exist without reference to real people—
however oblique, attenuated, or upside-down such reference may be (and
even though our notion of "real" people or "real" anything may be based
on some rather suspect conventions).[3] The writers discussed in this study
challenged, to a degree, conventional notions of character—but they never
doubted that people exist or that their characters simulated people existing.
Therefore I talk about the "character" of Clyde Griffiths, Melanctha Herbert,
et al. as if they had one. In a way, they do. The act of reading involves check-
ing the fictional creations against our notion of how human beings are, a
notion we derive at least as much from literature as from observation.[4] Even
the most deconstructive critic—e.g., Barthes in *S/Z*—reads this way. There is
a circular negotiation by which literature enriches our observations and our
observations enrich our understanding of literature.[5] I would have presumed
this was all self-evident, were it not currently under sustained and brilliant
attack.[6] In my conclusion I shall take up, briefly, the place of character in
contemporary fiction.

Finally, I want to forewarn the reader of a slightly unusual device I use in
my chapters: interpolating my own bracketed commentary within extended
quotations. For example, a writer like Howells obviously means to instruct
his readers morally; as I shall show in chapter 3 his fictions are, in a sense,
homilies. Reading Howells calls for constant moral awareness, not of grand,
conclusive issues but of the moment-by-moment temptations toward ill temper, resentment, and self-seeking, toward sins both of omission and commis-
sion. The reader is meant to respond moment by moment to the moral performance of Howells' style. The commentary I have interpolated within my
extended quotations from Howells is intended as such a response. Whether
mine are the exact readings Howells would have wanted I cannot say. I feel
no doubt that they represent the *type* of reading he wanted.[7] In the Whitman
chapter I interpolate commentary for a different reason—to emphasize the
radical discontinuity of the self in "Song of Myself." In such cases, I believe
that more usual methods of analysis would have deflected attention from the
performance for which these writers quite explicitly call.

The Ethics of Intensity in American Fiction

Introduction

1. Ethos vs. Pathos

In classical philosophical terms, the subject of this book is the displacement of ethos, as the principle of characterization, by pathos. The distinction between ethos and pathos is basic to Aristotle's view of characterization, both in literature and rhetoric. S. H. Butcher notes that in *The Poetics*: "By [ethe] are meant the characteristic moral qualities, the permanent dispositions of the mind, which reveal a certain condition of the will; [pathe] are the more transient emotions, the passing moods of feeling."[1] In English, Aristotle's ηθος [ethos] is translated as "character." For Aristotle character is mainly constituted by moral choice: "Ethos, as explained by Aristotle, is the moral element in character. It reveals a certain state or direction of the will. It is an expression of moral purpose, of the permanent disposition and tendencies, the tone and sentiment of the individual."[2] Aristotle's *Rhetoric* proclaims that, in characterizing the defendant in a trial, it is equitable to consider "not the momentary disposition of the agent, but his past character as invariably or usually displayed."[3] Aristotle goes on to say that one thing which indicates the quality of a character "is the revelation of moral purpose; for the quality of the *ethos* is determined by the quality of the purpose revealed, and the quality of this purpose is determined by its end."[4] Madeleine Doran, using these Aristotelian distinctions, shows how Othello's final speech is his attempt to dissociate his pathos of murderous jealousy from his ethos of noble soldier and to assert that his ethos is his true self.[5] In the *Poetics*, Aristotle considers ethos basic to genuine characterization: "Character is that which reveals moral purpose, showing what kinds of things a man chooses or avoids. Speeches, therefore, which do not make this manifest, or in which the speaker does not choose or avoid anything whatever, are not expressive of character."[6] By the same token, "any speech or action that manifests moral purpose of any kind will be expressive of character; the character will be good if the purpose is good."[7]

To the classicist critic Irving Babbitt, the greatest of the many sins of romanticism was its departure from the Aristotelian idea of character:

> The word character, one may note, is ambiguous, inasmuch as it may refer either to the idiosyncratic or to the universal human element in a man's dual nature. For example, an original genius like William Blake not only uses the word character in a different sense from Aristotle—he

cannot even understand the Aristotelian usage. "Aristotle," he complains, "says characters are either good or bad; now Goodness or Badness has nothing to do with Character. An apple tree, a pear tree, a horse, a lion are Characters; but a good apple tree or a bad is an apple tree still," etc. But character as Aristotle uses the word implies something that man possesses and that a horse or tree does not possess—the power namely to deliberate and choose. A man has a good or bad character, he is ethical or unethical, as one may say from the Greek word for character in this sense ($\eta\theta os$), according to the quality of his choice as it appears in what he actually does.[8]

Of course Babbitt's dichotomizing of all literary history into classicist truth and romanticist error is indefensibly simplistic and dogmatic. But, besides the fact that Babbitt's dogmatizing has a stylistic vigor not always found in more balanced criticism, his antagonism enabled his frequently acute and valid insights into the structure of the sensibility governed by pathos. Babbitt's comments are, therefore, useful, and I propose to draw on them without committing myself to his disputable judgments and evaluations. But I should emphasize that I use Babbitt not to distinguish between classical and romantic but to clarify the structural oppositions between ethos and pathos, limitation and expansion, choice and instinct, reason and emotion. Babbitt's unqualified assignment of the first item of all these pairs to classicism, and of the second to romanticism, may be dubious—but his analysis of the oppositions themselves is incisive.

For Babbitt, the romanticist is he who believes in unrestricted temperamental expansion, who identifies being with emotion, with intensity for its own sake: "Everything that limits temperamental expansion is dismissed as either artificial or mechanical; everything on the contrary that makes for the emancipation of temperament, and so for variety and difference, he welcomes as vital, dynamic, creative" (Babbitt, p. 52). "The romantic moralist . . . instead of building himself an island is simply drifting with the stream. For feeling not only shifts from man to man; it is continually shifting in the same man; so that morality becomes a matter of mood, and romanticism here as elsewhere might be defined as the despotism of mood" (p. 133). "In general the Rousseauistic reply to the Cartesian attempt to identify thought and being is the identification of being with emotion (*je sens, donc je suis*)" (p. 140). "The romanticist . . . bases . . . on the very intensity of his longing his claims to be an idealist and even a mystic" (p. 126). All this is very much to the point when we look at characters like Sister Carrie, Clyde Griffiths, Melanctha Herbert, and, most of all, the hero of "Song of Myself."

In short: "To dismiss like the romantic expansionist everything that limits or restricts the lust of knowledge or of power or of sensation as arbitrary and artificial is to miss true decorum and at the same time to sink, as a Greek would say, from ethos to pathos" (p. 162). Romantic expansionists, Babbitt argues, have inverted the traditional and proper notion of conscience as limitation and negation:

Goethe defines the devil as the spirit that always says no, and Carlyle celebrates his passage from darkness to light as an escape from the Everlasting Nay to the Everlasting Yea. We rarely pause to consider what a reversal of traditional wisdom is implied in such conceptions. In the past, the spirit that says no has been associated rather with the divine. Socrates tells us that the counsels of his "voice" were always negative, never positive. According to the ancient Hindu . . . the divine is the "inner check."   (p. 123)

So conscience is co-opted by the school of pathos:

The assertion of man's natural goodness is plainly something very fundamental in Rousseau, but there is something still more fundamental, and that is the shifting of dualism itself, the virtual denial of a struggle between good and evil in the breast of the individual. . . . The denial of the reality of the "civil war in the cave" involves an entire transformation of the conscience. The Conscience ceases to be a power that sits in judgment on the ordinary self and inhibits its impulses. It tends, so far as it is recognized at all, to become itself an instinct and an emotion.
                                                                        (p. 111)

In the writings of Whitman, both Jameses, Dreiser, and Stein there is a tendency to transform conscience from inner check into instinct and emotion. However, none of these writers completely denies the claim of conscience as inner check. In Henry James, Dreiser, and Stein the "civil war in the cave" is a major theme. If the value of Babbitt's criticism is the clarity with which he stated these oppositions, its defect is his failure to recognize that, for a writer, a tendency toward one pole entails less a denial of the other than a sustained tension between them. The opposition of pathos to ethos is dialectical. But for Babbitt, he who is not classicist saint must be romanticist sinner. Babbitt's insistence on total ideological purity turns practically all literature since 1800 into monochromatic instances of romantic error. He did not recognize that ethos survived, not only as a counterforce to pathos but sometimes, as in the mainstream Victorian novel, as the prevailing value.

2. Pragmatic Philosophers and Realistic Novelists

The parallel between pragmatic philosophy and realistic fiction is well established. C. S. Peirce and William James were developing the ideas which eventually became known as pragmatism at the same time that William Dean Howells and Henry James were working out, in criticism and practice, the bases of American realistic fiction. In these years, 1866 to 1871, the four saw a great deal of each other and, as E. H. Cady succinctly notes, they shared an evident affinity: "They tended, consciously or not, to use Occam's Razor and to insist on pluralism and relativity, on the fallibility and individuality of the human mind in an immensely complex world. In thought their destination was pragmatism. In literature, it was, and for closely related reasons, realism."[9]

Critics have specifically related two of Howells' late short stories to ideas of C. S. Peirce and William James.[10] Richard Hocks persuasively argues that Henry James was perfectly exact in his response to William's *Pragmatism* (1907): "I was lost in the wonder of the extent to which all my life I have (like Monsieur Jourdain) unconsciously pragmatized."[11] William James seems to confirm the affinity when, in a letter to Howells, he declares 1890 an *annus mirabilis* for philosophy and fiction: "The year which shall have witnessed the apparition of your 'Hazard of New Fortunes,' of Harry's 'The Tragic Muse,' and of *my* 'Psychology' will indeed be a memorable one in American literature!"[12] Later there was the teacher-student relationship of William James and Gertrude Stein. Even Dreiser, though strongly influenced by James's *bête noire*, Herbert Spencer, occasionally cites James.

It would be a mistake, however, to overstate the case for a specific *influence* of pragmatic philosophy on realistic fiction (or vice versa). Howells wrote the two stories for which an influence is argued after 1900, and Henry James did not discover he was unconsciously pragmatizing until 1907—his shock of recognition of William's philosophy postdates his greatest fiction. Howells might well have shared Henry James's distress, in 1872, at the insistence of his philosopher friends (and philosopher relative) on sticking to the question whereas "it gives me a headache merely to know of it."[13] Howells' enthusiastic review of William James's *Principles of Psychology* does not give the impression of much previous acquaintance with William's ideas, though James had laid the groundwork for *Principles* in a series of articles written in the seventies and eighties. Moreover, what most impressed Howells was not the innovative elements in *Principles* so much as its confirmation of a basically Victorian ethical vision:

> What a work like Mr. James's (if there is another like it) does for the unscienced reader is to give him the habit of looking at his own mental qualities and ingredients as materials of personality with which his conscience can then more hopefully deal, the more distinctly they are ascertained. It comes to an ethical effect, to suggestion for the ideal social life, with only rather more direct instruction than astronomy has.[14]

The evidence, then, suggests not a specific influence of pragmatic philosophy on literary realism but a set of parallels. We can thus draw on the philosophy in order to spell out certain implications of the fiction in much the same fashion as critics have paralleled existentialist philosophy to modernist fiction.[15] William James, G. H. Mead, and John Dewey articulate the philosophy and values implicit in pathos—especially the belief that relation and process are central to the function of consciousness. As Dewey points out, James's famous conception of a stream of consciousness "necessitates a consideration of relations as an immediate part of the field of consciousness, having the same status as qualities."[16] That is, relations are as real as things, the idea which governs James's *Essays in Radical Empiricism*:

To be radical, an empiricism must neither admit into its constructions any element that is not directly experienced, nor exclude from them any element that is directly experienced. For such a philosophy, *the relations that connect experiences must themselves be experienced relations, and any kind of relation experienced must be accounted as "real" as anything else in the system.*[17]   (James's italics)

In a sense relations are more real, there is more life in them: "Life is in the transitions as much as in the terms connected; often, indeed, it seems to be there more emphatically, as if our spurts and sallies forward were the real firing line of the battle, were the thin line of flame advancing across the dry autumnal field which the farmer proceeds to burn."[18] Moreover, certain functions and relations are mistakenly conceived to be substances. This is true of consciousness: "To deny plumply that consciousness exists seems so absurd on the face of it—for undeniably thoughts do exist—that I fear some readers will follow me no further. Let me then immediately explain that I mean only to deny that the word stands for an entity, but to insist most emphatically that it does stand for a function."[19] In sum:

> 1. Consciousness, as it is ordinarily understood, does not exist, any more than Matter, to which Berkeley delivered the coup de grace;
> 2. What does exist, and makes up the part of truth that the word "consciousness" covers, is the susceptibility of parts of truth to be related or known.[20]

As Ralph Barton Perry notes, James was engaged "in a determined effort to resolve certain *substantive* traditional thought into *relational* or *functional* difference."[21] Dewey, who acknowledged James's *Psychology* as the "spiritual progenitor"[22] of his own and G. H. Mead's work, described the central premises of his own early essays as "certain ideas of life activity, of growth, and of adjustment, which involve teleological and dynamic conceptions rather than ontological and static ones." The "conception of process" was the key idea.[23] The American democratic experience was, Dewey later said, essentially processual:

> Democracy is the faith that the process of experience is more important than any value attained, so that special results achieved are of ultimate value only as they are used to enrich and order the ongoing process. Since the process of experience is capable of being educative, faith in democracy is all one with faith in experience and education.[24]

Though James developed his metaphysics of process most fully in his late writings, his emphasis on "the relational or transitive state" was one of the most original and important aspects of *Principles of Psychology*.[25] In *Principles* James declares that, because there is a lack of terms to describe relational and transitive experiences, the error has been made

> of supposing that where there is no name, no entity can exist. All

dumb or anonymous psychic states have, owing to this error, been coolly suppressed; or, if recognized at all, have been named after the substantive perception they led to, as thoughts 'about' this object or 'about' that, the stolid word *about* engulfing all their delicate idiosyncracies in its monotonous sound.[26]

In the light of this diatribe against the substantive, William's complaints about his brother's literary style (see chapter 4) seem ironic: the difficulty of Henry's style was precisely his tendency to articulate dumb or anonymous psychic states while coolly suppressing the substantive results.[27] William James's redirection of psychology toward process and relation parallels the change in contemporary fiction which Gordon O. Taylor describes as a shift "from a notion of static, discrete mental states requiring representational emphasis on the conventional nature of particular states, toward a concept of organically linked mental states requiring representational emphasis on the nature of the sequential process itself."[28]

William James's concentration on process led him to such extraordinary analyses as that of "the waxing and waning" of images (*Principles*, I, 253). The self too may wax or wane. The loss of some possession that we have appropriated to our identity may cause "a sense of the shrinkage of our personality, a partial conversion of ourselves to nothingness" (*Principles*, I, 293). Expansion vs. shrinkage: this is the very paradigm of self so bitterly attacked by Babbitt. James, however, saw difficulties in the "expansive," "sympathetic" type of nature: "The outline of their self often gets uncertain enough" (*Principles*, I, 313); besides, the universality of their embrace of the world blurs out moral distinctions. But this is mild criticism as contrasted to William's assault on the narrow, negating self—represented in extreme form in the philosophy of stoicism:

> This Stoic fashion, though efficacious and heroic enough in its place and time, is, it must be confessed, only possible as an habitual mood of the soul to narrow and unsympathetic characters. It proceeds altogether by exclusions. If I am a Stoic, the goods I cannot appropriate cease to be *my* goods, and the temptation lies very near to deny that they are goods at all. We find this mode of protecting the Self by exclusion and denial very common among people who are in other respects not Stoics. All narrow people *intrench* their Me. They *retract* it,—from the region of what they cannot securely possess. People who don't resemble them, or who treat them with indifference, people over whom they gain no influence, are people on whose existence, however meritorious it may intrinsically be, they look with chill negation, if not with positive hate. Who will not be mine I will exclude from existence altogether; that is, as far as I can make it so, such people shall be as if they were not. Thus may a certain absoluteness and definiteness in the outline of my Me console me for the smallness of its content.   (*Principles*, I, 312-313)

Although James never put it so directly, the logic of his processual philosophy leads toward Dewey's flat dictum that "Growth itself is the only moral 'end.' "[29]

It is no surprise that James is one of Babbitt's romanticist malefactors:

> It is . . . significant that the humanist[30] can agree with nearly every line of James's chapter on habit [in *Principles*] and that he disagrees very gravely with James in his total tendency. That is because James shows himself, as soon as he passes from the naturalistic to the humanistic level, wildly romantic. Even when dealing with the "Varieties of Religious Experience" he is plainly more preoccupied with the intensity than the centrality of this experience.   (Babbitt, p. 290)

There is a quite genuine basis to Babbitt's attack, both for its antagonism toward intensity and its ascription to James of a belief in the virtue of intensity. M. H. Abrams has shown how intensity, in romanticist criticism, came "to rival, and sometimes supersede, older terms like 'nature,' 'truth,' and 'universality' as a first order criterion for poetic value."[31] If, as Keats said, "the excellence of every art is its intensity," and if, as Mill said, all genuine poems must be "short poems; it being impossible that a feeling so intense . . . should sustain itself at its highest elevation for long together," then it follows that passion rather than plot is what matters in literature. Abrams notes that "Aristotle had said that plot is the soul of tragedy, but Coleridge held that 'Passion must be the Soul of Poetry. . . .' "[32] In Babbitt's terms all this is part of the sinking from ethos to pathos: "The genuine classicist always puts his main stress on design or structure; whereas the main quest of every type of romanticist is rather for the intense and vivid and arresting detail" (p. 56). As with literary structure, so with character structure: "Rousseau would put in the place of form a fluid emotionalism" (p. 110). These are, Babbitt believes, the inevitable results of valorizing intensity in art and character.

James does, in fact, valorize intensity; in a remarkable passage in *Principles of Psychology* he goes to the extreme of identifying intensity with reality:

> Speaking generally, the more a conceived object *excites* us, the more reality it has. The same object excites us differently at different times. Moral and religious truths come 'home' to us far more on some occasions than on others. As Emerson says, "There is a difference between one and another hour of life in their authority and subsequent effect. Our faith comes in moments . . . yet there is a depth in those brief moments which constrains us to ascribe more reality to them than to all other experiences." The 'depth' is partly, no doubt, the insight into wider systems of unified relation, but far more often than that it is the emotional thrill.   (*Principles*, II, 307)

Writing to Henry, William declared "It is the amount of life which a man feels that makes you value his mind."[33] John Dewey, summarizing James's reconstruction in philosophy, not only argues for the primary reality of process but rather casually identifies reality and energy: "And change rather than fixity is now a measure of 'reality' or energy of being; change is omnipresent."[34] Interestingly, Dewey is dubious enough about the word "reality" to put it in quotation marks; the validity of the energy of being he takes for granted.

Intensity, then, is for James a criterion of value. But James had a thoroughly ambivalent attitude toward intensity and pathos. His ethical philosophy incorporated into his vision of process and relation an emphasis on traditional self-discipline to which even Babbitt could grant his imprimatur. In *Principles* this ethical emphasis is strongest in the famous chapter on habit, a chapter Babbitt could "agree with nearly every line of." And James's attacks on the use of intensity as a criterion are as striking as his own use of it as a criterion. James vigorously dissented from Oliver Wendell Holmes's forthright praise of intensity and energy of being. Holmes declared:

> The rule of joy and the law of duty seem to me all one. I confess that altruistic and cynically selfish talk seem to me about equally unreal. . . . From the point of view of the world the end of life is life. Life is action, the use of one's powers. As to use them to their height is our joy and duty, so it is the one end that justifies itself. . . . Life is an end in itself, and the only question as to whether it is worth living is whether you have enough of it.[35]

Dreiser's Frank Cowperwood would certainly have agreed, but William James thought the speech rather injudicial:

> It's all right for once, in the exuberance of youth, to celebrate mere vital excitement, *la joie de vivre*, as a protest against humdrum solemnity. But to make it systematic, and oppose it, as an ideal and a duty, to the ordinarily recognized duties, is to pervert it altogether—especially when one is a Chief Justice. . . . Mere excitement is an immature ideal, unworthy of the Supreme Court's official endorsement.[36]

Perry notes that James's dissent "derives . . . significance from the fact that James himself seemed so often to be preaching the same gospel—of action for the action's sake."[37] Certainly James's reaction is more than slightly inconsistent with the notion in *Principles* that "the more a conceived object *excites* us, the more reality it has."[38]

James himself valued reality over consistency. In *Pragmatism* James analyzed, by means of a deliberately undignified metaphor, how new knowledge is mediated by old:

> Our minds thus grow in spots; and like grease-spots, the spots spread. But we let them spread as little as possible: we keep unaltered as much of our old knowledge, as many of our old prejudices and beliefs, as we can. We patch and tinker more than we renew. The novelty soaks in; it stains the ancient mass; but it is also tinged by what ab-

sorbs it. Our past apperceives and co-operates; and in the new equilibrium in which each step forward in the process of learning terminates,
it happens relatively seldom that the new fact is added *raw*. More
usually it is embedded cooked, as one might say, or stewed down in
the sauce of the old.

New truths thus are the resultants of new experiences and of old
truths combined and mutually modifying one another.[39]

Process and relation form the grease spot that spreads through James's traditional ethical set. Ultimately the processual vision reconstitutes ethics, establishing them on a relativistic and expansionary basis:

> In point of fact there are no absolute evils, and there are no non-moral
> goods; and the *highest* ethical life—however few may be called to bear
> its burdens—consists at all times in the breaking of rules which have
> grown too narrow for the actual case. There is but one unconditional
> commandment, which is that we should seek incessantly, with fear and
> trembling, so to vote and to act as to bring about the very largest total
> universe of good that we can see. Abstract rules indeed can help; but
> they help the less in proportion as our intuitions are more piercing, and
> our vocation is the stronger for the moral life. For every real dilemma is
> in literal strictness a unique situation; and the exact combination of
> ideals realized and ideals disappointed which each decision creates is
> always a universe without a precedent, and for which no adequate pre-
> vious rule exists.[40]

This is at an opposite extreme from Babbitt's absolutist ethics, an ethics
Babbitt did not hesitate to apply even where patently absurd, as in the following remarkable passage:

> The endless twisting and dodging and proneness to look for scapegoats
> ... is surely the least reputable aspect of human nature. Rousseau
> writes to Madame de Francueil ... that it was her class, the class of the
> rich, that was responsible for his having had to abandon his children.
> ... A man may thus dodge his duties as a father, and at the same time
> pose as a paladin of humanity. Rousseau is very close here to our most
> recent agitators. If a working girl falls from chastity, for example, do
> not blame her, blame her employer. She would have remained a model
> of purity if he had only added a dollar or two to her wage.
>
> (Babbitt, p. 129)

Babbitt is, of course, quite right about Rousseau—but his application of abstract rule to the working girl is an extraordinary instance of moral strabis-
mus. James's relativistic ethics allowed him to distinguish a self-serving rationalization from a desperate moral plight. Indeed, James's emphasis on process
enabled sophisticated analysis of the mechanism of rationalization, the
analysis found in his chapter on habit that Babbitt assented to and that
Howells saw as strengthening the conscience.

In *A Modern Instance* Howells characterizes Bartley Hubbard through a processual analysis of Bartley's ethical choices. Howells' analysis reads like an application of James's *Principles* though, in fact, it was published eight years earlier. More usually, however, a processually oriented vision entails a certain blurring of the traditional ethical suppositions and a displacement of ethos by pathos. This too keys with William James's philosophy. But we shall see, even in writers whose dominant mode is pathos and process, a recurrence of James's own ambivalence about the traditional ethical views so evident in the "habit" chapter of *Principles*, and the ethics of intensity which he generally implied and frequently denied throughout his writings.

1. The Ethical Imperative: "Self, Self, Self" in Victorian Fiction

Babbitt's argument that pathos is central to romantic and post-romantic Western literature is flawed by his failure to distinguish romanticism from Victorianism. The Victorian moment of the dialectic swung as much toward ethos as did the romantic moment toward pathos, and the mainstream Victorian novel is the most impressive embodiment of the nineteenth-century version of ethos. Moreover, as Daniel Walker Howe shows, "Victorianism was a transatlantic culture" that "was experienced more intensely in the United States than in Victoria's homeland."[1] Though there were strong countercurrents to Victorian values in America as in England, American Victorianism "exercised a kind of hegemony . . . particularly over the printed word."[2] American writing was largely judged by the norms of English Victorian literature; the writers who accorded least with those norms had also the smallest American audience—e.g., Melville and Whitman.[3] Howells and Henry James both shared certain Victorian assumptions, but found it necessary to criticize the Victorian literary giants in order to free up space for their own writing. They were well aware to whom they would be adversely compared.[4] Though Howells' quarrel with Victorian fiction seems relatively minor,[5] the other writers in this study consciously departed from the ethical viewpoint encoded in Victorian fiction. This rejection is especially visible in their revisions of the great Victorian theme of self, the theme that is the subject of this chapter.

1. "Self"

"Oh, self, self, self! At every turn nothing but self!"[6] cries old Martin Chuzzlewit, thus summing up both the ethos of the Chuzzlewit family and precisely what Dickens is trying to attack in his novel about the Chuzzlewits. Martin's outcry could serve as a motto for some of the greatest nineteenth-century English novels—not only those of Dickens, but also of Austen, Thackeray, Eliot, Trollope, and Meredith. A. N. Kaul points out that Hawthorne echoes Dickens' line in Zenobia's passionate denunciation of Hollingsworth in *The Blithedale Romance*:[7]

> "It is all self!" answered Zenobia, with still intenser bitterness. "Nothing else; nothing but self, self, self. The fiend, I doubt not, has made his choicest mirth of you, these seven years past, and especially in the mad

summer we have spent together. I see it now! I am awake, disenchant-
ed, disenthralled! Self, self, self!"[8]

In both Dickens' novel and Hawthorne's, selfishness is *the* theme. Henry
James saw the central idea of *The Blithedale Romance* as "the suggestion
that such a company could be bound together more by its delusions, its
mutual suspicions and frictions, than by any successful surrender of self."[9]

That the pejorative meaning of "self," as instanced above by Dickens and
Hawthorne, became archaic in the early twentieth century is a clue to a major
shift in values. This Victorian usage of "self" is precisely defined by the
OED: "One's personal welfare and interests as an object of concern: chiefly
in bad sense; selfish or self-interested motives, selfishness."* The range of
citations goes from 1680—"Self is the great anti-Christ and anti-God in the
world"—to 1906—"Self is their god and selfishness their religion."[10] After
1906 it would seem that "self" was no longer so great a worry as to demand
personification.

But for the Victorians "self" rampant was a major cultural threat. Most of
the great Victorians could have titled one of their novels *The Egoist*. Scott,
perhaps the least interested in the theme of "self," created in Jeanie Deans
one of the most impressively unselfish heroines of the century. In his preface
to another of his novels he deprecates didacticism but claims that fictions like
his own quite naturally teach self-denial: "I am, I own, no great believer in
the moral utility to be derived from fictional compositions; yet, if in any case
a word spoken in season may be of advantage to a young person, it must
surely be when it calls upon him to attend to the voice of principle and self-
denial, instead of that of precipitate passion."[11]

If Scott's "Big Bow-wow" style was best adapted to a heroic scale of
action, Jane Austen's novels could, as Scott said, splendidly inculcate "the
kind of moral . . . which applies equally to the path of common life."[12]
Current critics show that the major action in *Pride and Prejudice* is Elizabeth
Bennett's need to "exorcise her egoism"[13] and that the theme of *Emma* is
"the virtue of overcoming selfishness and self-centeredness."[14] *Mansfield Park*
exemplifies the theme of self-denial with an extremity disturbing to modern
readers.

This is not to say that we find in the Victorian novelists a uniform attitude
toward, or even a universally agreed-upon definition of, "self." But we do
find various forms of a central, recurrent theme: a "movement from blinding
subjectivism through moral suffering to a more relatively self-denying objec-
tivity."[15] The heroes and heroines who follow this progress range from Emma
Woodhouse to the young Martin Chuzzlewit to Gwendolyn Harleth. Some
characters never so much as begin the ascent—such as Rosamund Vincy, who
is "the standard egoist of Victorian fiction."[16] But this standard egoist is a
paradigmatic figure; the pattern allows for variations as different as Sir
Willoughby Patterne, Quilp, and Grandcourt. And, finally, some characters

---

*Hereafter "self" in quotation marks will have this special meaning.

are born good and need never make the ascent: e.g., Dobbin, too many of Dickens' characters, and, to the detriment of the novel named after him, Daniel Deronda. This last is an instance of the danger of putting a selfless character at the center of a novel.

2. Religious Humanism

There is no completely satisfactory explanation for Victorian writers' near-obsessive fascination with the menace of "self." But J. Hillis Miller is surely right in believing that one important factor was the failure of religious authority in the nineteenth century: "the vanishing of any extrahuman foundation for man, nature, or society." What shows in the Victorian novel is that "when God vanishes, man turns to inter-personal relations as the only source of meaning and value in the world." Human subjectivity becomes the "foundation of all things, the only source of meaning and value in the world." It appears that we must all love one another or die: "All these novelists concentrate on the theme of love, and all in one way or another see the relation of the self to the other as an attempt to satisfy religious longings in a world where relations to God are blocked." No wonder, then, that "self" becomes the arch-enemy in a cultural situation where "society is generated and sustained by individual acts of self-denying, self-creating love."[17]

Victorian fiction reflects Victorian religious humanism. Matthew Arnold, in his Hebraic mood, acknowledged that conduct, not culture, is three-fourths of human life.[18] Yet he also reassuringly proclaimed that the true mystery of Christianity is not the absurd irrationality of the Trinity—"What we call the fairy-tale of the three Lord Shaftesburys"[19]—but the more assimilable doctrine of "the sweet reasonableness of Jesus."[20] Arnold thus reinvents a Christ who would do for Englishman or Jew. He resolves any lingering doubts with an authoritative-sounding definition of righteousness: "The method and secret of Jesus, that is to say, conscience and self-renouncement, *are* righteousness" (Arnold's italics).[21]

Religion reduced to "ethics heightened"[22] and ethics defined in terms of self-renunciation is (with notable exceptions) a program as characteristic of Victorian fiction as of Arnold's exhortatory essays. Too often Arnold merely states the necessity of ethics, duty, and self-renunciation, as if the conduct these virtues entail were obvious. The novelists had the more difficult problem of carrying out acts of repugnant self-assertion, noble self-abnegation, and meliorative self-awareness across three volumes. They managed the task by translating the great Christian conversion plot into humanistic terms: "The typical conversion of the great Victorian novel is not a religious conversion but a turning from self-regard to love and social responsibility."[23] An 1854 review of *Bleak House* noted the total lack of a concept of "the supernatural and eternal world"[24] behind the phenomenal world of Dickens' self-seekers and self-abnegators. A modern critic of *Great Expectations* shows that while the ethics of the novel are Christian its vision is not finally religious; the narrator does not see beyond this world.[25]

It is in George Eliot that the conversion of religion into humanistic ethics is most self-aware, responsible, and intense. Her 1854 translation of Feuerbach's *The Essence of Christianity*[26] is a manifesto of religious humanism. Humanism's conversion of religion into ethics is based on the belief that religion is itself a projection of human desires and powers. Feuerbach says (in Eliot's translation): "All the attributes of the divine nature are . . . attributes of the human nature."[27] Thus "the revelation of God is nothing else than the revelation, the self-unfolding of human nature."[28] The essence of Feuerbach's philosophy is an attempt to save the appearances in the realm of ethics. If ethics are *prior* to religious embodiments of them, as Feuerbach maintains, they are not dependent on religious support. Since God is a projection of ideal human qualities, He can abscond without necessarily making off with the ethical assets: "The fact is not that a quality is divine because God has it, but that God has it because it is in itself divine."[29] So *caritas* needs no deific guarantee. (As Samuel Butler put it: "An honest God's the noblest work of man.") Feuerbach declares:

> Love to man must be no derivative love; it must be original. If human nature is the highest nature to man, then practically also the highest and first law must be the love of man to man. *Homo homini Deus est:*—this is the axis on which revolves the history of the world. The relations of child and parent, of husband and wife, of brother and friend—in general, of man to man—in short, all the moral relations are per se religious. Life as a whole is, in its essential substantial relations, throughout of a divine nature.[30]

At his worst, Feuerbach sounds, in Eliot's translation, rather like a Teutonic redaction of "A Christmas Carol," with warm gushes of familial *Gemütlichkeit* substituting for the millennium of Christian tradition. Eliot herself was made of sterner stuff, as her more Hebraic version of humanism shows:

> On a famous occasion when George Eliot mentioned the three words which had so long been "inspiring trumpet-calls of men,—the words God, Immortality, Duty—" she "pronounced, with terrible earnestness, how inconceivable was the *first*, how unbelievable was the *second*, and yet how peremptory and absolute the *third*." It is partly because the first two words have lost their meaning that the third is given such passionate affirmation, in her novels and in contemporary society.[31]

Duty, in effect *means* the renunciation of "self."

3. Renunciation

Renunciation is the difficult solution to the problem of "self." It affords a rare moment of peace to the tumultuous spirit of Maggie Tulliver: "She was experiencing some of that peaceful melancholy which comes from the renunciation of demands for self, and from taking the ordinary good of existence . . . as a gift above expectation."[32] In fact, "renunciation, for George Eliot, is the essential part of virtue; and it is the chief moral reality implied by her whole outlook."[33] So too with Dickens, who shared with his readers "a delight in stories of renunciation in which one character gives up happiness for the sake of another."[34] Sidney Carton attains secular canonization[35] through renunciation: "Self becomes in this novel, both figuratively and literally, sacrificed in the interests of others, but in that way self also becomes both purged of self-regard and immortally ennobled."[36]

But world-champion renouncers like Sidney Carton and Esther Summerson excite a suspicion that self-renunciation can become an elaborately self-ennobling *role*. George Eliot relieves such suspicions partly by her psychologically acute recognition of them. Walter Houghton notes how Eliot carefully qualifies the heroic impulses of Dorothea Brooke and Maggie Tulliver:

> Dorothea was "enamored of intensity and greatness." If she yearned to renounce her self in a noble cause, it was really the vision of playing a great role, and not a vivid sense of the objective, that captured her imagination. George Eliot had pointed this out in the case of Maggie Tulliver: "From what you know of her, you will not be surprised that she threw some exaggeration and willfulness, some pride and impetuosity, even into her self-renunciation: her own life was still a drama for her, in which she demanded of herself that her part should be played with intensity."[37]

An even greater problem with self-renouncing characters is that, except in such stirring but innately one-shot situations as Sidney Carton's, it is difficult to do much with a character whose main virtue consists of making refusals. Stanley Marcus attributes the passivity of Oliver Twist and other Dickens heroes and heroines to the writer's association of goodness with the inability to do anything for oneself—except to endure, free from the taint of a willful or self-interested participation in one's fate.[38] In other words, virtue seems opposed to *virtù*. In *The Old Curiosity Shop* the conflict between Little Nell and Quilp opposes a goodness and purity validated by their very debility to a self-assertiveness and energy of being essentially demonic:

> In almost every one of its representations this energy appears as subterranean, repressed, uncivilized, and violently antagonistic to society and moral order. Yet its source is also the essential energy of life, and Nell's utter alienation from it drains her of the power to survive; for to allow Nell any trace of that energy would for Dickens have been tantamount to polluting her.[39]

Another critic argues that "an energetic excess of being in realistic fiction is inevitably compromised or punished in its heroes; it is tolerated only in the minor figures of fiction, in the degraded form of amusing eccentricities."[40] The superiority of Fanny Price to Mary Crawford and her brother in *Mansfield Park* is based on the "identification of true being—as opposed to the theatrical self-diffusions of the Crawfords—with self-effacement."[41] No wonder that to V. S. Pritchett *Wuthering Heights* is such a relief from the usual

Victorian novel: "How refreshing to see the open skirmishing of egoism."[42]

But perhaps modernists have overreacted so much to the excesses of the Victorian repudiation of "self" that they could be fairly accused of putting their own faith in a "naked, violent assertion of the self."[43] Lionel Trilling energetically defends Fanny Price's debility as a legitimate sign that "she is a Christian heroine," "one of the poor in spirit."[44] Trilling accuses his contemporaries when he notes that the word "duty"

> grates upon our moral ear. We do what we should do, but we shrink from giving it the name of duty. "Cooperation," "social-mindedness," the "sense of the group," "class solidarity"—these locutions do not mean what duty means. They have been invented precisely for the purpose of describing right conduct in such a way as *not* to imply what duty implies—a self whose impulses and desires are very strong, and a willingness to subordinate these impulses and desires to the claim of some external nonpersonal good. The new locutions are meant to suggest that right action is typically to be performed without any pain to the self.[45]

In contrast, the Victorians "thought that morality was terribly hard to achieve, at the cost of renunciation and sacrifice."[46]

It may be that Trilling and Marcus are both right: one emphasizes the validity and the other the limitations of the Victorian ethos of renunciation.

4. The Psychology of "Self"

The theme of egoism in Victorian fiction called forth an impressive subtlety and complexity. In examining the Egoist's Progress, Victorian novelists developed a dialectic of egoism and became experts on the ethical consequences of selfishness. *Vanity Fair* parallels Becky Sharp's hard selfishness to the more insidious, softer selfishness of Amelia Sedley. *Jane Eyre* contrasts Edward Rochester's undisguised egoism to the more perverse egoism of St. John Rivers,[47] an egoism the more repellent because of its associations with the Victorian virtues of austere duty and the doctrine of work. A nineteenth-century critic of *Jane Eyre* noted its "unresolved discord": "At one moment . . . we seem to be drifting toward the solution that strong passion is the one really good thing in the world" but, at another, "Duty is supreme."[48] A modern critic might call such discord a "gap of indeterminacy,"[49] which forces the reader to participate in a moral action by deliberately withholding judgment—except that, in the end, it turns out that Jane Eyre's duty is to follow her passion. This very clever resolution has been adopted by all succeeding gothic romancers.

If Brontë's ending appears somewhat factitious (if marvelously pleasing), it is because she herself so acutely analyzed St. John Rivers' typically Victorian attempt to solve the conflict of passion and duty by confusing the former with the latter. It would not be too much to say that the psychology of the great Victorian novelists was an analytic designed to unmask the various rationalizations of "self." When these novelists moved into a character's mind it was almost always to reveal him either unconsciously displaying his self-deceptions or beginning to become aware of and to exorcise them.[50]

Such investigations of consciousness generally took the form of a reverie structured in terms of an almost allegorized debate between "self" and conscience—a realistic version of the medieval psychomachia. Scott's *Rob Roy* offers a nicely illustrative passage which has only moved halfway from allegory. Passion and Duty contend as Frank Osbaldistone attempts to answer his own questions about the propriety of his jealous spying on Diana Vernon:

> Passion and self-will were ready with their answers to these questions. In detecting this secret, I was in all probability about to do service . . . to Miss Vernon, whose frank simplicity of character exposed her to so many risks in maintaining a private correspondence, perhaps with a person of doubtful or dangerous character. If I seemed to intrude myself on her confidence, it was with the generous and disinterested (yes, I even ventured to call it the *disinterested*) intention of guiding, defending, and protecting her against craft,—against malice,—above all, against the secret counsellor whom she had chosen for her confidant. Such were the arguments which my will boldly preferred to my conscience, as coin which ought to be current; and which conscience, like a grumbling shopkeeper, was contented to accept, rather than come to an open breach with a customer, though more than doubting that the tender was spurious.[51]

Two aspects of this passage are paradigmatic of the Victorian analysis of the psychology of selfishness. First, the level of mind examined is in a shadowland between conscious and unconscious—Frank is fooling himself but somewhere in his mind he knows perfectly well that he is fooling himself; he is aware of his own self-deception. And second, Scott's description of Frank's consciousness is completely keyed to ethical intention. In trying to outflank ethics Frank must think in terms of ethics, as when he tries to persuade himself that his sneaking about is "disinterested."

These two aspects are, of course, intrinsically connected, since ethical judgment presumes the freedom to choose between right and wrong, which presumes the ability to understand which is which. In Jane Austen and George Eliot the ethical intention is less blatant and the characters' awareness of what they are really up to evolves much more gradually, but the basis is there: consciousness is ethically structured and characters choose to fool themselves. The irony of Scott's depiction of a self-deluder is identical in structure, if far thinner in texture, to that which Austen uses in *Emma* "to elucidate the complex processes of Emma's sophisticated, if erring, intelligence and her refined, if self-misunderstood, sentiments."[52]

5. The Analysis of "Self": *Romola*

The ethical psychology of the Victorians recalls, not Freud and Jung's psychology of the unconscious, but Sartre's psychology of total consciousness and complete responsibility. A modern critic observes of George Eliot: "No one has been a finer analyst of what an existentialist would call 'bad faith,' the twists and turns of the corrupted self as it seeks to evade truth and responsibility."[53] In the 1880s a reviewer noted Eliot's influence on the fiction of her time: "Within the past twenty-five or thirty years English fiction has taken on itself an introspective hue, and the taste of readers of fiction is all for analysis of character and motive, while the taste of the period immediately preceding was entirely for the display of character and motive in action."[54]

The difference is that between Dickens' emphasis on dramatic action and the prevalence of analysis in Eliot and James. Barbara Hardy shows that all three employ the Victorian convention of the change of heart from selfishness to love, but "where George Eliot and James transcribe the moral process in slow motion and loving detail, allowing for its irregular pulse, its eddy, its wayward lapse and false start, Dickens shows it as quick, simple, and settled."[55] What Eliot and James share is an interest in process as such. Many of Eliot's modern critics have emphasized her mastery in the representation of gradual process:

> To the slow mounting of temptation George Eliot returns again and again. It is a temptation like this which makes Arthur Donnithorne seduce Hetty and Hetty abandon her child; Maggie and Stephen Guest yield to a similar erosive process. . . . It is through this kind of slow weakening, even, that Gwendolyn Harleth fails to throw the rope to her drowning husband. . . . Romola, of course, is more than anything else an account of how Tito sins more and more deeply without ever really intending evil at all. No one, in the moment of yielding, fully sees the significance of his act; insight is dulled by the pressure of circumstance.[56]

Eliot shows that "events move slowly and steal upon us unawares," "that the obscure is often crucial," that we become gradually enmeshed in circumstance.[57] Nevertheless, she holds her characters fully as accountable for their yielding to "passion and self-will" as does Scott.

Romola, in particular, exemplifies the ethical tendency of Victorian fiction in its severe analysis of Tito Melema, a character who is "self" itself. Probably now the least-read of Eliot's novels, *Romola* is set in the Florence of Savonarola. The novel's heroine, Romola, daughter of a classical scholar, is caught between her father's Hellenism and Savonarola's extreme Hebraism. The conflict is exacerbated by her marriage to Tito, whose very function in the novel is to be the "recipient of a brilliant but corrupt Hellenic tradition."[58] What so impressed some readers of *Romola* and so enraged others was Eliot's careful tracking of the process of Tito's decline.

It should be emphasized that Tito is not a cardboard Victorian villain. He is presented analytically rather than melodramatically, despite the fact that he is engaged in two classically melodramatic pursuits: the seduction of an

innocent maiden and the secret betrayal of a benefactor. But Tito is never determined to prove a villain; he takes no malicious enjoyment in victimizing
others. His acts of treachery and deception are drifted into, half-accidentally,
to avoid trouble—never chosen unequivocally for their own sake. He con-
tinues his illicit relationship with the naïve Tessa at least partly out of good
nature: "It would have been brutal to leave her, and Tito's nature was all
gentleness."[59] The sentence is, of course, ironic, but Tito's rationalization is
all the more insidious in that it is not a total inversion of the truth: "the
elements of kindness and self-indulgence are hard to distinguish in a soft
nature like Tito's."[60] His betrayal of his patron and benefactor, Baldassare
Calvo, is no conscious, active, principled (as it were) malignity. It is the unintended result of a series of seemingly small refusals actively to seek out and
rescue Baldassare from captivity. Tito, in a prolonged self-colloquy, rational-
izes that if he were certain Baldassare were still alive he would try to aid him.
But this leads to the next step: his need to conceal from others what, despite
all rationalizations, he knows to be disgraceful behavior.

The purpose of Eliot's remarkable analysis of Tito is to hold him strictly
accountable for thus cultivating unawareness. The emphasis is not on Tito's
actions but on the growing corruption of his consciousness, his self-confirmation in bad faith:

> The contaminating effect of deeds often lies less in commission than
> in the consequent adjustment of our desires—the enlistment of our self-
> interest on the side of falsity. . . .
> Besides, in this first distinct colloquy with himself the ideas which
> had previously been scattered and interrupted had now concentrated
> themselves; the little rills of selfishness had united and made a channel,
> so that they could never again meet with the same resistance. Hitherto
> Tito had left in vague indecision the question whether, with the means
> in his power, he would not return and ascertain his father's fate; he had
> now made a definite excuse to himself for not taking that course; he
> had avowed to himself a choice which he would have been ashamed to
> avow to others; and which would have made him ashamed in the re-
> surgent presence of his father. But the inward shame, the reflex of that
> outward law which the great heart of mankind makes for every indi-
> vidual man, a reflex which will exist even in the absence of the sympa-
> thetic impulses that need no law, but rush to the deed of fidelity and
> pity as inevitably as the brute mother shields her young from the at-
> tack of the hereditary enemy—that inward shame was showing its
> blushes in Tito's determined assertion to himself that his father was
> dead, or that at least search was impossible.[61]

Suddenly faced with the enslaved Baldassare, Tito makes the great denial,
proclaiming him "*Some madman*, surely."[62] This denial, far from being an act
of premeditated malignity, is the result of Tito's habitual avoidance of clear-
cut moral choice. So far as calculated villainy goes, Tito would have been
better off, as he later reflects, to acknowledge Baldassare and claim he had

believed him dead. But he blurts out a characteristic non-acknowledgment, illustrating that, from the ethical point of view, character is choice, especially for a character who chooses to evade choice: "Tito was experiencing that inexorable law of human souls, that we prepare ourselves for sudden deeds by the reiterated choice of good or evil which gradually determines character."[63] Tito, with his "unconquerable aversion to anything unpleasant,"[64] is at the mercy of his self-indulgent temperament, his momentary impulses, his chosen refusal consciously and honestly to choose. So he is always, characteristically, caught in the flux of "one of those lawless moments which come to us all if we have no guide but desire."[65]

6. The Reaction from Analysis: The Cat on the Vivisection Table

By the eighties, and on into the nineties, readers were becoming increasingly irritated with the inexorable ethical analysis of such novels as *Romola*. In 1873 Henry James complained that "Romola sins by excess of analysis."[66] In 1885 James observed of George Eliot that what constituted "half the beauty of her work" was also a major limitation of it: "The philosophic door is always open, on her stage, and we are aware that the somewhat cooling draught of ethical purpose draws across it."[67] This is a gentle demurrer compared to the language of the 1887 reviewer who welcomed the fiction of Hall Caine (!) as an alternative to the "long-spun mental anatomizing" of Eliot and the analytical school.[68] By the nineties ethics and analysis were less in vogue than passion and self-will.[69]

Even a sympathetic modern critic of Eliot has declared that she frequently "sees her characters as something close to what today we would call a 'case.' "[70] Eliot has been accused of treating Gwendolyn Harleth punitively.[71] Tito Melema, a marvelous creation, is, unarguably, a punitively treated case history of "self."

In attacking "self" the Victorian novelists did not always avoid the danger of attacking *self*. Critics have shown that Dickens distrusted emotional energy (see section 3 above), but the difficulty is most beautifully argued in Henry James's "The Lesson of Balzac." James draws on Taine's comment "Balzac aime sa Valérie" and on Taine's contrast of how Balzac participated in the reality of his "awful little Madame Marneffe" (Valérie Marneffe) with how Thackeray shrank from a full development of Becky Sharp:

> Balzac loved his Valérie then as Thackeray did not love his Becky. . . .
> all his [Balzac's] impulse was to *la faire valoir*, to give her all her
> value, just as Thackeray's was the opposite one, a desire positively to
> expose and desecrate poor Becky—to follow her up, catch her in the
> act, and bring her to shame: though with a mitigation, an admiration,
> an inconsequence, now and then wrested from him by an instinct
> finer, in his mind, than the so-called "moral" eagerness. The English
> writer wants to make sure, first of all, of your moral judgment; the
> French is willing, while it waits a little, to risk, for the sake of his subject and its interest, your spiritual salvation.[72]

Wolfgang Iser sees the relationship of Thackeray's negative characters to his moral intention as the strength of his fiction. By preventing sympathy with a hero, Thackeray forces the reader into ethical judgment: "Leaving the reader perfectly miserable after his reading indicates that such a novel is not going to offer him pictures of another world that will make him forget the sordid nature of this one; the reader is forced, rather, to exercise his own critical faculties in order to relieve his distress by uncovering potential alternatives arising out of the world he has read about."[73] As Thackeray put it, "My object . . . is to indicate, in cheerful terms, that we are for the most part an abominably foolish and selfish people. . . . all eager after vanities. . . . I want to leave everybody dissatisfied and unhappy at the end of the story—we ought all to be at our own and all other stories."[74]

But Henry James was not the only reader disturbed at the expense of spirit involved in tracking the worthless soul through three volumes to its foul mousehole. A letter written by William Butler Yeats in 1887 expresses his distaste for George Eliot's Victorian ethos in a polemic so intemperate, unfair, extreme, and invigorating as to deserve quotation in full:

> My dear Gregg, I have read only four books of George Eliot's—*Silas Marner—Romola—Spanish Gypsy*—and a volume of selections. I don't mean to read a fifth.
> Reasons why:
> *Firstly*. Tito, her most famous character, is as interesting as a cat on the vivesection [*sic*] table. In him there is none of that beauty that Hugo gave to everything he touched, not only to Esmeralda but to the hunchback. In literature nothing that is not beautiful has any right to exist. Tito is created out of anger, not love.
> *Secondly*. She understands only the conscious nature of man. His intellect, his morals,—she knows nothing of the dim unconscious nature, the world of instinct, which (if there is any truth in Darwin) is the accumulated wisdom of all living things from the monera to man, while the other is at the very most the wisdom gathered during four score years and ten.
> *Thirdly*. Her beloved analysis is a scrofula of literature. All the greatest books of the world are synthetic, homeric.
> *Fourthly*. She has morals but no religion. If she had more religion, she would have less morals. The moral impulse and the religious destroy each other in most cases.
> *Fifthly*. I never met a George Eliotite who had either imagination or spirit enough for a good lie.
> *Sixthly*. In the *Spanish Gypsy* there are seven arguments of about fifty pages each. This is the way she describes passion.
> *Seventhly*. She is too reasonable. I hate reasonable people, the activity of their brains sucks up all the blood out of their hearts.
> I was once afraid of turning out reasonable myself. The only business of the head in the world is to bow a ceaseless obeisance to the heart.   Yours sincerely   W. B. Yeats[75]

Except for the second and, to some degree, the sixth point, Yeats describes Eliot's fiction accurately enough, however outrageous his evaluation. Eliot is punitive to her characters, she is analytical, she does reduce religion to morality, she is (horror of horrors) reasonable. Had Yeats read *Adam Bede*, *Middlemarch*, and *Daniel Deronda* carefully he might have admitted that Eliot understood well "the dim unconscious nature, the world of instinct," though she examines it (analytically, of course) where it impinges on the consciousness and is thus open to ethical judgment.

Yeats's letter is a classic protest of passion against ethics. Yeats finds Eliot's religious humanism not merely unconvincing but repellent, and his own poetry shows the emergence of a new paradigm based on the glorification of passion over ethics, on the flowering of self rather than the repudiation of "self." His response to Eliot parallels that of Nietzsche, who went further than anyone in the defense of the unreconstructed self:

> Yet Zarathustra did not come to say to all these liars and fools: "What do *you* know of justice? What *could* you know of virtue?"
>
> Rather, that you, my friends, might grow weary of the old words you have learned from the fools and liars.
>
> Weary of the words: reward, retribution, punishment, and revenge in justice.
>
> Weary of saying: what makes an act good is that it is unselfish.[76]

Given such a point of view, Nietzsche's opinion of Eliot is predictable: she exemplifies the bankruptcy of religious humanism, of the delusion that Christian morality is not dependent on Christian faith:

> *G. Eliot*. They are rid of the Christian God and now believe all the more firmly that they must cling to the Christian morality. That is an English consistency; we do not wish to hold it against little moralistic females à la Eliot. In England one must rehabilitate oneself after every little emancipation from theology by showing in a veritably awe-inspiring manner what a moral fanatic one is. That is the penance they pay there.
>
> We others hold otherwise. When one gives up the Christian faith, one pulls the right to Christian morality out from under one's feet....
>
> When the English actually believe that they know "intuitively" what is good and evil, when they therefore suppose that they no longer require Christianity as the guarantee of morality, we merely witness the *effects* of the dominion of the Christian value judgment and expression of the strength and depth of this dominion: such that the origin of English morality has been forgotten, such that the very conditional character of its right to existence is no longer felt. For the English, morality is not yet a problem.[77]

Though his *übermensch* was a far less convincing model than English morality, Nietzsche acutely perceived the weakness in the moral foundations of classic Victorian fiction. It may be, in a paradox expressive of English character, that we owe the wonderful richness of nineteenth-century English fiction to the obsolescence of its moral base.

2. Whitman's Body:
Kinesthetic Imagery and Sexual Pathos
in "Song of Myself"

In section 21 of "Song of Myself" the persona announces, with sublime rhetorical confidence: "I am the poet of the Body and I am the poet of the Soul."[1] Apparently bolstered by this and other assurances ("I accept Time absolutely," "I accept reality" [pp. 40–41]), the persona proceeds to a full confession of its identity, with a stress on the body in section 24: "Walt Whitman, a kosmos, of Manhattan the son, / Turbulent, fleshy, sensual, eating, drinking, and breeding" (p. 41). This seems a definite enough identity yet, as Richard Chase points out, "to compare 'Song of Myself' with *Dichtung und Wahrheit* or with Rousseau's *Confessions* or Wordsworth's *Prelude* is to be struck with how sparsely Whitman has represented himself, how small is the volume of the concrete natural and social particularity of the author's life." Whitman's life as a whole "might be called an evasion according to plan."[2] Whitman himself said, in an anonymous review of the first edition of *Leaves of Grass*: "The . . . poems have each distinct purposes, curiously veiled. Theirs is no writer to be gone through with in a day or a month. Rather it is his pleasure to elude you and provoke you for deliberate purposes of his own."[3] Over twenty-five years later Whitman told Edward Carpenter:

> What lies behind "Leaves of Grass" is something that few, very few, only one here and there, perhaps oftenest women, are at all in a position to seize. It lies behind almost every line; but concealed, studiedly concealed; some passages left purposely obscure. There is something in my nature *furtive* like an old hen! . . . Sloan Kennedy calls me "artful" —which about hits the mark. I think there are truths which it is necessary to envelope or wrap up.[4]

In fact, the self of "Song of Myself" is strangely insubstantial, especially in the representation of its body. For Whitman idealizes and spiritualizes the self not by denying its physicality but by making that physicality mysterious and even, paradoxically, impalpable. This he does by emphasizing the kinesthetic rhythms of the body over its external form. As a result he deliberately blurs the boundaries between the self and the world and the relationship between the self and others as it is traditionally conceived, while foregrounding the usually unnoticed processes by which the self begins to bring its disparate impulses into relation and coherence. And the whole is based not on the world as ethos—that is, the world structured by social status and moral choice—but on the world as pathos—the world structured by the flow of libidinal energy. The intensity of the energy is itself a value and a relational principle. In the course of this chapter I shall show how Whitman, in his poetry, enacts his revolutionary revision of the perceptual world in terms of kinesthesia, discontinuity, and dissociation, and then reformulates in terms of pathos the relationship with others that he has deconstructed in terms of ethos.

1. Dissociations

Whitman announces the evasion of ethos through an image in the second section of his poem:

> Houses and rooms are full of perfumes, the shelves are crowded with
>   perfumes,
> I breathe the fragrance myself and know it and like it,
> The distillation would intoxicate me also, but I shall not let it.
>
> The atmosphere is not a perfume, it has no taste of the distillation, it
>   is odorless,
> It is for my mouth forever, I am in love with it, I will go to the bank by
>   the wood and become undisguised and naked,
> I am mad for it to be in contact with me.   (p. 25)

Houses and rooms represent the world of ethos, of social place and definition. The perfumes are artificial not in the sense that they have no connection with nature but that they are "distillations" of human experience while the poem's persona asserts he will start fresh with an undistilled atmosphere. He also rejects such poetic distillations as internal rhyme (rooms/perfumes) for a line that follows, in its caesurae and renewals, the rhythm of the breath. He is now ready to present the reader with a performance, unprecedented in American poetry, of the self's relation to the undistilled atmosphere:

> The smoke of my own breath
> Echoes, ripples, buzz'd whispers, love-root, silk-thread, crotch and vine,
> My respiration and inspiration, the beating of my heart, the passing of
>   the blood and air through my lungs,
> The sniff of green leaves and dry leaves, and of the shore and dark-
>   color'd sea rocks, and of hay in the barn,
> The sound of the belch'd words of my voice loos'd to the eddies of the
>   wind,
> A few light kisses, a few embraces, a reaching round of arms,
> The play of shine and shade on the trees as the supple boughs wag,
> The delight alone or in the rush of the streets, or along the fields and
>   the hill-sides,
> The feeling of health, the full-noon trill, the song of me rising from bed
>   and meeting the sun.   (pp. 25–26)

What is revolutionary in this passage is not the visual images, which are un-remarkable, but the quite extraordinary kinesthetic images. Nature is not simply external, seen with the eyes; it is part of the poet's being, his "respira-tion and inspiration." In "The sniff of green leaves and dry leaves" the per-sona's intake of breath structures a line that goes out and out and out from the leaves at "the bank by the wood" to the seashore and finally circles back to the barn. In effect the persona breathes the continental atmosphere in his poetic inspiration. In the next line we return to the persona's body with some emphatic belches, but these again are diffusing his breath of life (these lines) into the ecosystem. The "belch'd words," though diffused, cannot be lost since they are "loos'd to the eddies of the wind." The line is a *tour de force*, in which radical transcendental doctrines of circularity and unity are vitalized with a tough comic vulgarity (i.e., the introduction of "belch'd" into Ameri-can poetic diction and, indeed, its use as a synonym for poetic "respira-tion").[5] The Emersonian Me has not so much leaped over as belched through the separation from the Not-Me.

The language here and throughout "Song of Myself" does not refer to, so much as enact, a world of tactile energies. Words themselves are tactile, as Whitman asserts in *An American Primer*: "These words are alive and sinewy,—they walk, look, step, with an air of command. . . . Kosmos words . . . are showing themselves, with foreheads, muscular necks and breasts. These glad-den me. I put my arms around them—touch my lips to theirs."[6] The words of "Song of Myself" should affect the reader in a similarly tactile manner: "My words itch at your ears till you understand them" (p. 65). The palpability of words contrasts with the impalpability of things, leading to an obscurity Whitman acknowledged and justified in his 1876 preface:

> In certain parts, in these flights . . . I have not been afraid of the charge
> of obscurity . . . because human thought, poetry or melody, must leave
> dim escapes and outlets—must possess *a certain fluid, aerial character*,
> akin to space itself, obscure to those of little or no imagination, but in-
> dispensable to the highest purposes. Poetic style, when addressed to the
> Soul, is *less definite form, outline, sculpture*, and becomes vista, music,
> half-tints, and even less than half-tints. True it may be architecture, but
> again it may be the forest wild-wood, or the best effects thereof, at twi-
> light, the waving oaks and cedars in the wind, and the *impalpable*
> odor.[7]

Libido is invested in this fluidity of language: "Echoes, ripples, buzz'd whispers, love-root, silk-thread, crotch and vine." Here visual, auditory, and tactile images come together in an odd combination to intimate sensuality. The line shows a radical dissociation of language. Where do these "echoes, rip-ples, and buzz'd whispers" come from, and what is their relation to "love-root, silk-thread, crotch and vine"? The sounds seem to come out of two quite different contexts; they are coupled together as fortuitously as an um-brella might be with a sewing machine. On the one hand they suggest myste-rious sexual intrigues being subtly plotted, partly overheard, and passed on as whispered hints and gossip within a large, crowded drawing room. (Whitman might have derived this mini-plot from one of the Italian operas he adored.)[8] But on the other hand, the sounds also evoke an outdoor setting—the ripple of water, the susurrus of insect wings. Even the phallus and pubic hair that the poet undisguises have the vegetal qualities of roots, Spanish moss, vines, the crotch of the oak where branch joints off from trunk. The strange associations depend upon the original dissociation—the passage is a catalogue of sense impressions, united only by the poet's imagination, rather than a single coherent scene described by a poet-observer. Thus Whitman can describe in the same passage the delight of aloneness and "A few light kisses, a few embraces, a reaching round of arms." Whose arms? A phantom participant's,[9] for there are only two characters in Whitman's epic—reader (see section 2 below) and persona, and the persona is, for all his expression of a new sensuous immediacy, curiously phantomlike.

In the 1876 preface Whitman describes *Leaves of Grass* as "a radical utterance out of the abysms of the Soul, the Emotions and the Physique."[10] The definition is literally true of the work's technique, which by radical dissociations expresses the usually preconscious abysm of the self. It is as Roy Harvey Pearce has demonstrated: Whitman "gives the world a new meaning—transforming it by alienating it from itself."[11] William James saw dissociation as essential to reasoning;[12] he argued that "Genius, in truth, means little more than the faculty of perceiving in an unhabitual way" (*Principles*, II, 110). The artist evidences a particular form of this dissociative genius:

> The whole education of the artist consists in his learning to see the presented signs as well as the represented things. No matter what the field of view *means*, he sees it also as it *feels*—that is, as a collection of patches of color bounded by lines—the whole forming an optical diagram of whose intrinsic proportions one who is not an artist has hardly a conscious inkling. The ordinary man's attention passes *over* them to their import; the artist's turns back and dwells *upon* them for their own sake.   (*Principles*, II, 243)

Paradoxically the artist, by dissociating everyday perception, makes a sophisticated regression to the prior stage of what Anton Ehrenzweig terms "oceanic dedifferentiation."[13]

Artistic dissociation is a creative displacement[14] of the center of consciousness in favor of its margins as William James analyzed it:

> My present field of consciousness is a center surrounded by a fringe that shades insensibly into a subconscious more. I use three separate terms here to describe this fact; but I might as well use three hundred, for the fact is all shades and no boundaries. Which part of it properly[15] is in my consciousness, which out? If I name what is out, it has already come in. The center works in one way while the margins work in another, and presently overpower the center and are central themselves.[16]

James himself inverts center and margins by emphasizing the effect on humans of the subjective attributes of objective nature; these attributes may be subjective because they do not affect the rest of physical nature,[17] but

> they are not inert as regards that part of physical nature which our own skin covers. It is those very appreciative attributes of things, their dangerousness, beauty, rarity, utility, etc., that primarily appeal to our attention. In our commerce with nature these attributes are what give emphasis to objects; and for an object to be emphatic, whatever spiritual fact it may mean, means also that it produces immediate bodily effects upon us, alterations of tone and tension, of heartbeat and breathing, of vascular and visceral action.[18]

Things not contiguous to each other can be related by our appropriation of them:

> though in that group it be true that things do not act on one another by their physical properties, do not dent each other or set fire to each other, they yet act on each other in the most energetic way by those very characters which are so inert extracorporeally. It is by the interest and importance that experiences have for us, by the emotions they excite, and the purposes they subserve, by their affective values, in short, that their consecution in our several conscious streams, as "thoughts" of ours, is mainly ruled. Desire introduces them; interest holds them; fitness fixes their order and connection.[19]

That is, things separate in themselves are kinesthetically united.

Such kinesthetic response is not a minor activity of the self; arguably it is the self:

> The sense of my bodily existence, however obscurely recognized as such, may then be the absolute original of my conscious selfhood, the fundamental perception that I am. All appropriations may be made to it, by a Thought not at the moment immediately cognized by itself.
>
> Its [the moment of consciousness'] appropriations are therefore less to itself than to the most intimately felt part of its present Object, the body and the central adjustments, which accompany the act of thinking, in the head. These are the real nucleus of our personal identity. . . . They are the kernel to which the represented parts of the Self are assimilated, accreted, and knit on.   (Principles, I, 341; James's italics)

Awareness itself is kinesthetic in quality:

> be we never so abstracted from distinct outward impressions, we are always inwardly immersed in what Wundt has somewhere called the twilight of our general consciousness. Our heart-beats, our breathing, the pulses of our attention, fragments of words or sentences that pass through our imagination, are what people this dim habitat. Now, all these processes are rhythmical, and are apprehended by us, as they occur, in their totality; the breathing and pulses of attention, as co-

herent successions, each with its rise and fall; the heart-beats similarly, only relatively far more brief; the words not separately, but in connected groups. In short, empty our minds as we may, some form of *changing process* remains for us to feel, and cannot be expelled.

(Principles, I, 620)

Ralph Barton Perry has noted James's own kinesthetic tendency: James "said of himself, 'I'm a motor. . . .' He meant . . . that he was one of those who 'in memory, reasoning, and all their intellectual operations,' make use of 'images derived from movements' rather than from sight, hearing, or touch."[20] Whitman was such another; the genius of Whitman and James lay in their ability to dissociate the conventional model of human consciousness from static, spiritual integrality into kinesthetic process.

The radical dissociations in Whitman's poem may be seen more clearly if we contrast it to a more traditional American poem, Whittier's "Snow-Bound." "Snow-Bound" is, like "Song of Myself," a transaction between fantasy and reality; its real scene is the inner space, the fantasy world, of Whittier's memory. As Roy Harvey Pearce notes:

> there is a fantasy within the fantasy, memory within memory. We are told in succession, how the adults in the family each recalled his own history, a snow-bound state within a snow-bound state; and we sense, however dimly, the power of an infinite regression into the comforts of fantasy, even as we know that all this is fantasy (or, if you like, memory softened) and therefore at best offers us only temporary surcease from the trials of our day-to-day lives.[21]

If there is memory within memory, so is there a continuity and connectedness among present, past, and future (the poet's sense of his mortality). Transitions are made gracefully, with no jars or jaggedness. The characters and setting of the poem represent particular people in a particular place at a particular time, not a collage of images separate in time and space, bound *only* by the poet's imagination. The characters are not, for the most part, sharply individualized but, bathed in the warmth of Whittier's affection, they are thoroughly credible:

> There, too, our elder sister plied
> Her evening task the stand beside;
> A full, rich nature, free to trust,
> Truthful and almost sternly just,
> Impulsive, earnest, prompt to act,
> And make her generous thought a fact,
> Keeping with many a light disguise
> The secret of self-sacrifice.[22]

There is a more complex characterization—a quite brilliant one, in fact—of the one member of the snow-bound circle toward whom Whittier feels some ambivalence:

She sat among us, at the best
A not unfeared, half-welcome guest,
Rebuking with her cultured phrase
Our homeliness of words and ways.
A certain pard-like, treacherous grace
Swayed the lithe limbs and drooped the lash,
Lent the white teeth their dazzling flash;
And under low brows, black with night,
Rayed out at times a dangerous light;
The sharp heat-lightnings of her face
Presaging ill to him whom Fate
Condemned to share her love or hate.
A woman tropical, intense
In thought and act, in soul and sense,
She blended in a like degree
The vixen and the devotee,
Revealing with each freak or feint
The temper of Petruchio's Kate,
The rapture of Siena's saint.   (pp. 495–496)

Notable in both these portraits is Whittier's stress on ethos, as opposed to pathos. The characters are sharply delineated in social and moral terms, but the poet makes no real attempt to penetrate their inward life, not even that of the passionate guest. As Whittier puts it: "The outward, wayward life we see, / The hidden springs we may not know" (p. 496).

Also notable is that, as each portrait proceeds, the action of the winter idyll stops to isolate the character, presenting his or her essential nature caught in the amber of poetic recollection. Since the real present of the poem is the moment of his recollection, Whittier can convey a sense of fatality by carrying his portrayal beyond the transient peace of the idyll—as he does in describing the strange Holy-Land wanderings of the passionate guest. At the same time, the characters are held within the past perfect (as it were) of the snow-bound idyll, through the communal scenes of storytelling and through devices within the portrayal. For instance, the sketch of the passionate guest ends in the Holy Land but begins with an account of the discomfort her presence induces in the family circle. And the poet makes a very shrewd transition at the end of this sketch. After hoping for God's mercy on this erring but pitiful woman—"That He remembereth we are dust!"—he turns to "the great logs, crumbling low," sending out "a dull and duller glow" (p. 496). Thus we return to the snow-bound scene, the image of mortal dust transmuting into crumbling logs which are themselves emblematic of the passing of time.

In contrast to Whittier, Whitman is more interested in "the hidden springs" than in "the outward, wayward life we see": Whitman concentrates on pathos, largely ignoring or even denigrating ethos; he substitutes the juxtaposition of discontinuous experiences, bound together only by the poet's fluid consciousness, for narrative continuity and clear time transitions;

and he presents only two real characters, reader and persona—and the persona is a curiously enigmatic figure that lacks any clear definition in moral and social terms.[23] In general, as we move from Whittier's poetry to that of Whitman, we lose the sense of a coherent, ordered world with clear social relations among people. John Jay Chapman's extreme statement seems, in one sense, exact: "in all that concerns the human relations Walt Whitman is as unreal as, let us say, William Morris, and the American mechanic would probably prefer Sigurd the Volsung, and understand it better than Whitman's poetry."[24] The statement is exact, that is, in reference to conventional social relationships. What "Song of Myself" substitutes for the conventional social relationship is a sensuously immediate world, in which a highly sensitized self interacts with an imagined reader. The security and fixity of social definition are lacking, but the self establishes in their place other, more protean and intense, relationships.

These differences show clearly if we examine some Whitman images and the connections among them:

> The little one sleeps in its cradle,
> I lift the gauze and look a long time, and silently brush away flies with
>   my hand.
> The youngster and the red-faced girl turn aside up the bushy hill,
> I peeringly view them from the top.
>
> The suicide sprawls on the bloody floor of the bedroom,
> I witness the corpse with its dabbled hair, I note where the pistol has
>   fallen.   (p. 30)

The individual images are very fine, very sharply and truly realized. But there is no sense of a spatially and chronologically continuous world in which they cohere. The images, then, *depend* on the poetic observer; without Whitman they would pop into non-being like a tree without a Berkeley or an Alice without a red king. This may be literally true of Whittier's world as well, but as we perceive it that world may have needed a recorder but not a creator—it did not need Whittier to exist. Indeed, while Whittier is strongly present as memorializer and recorder of his world, in the snow-bound scene itself he is only briefly seen and never heard, as befits a New England boy. In contrast, Whitman's presence is emphasized in his images: he brushes away flies, peeringly views, notes and witnesses. Again, the connection of the poet-observer with his momentary characters is, at the least, equivocal: who is the suicide, what is the poet doing at the scene? There may be perfectly logical answers to such questions; what is important is that the poet is not concerned to give them. The language itself, with its brilliant idiosyncrasies—"peeringly," "dabbled"—asserts the poet's personal vision. As in much modernist poetry, traditional forms of coherence are sacrificed for intensity, and sharp juxtaposition substitutes for conventional spatial and chronological transition and continuity.

This is not to say that the juxtapositions lack a principle of order. Moreover, the order is temporal and spatial, though it is metaphorically sustained as opposed to the usual metonymical progression of narrative mimesis. The temporal order which unifies the three images is the progression from birth to sexual encounter to death—all witnessed by the persona. But when and where does this witnessing take place? For the reader, at least, it is clear that the images are simultaneous. They may represent three separate events involving three disparate people but they also represent a given moment of city life, a moment which encapsulates the rhythmical recurrences of a human existence urged on and sometimes hastened to destruction by the force of desire. Visually, the kinship is not with the medieval panel painting, which shows stages of a narrative, but with the modern collage, which shows typical events happening all at once. The poet's witnessing, then, takes place in the temporality of his consciousness, which metaphorically relates typical instances to the underlying rhythm of desire. Similarly, the spaces the images occupy are not contiguous but are unified by the poet's construction of a linguistic space.[25] Each image takes two lines. The first line of each image consists of a subject, a verb of action which also suggests location, and a prepositional phrase which establishes the location—e.g., "The suicide/sprawls/on the bloody floor of the bedroom." This purely arbitrary grammatical parallelism, like the metaphors which reflect the life cycle, creates a unity that is not represented but constructed by the poet's consciousness.

If the poet's temporal and spatial location are problematic when he witnesses others, they are even more so when he celebrates himself. This is so despite his many insistences on his physical presence:

> Who goes there? Hankering, gross, mystical, nude;
> How is it I extract strength from the beef I eat?
> Having pried through the strata, analyzed to a hair, counsel'd with
>   doctors and calculated close,
> I find no sweeter fat than sticks to my own bones.   (p. 38)

But "mystical" in the first line, with the careful scientific analysis of various strata of fat in the last two, gives us a body as surreal as it is real. Even as a participant Whitman is phantasmal:

> The big doors of the country barn stand open and ready,
> The dried grass of the harvest-time loads the slow-drawn wagon,
> The clear light plays on the brown gray and green intertinged.
> The armfuls are pack'd to the sagging mow.
>
> I am there, I help, I came stretch'd atop the load,
> I felt its soft jolts, one leg reclined on the other,
> I jump from the cross-beams and seize the cloves and timothy,
> And roll head over heels and tangle my hair full of whisps.   (p. 30)

Whitman's ghostly self gets a free ride on the wagon and sensuously enjoys it, but the "I help" is a joke.

At other points the poet's body is more obviously extraordinary:

> Sure as the most certain sure, plumb in the uprights, well entretied,
>   braced in the beams,
> Stout as a horse, affectionate, haughty, electrical,
> I and this mystery here we stand.   (p. 26)

Once more the imagery both solidifies and dematerializes the body. The horse
and the carpentry images, each present a substantial body—but the combination of the two! For an actual visual equivalent of this odd set of images one
would have to wait for Max Ernst with his elephant of the Celebes. To top it
all off, this strangely described "I" is to be seen standing with "this mystery."
The effect is informal—Whitman posed with his arm over "this mystery's"
shoulders. Whitman and the mystery interchange qualities, the one becoming
more abstract, the other more concrete.

Whitman himself quite precisely defines the theory behind this linguistic
maneuver, in an anonymous review of the 1855 *Leaves*:

> The theory and practice of poets have hitherto been to select certain
> ideas or events or personages, and then describe them in the best man-
> ner they could, always with as much ornament as the case allowed.
> Such are not the theory and practice of the new poet. He never presents
> for perusal a poem ready-made on the old models, and ending when
> you come to the end of it; but every sentence and passage tells of an in-
> terior not always seen, and exudes an impalpable something which
> sticks to him that reads, and pervades and provokes him to tread *the
> half-invisible road where the poet, like an apparition,* is striding fear-
> lessly before. If Walt Whitman's premises are true, then *there is a sub-
> tler range of poetry than that of the grandeur of acts and events,* as in
> Homer, *or of characters,* as in Shakespeare—poetry to which all writing
> is subservient, and which confronts the very meanings of the works of
> nature and competes with them.[26]

In Whitman's theory, as Charles Feidelson points out: "A poem . . . instead of referring to a completed act of perception, constitutes the act itself,
both in the author and in the reader."[27] Whitman's verbal creation of the
chumminess between his persona and the mystery is an act of imagination
which competes with the meanings of the works of nature. "*Verbal* creation,"
let me stress, since the image, though created from reliable materials (plumb
in the uprights, etc.), is not mimetic—at least in any visual fashion.

No more conventional is the image of the self in section 4, which comes
after the catalogue of sociological, conditioning factors that concludes "These
come to me days and nights and go from me again, / But they are not the Me
myself":

> Apart from the pulling and hauling stands what I am,
> Stands amused, complacent, compassionating, idle, unitary,
> Looks down, is erect, or bends an arm on an impalpable certain rest,
> Looking with side-curved head curious what will come next,
> Both in and out of the game and watching and wondering at it. (p. 27)

Here the image is easily visualizable—it seems, in fact, an exact verbal equivalent of the "carpenter portrait" included in the 1855 edition, which shows
Whitman in an informal, relaxed pose, head side-curved, arm bended with
fist on hip. But how can a "certain" rest be "impalpable"? This self is simultaneously material and yet free from any conditioning by sociological or
physical (e.g., gravity) forces. The seemingly material body is, in fact, a
personified aspect of consciousness, emblematic of the detached, disinterested self, the *free* self.

Whitman's spatial and temporal dissociations, however much they may
lose in traditional human relatability, free the self from all hierarchical fixi-
ties. As Hayden White declares:

> The avant-garde insists on a transformation of social and cultural prac-
> tice that will not end in the substitution of a new elite for an old one, a
> new protocol of domination for the earlier ones, nor the institution of
> new privileged positions for old ones— whether of privileged positions
> in space (as in the old perspectival painting and sculpture), of privileged
> moments in time (as one finds in the older narrative art of fiction and
> in conventional historiography), of privileged places in society, of
> privileged areas in the consciousness (as in the conservative, that is to
> say, orthodox Freudian psychoanalytic theory), of privileged parts of
> the body (as the genitally organized sexual lore insists is "natural"), or
> of privileged positions in culture (on the basis of a presumed "superior"
> taste) or in politics (on the basis of a presumed superior "wisdom").[28]

In this perspective Whitman might be seen not as the last American romanticist but as the second American surrealist.[29]

2. Reconstitutions

Having presented a double portrayal of the self as both material and de-
materialized, "a man cohered out of tumult and chaos,"[30] Whitman can
make the doubling explicit in section 5:

> I believe in you my soul, the other I am must not abase itself to you,
> And you must not be abased to the other.
> Loafe with me on the grass, loose the stop from your throat,
> Not words, not music or rhyme I want, not custom or lecture, not
>   even the best,
> Only the lull I like, the hum of your valvèd voice.
>
> I mind how once we lay such a transparent summer morning
> How you settled your head athwart my hips and gently turn'd over
>   upon me,
> And parted the shirt from my bosom-bone, and plunged your tongue
>   to my bare-stript heart,
> And reach'd till you felt my beard, and reach'd till you felt my feet.
>   (pp. 27–28)

The elusive identity of "the other I am" is less important than the fact that, in the passages previously discussed, Whitman has established the authority to effect such a startling dissociation. He has created a poetic world in which such dissociation appears thoroughly natural. The soul materializes in this passage (in the culmination of the passage it makes love to the poet), but in such a way as to become interfused with the body. The soul expresses itself not in the sociological terms rejected in section 4, not in abstractions or commonplaces—"not words," "not custom or lecture"—but in rhythm: "Only the lull I like, the hum of your valvèd voice." The image evokes the awareness that one can sense the emotional values of a conversation better by standing some distance away and taking in the tone of the voices undistracted by the words themselves; people reveal themselves less through their choice of words than through their gestures and tone of voice. Literature has been defined as verbal gesture, set apart from other forms of language by its emphasis on the tactile effect of words and on the rhythmic effects of verbal groupings.[31] In "Song of Myself" the self is defined less in terms of its ideas and opinions, its ethical and moral *notions*, than in terms of its rhythmical flow. Whitman does not abjure authoritative, even dogmatic, assertions, but what he most frequently asserts is the primacy of physical sensation and animal instinct over traditional social ethos:

> Logic and sermons never convince,
> The damp of the night drives deeper into my soul.   (p. 46)
> I think I could turn and live with animals, they're so placid and
>   self-contained,
> I stand and look at them long and long.
> They do not sweat and whine about their condition,
> They do not lie awake and weep for their sins,
> They do not make me sick discussing their duty to God,
> Not one is dissatisfied, not one is demented with the mania of owning
>   things.
> Not one kneels to another, nor to his kind that lived thousands of
>   years ago,
> Not one is respectable or unhappy over the whole earth.   (p. 47)

Thus attacks on Whitman's ideology seem somewhat beside the point. "Lull" and "hum" are unarguable since in their assonance they act themselves out, they *realize* themselves. One might as well argue with a rock or a river. "I will have purposes as health or heat or snow has and be as regardless of observation."[32] Thus, in the first passage quoted in this section, sexual desire is performed rather than argued: the suspirated repetitions of "and" are libidinally governed—they are almost panted—while they also mark the breath pauses between the several kinesthetic exertions of parting, plunging, and reaching.

Breath is a persistent metaphor in Whitman's theoretical writings. In the 1855 preface he proclaims that if the poet "breathes into anything that was before thought small it dilates with the grandeur and life of the universe."[33]

In "Democratic Vistas" Whitman celebrates "the image-making faculty, coping with material creation, and rivaling, almost triumphing over it," which can "alone, when all the other parts of a specimen of literature or art are ready and waiting . . . breathe into it the breath of life, and endow it with identity."[34] Breath here creates identity, is the ground of imagery in keeping with the kinesthetic basis of Whitman's creation: "the pulsations in all matter, all spirit, throbbing forever—the eternal beats, eternal systole and diastole of life in things."[35] In "Song of Myself" the poet performs a quasi-Christian miracle of salvation through the dilation of his breath:

> To any one dying, thither I speed and twist the knob of the door,
> Turn the bed-clothes toward the foot of the bed,
> Let the physician and the priest go home.
>
> I seize the descending man and raise him with resistless will,
> O despairer, here is my neck,
> By God, you shall not go down! hang your whole weight upon me.
>
> I dilate you with tremendous breath, I buoy you up,
> Every room of the house do I fill with an arm'd force,
> Lovers of me, bafflers of graves.   (p. 57)

The greatest of Whitman's poetry enacts William James's conviction that the stream of thinking is the stream of breathing and that consciousness, *spiritus*, is literally, not metaphorically, the breath:

> Let the case be what it may in others, I am as confident as I am of anything that, in myself, the stream of thinking (which I recognize emphatically as a phenomenon) is only a careless name for what, when scrutinized, reveals itself to consist chiefly of the stream of my breathing. The "I think" which Kant said must be able to accompany all my objects, is the "I breathe" which actually does accompany them. There are other internal facts besides breathing (intracephalic muscular adjustments, etc., of which I have said a word in my larger Psychology), and these increase the assets of "consciousness," so far as the latter is subject to immediate perception; but breath, which was ever the original of "spirit," breath moving outward, between the glottis and the nostrils, is, I am persuaded, the essence out of which philosophers have constructed the entity known to them as consciousness.[36]

In short, *Spiro ergo sum*, a radical reversal of Descartes.

As Jacques Derrida interprets Rousseau, the concept of a "speaking and singing breath, breath of language which is nonetheless inarticulate" is Rousseau's way to escape the splintering of immediate identity by articulation:

> It is on this onto-theological model that Rousseau regulates his repetitions of origin. With this exemplary model of a pure breath (*pneuma*) and of an intact life, of a song and an inarticulate language, of speech

without spacing, we have, even if it is placeless [*atopique*] or utopian, a paradigm suitable to our measure. . . . It is the *neume*: pure vocalization, form of an inarticulate song without speech, whose name means breath.

For Rousseau "this limit of origin is indeed that of a pure presence, present enough to be living, to be felt in pleasure [*jouissance*] but pure enough to have remained unblemished by the work of difference, inarticulate enough for self-delight [*jouissance de soi*] not to be corrupted by interval, discontinuity, alterity." This "pleasure [*jouissance*] of a continuous and inarticulate presence"[37] is attained in Whitman by way of a deconstruction of conventional time and space which allows for the construction of an internal time of desire and fantasy, for time measured by breath.

It was this immediacy in Whitman to which D. H. Lawrence strongly responded:

Give me the still, white seething, the incandescence and coldness of the incarnate moment: the moment, the quick of all change and haste and opposition: the moment, the immediate present, the Now. . . . The source, the issue, the creative quick. . . . This is the unrestful, ungraspable poetry of the sheer present, poetry whose very permanency lies in its wind-like transit. Whitman's is the best poetry of this kind. . . . The clue to all his utterance lies in the sheer appreciation of the instant moment, life surging itself into utterance at its very well-head. . . . The quivering nimble hour of the present, this is the quick of Time. This is the immanence. The quick of the Universe is the *pulsating, carnal, self.*[38]

Whitman claimed as much for himself: "I chose the fundamentals for *Leaves of Grass*—heart, spirit: the *initiating passions of character.*"[39]

The self's rhythm is, of course, the rhythm of the poem, "Song of Myself," "a language fann'd by the breath of Nature."[40] Since Whitman abjures set, prefabricated forms, he bases his poetic rhythms on his physical rhythms, the respiration and inspiration of his breath. In the valvèd divisions of the breath, with its hum and lulls, arbitrary divisions of the self into body and soul, material and immaterial, break down and are merged into a flowing unity. William Carlos Williams, though he underestimated the formal and technical control of Whitman's verse, could still contrast Whitman's commitment to his verse line with that of the young ephebes who "do not believe in seeking within the literary forms, the lines, the foot, the way in which to expand their efforts to know the universe, as Whitman did."[41] Charles Olson's vision of "projective verse" is clearly in the line of descent from Whitman:

If I hammer, if I recall in, and keep calling in, the breath, the breathing as distinguished from the hearing, it is for cause, it is to insist upon a part that breath plays in verse which has not (due, I think, to the smothering of the power of the line by too set a concept of the foot) has not been sufficiently observed or practiced, but which has to be if verse is to advance to its proper force and place in the day, now, and ahead. I take it that PROJECTIVE VERSE teaches, is, this lesson, that that verse will only do in which a poet manages to register both the acquisitions of his ear *and* the pressures of his breath.[42]

This is why the early kinesthetic passage I began by analyzing is so important. It establishes the physical presence of the body rhythms, including the rhythms of the breath that are the base reality of the poem.

But, as we have seen, in order to reach a basic unity the poem proceeds by means of radical dissociations. The affirmation of the kinesthetic energy of the body electric comes about partly through the dissolution of its clear outlines, while the affirmation of the pathos of the rhythms of emotion involves a dissociation of the self from the ethos that governs social and moral identity. For instance, in the climactic passage in section 5, all the action, motion, and response—all the panting, plunging, and reaching—take place not between two separate individuals in the public world but within the self, albeit the self multiplied into "a theater of simultaneous possibilities" or "a microcosm of struggling identities."[43] To this internal drama we might contrast Whittier's tenderness for his flesh-and-blood sister.

In a sense, then, Whitman's "Song" is the first truly real and alive American poem. In it the poet manages to register both the acquisitions of his ear *and* the pressures of his breath, "thereby reaching the immediate present"; at points he seems actually to replace the *cogito* with the *spiro* as the principle of identity. But in the sense in which reality is sociologically defined as, in Daniel Bell's words, "a confirmation by significant others"—as a group construction, interstitched by human relations—Whitman's world is strangely thin and insubstantial. Roy Harvey Pearce notes that, in the poems of *Leaves*:

> The structure is one of relationship, in which the poet, through his control of two or more points of view, manages to pull his world together. Yet the relationship is of a particularly limited sort. The points of view are always aspects of the poet's creative self and are manipulated as such; they are in no sense dramatic, much less novelistic. Whitman has little or none of that final sense of "otherness" which makes for major fiction.[44]

Edwin Haviland Miller also emphasizes Whitman's incomplete realization of the other:

> There is perhaps overemphasis upon the self when things are no longer things but narcissistic reflections. In the hundreds of poems written by the man who liked to proclaim himself the poet of democracy, no one emerges as an identifiable individual. Whitman's people are not even granted the dignity of a name, but are reduced to gestures characteristic of their trades and pursuits.* They are objects in an egocentric landscape. Naturally these muscular gestures are not capable of dialogue.

---

*Which is to say, they are apprehended, like the persona's self, kinesthetically. Personal names can be a perfume of social definition and place.[45]

Whitman replaces meaningful social interaction with a lovely, seductive monologue, although his art is intended to create the illusion of a dialogue. The reader, like the poet, however, only talks to himself.[46]

Does Whitman's great experimental breakthrough lead merely to narcissism and solipsism? In a sense, yes—as we see especially in relation to the poem's sexual theme. But it is just here, in the sexual theme, that the solipsism becomes inverted, and creates startling new possibilities of relatedness between poet and reader. Such a relation is necessarily based on the reader, like the poet, talking only to himself.

The sexuality of "Song of Myself" is, of course, markedly narcissistic.[47] I have already noted the images of bodiless arms embracing Whitman, of soul making love to poet. The strangest instance of narcissistic sexuality, however, occurs in sections 27 and 28. The poet introduces the episode with a boast about his sensitivity:

> Mine is no callous shell,
> I have instant conductors all over me whether I pass or stop,
> They seize every object and lead it harmlessly through me.
>
> I merely stir, press, feel with my fingers, and am happy,
> To touch my person to someone else's is about as much as I can stand.
>   (p. 45)

The expectations this passage sets up are quite misleading, for in the subsequent passage, which gives what should be the concrete example of this generalized sensitivity, nothing works out. The conductors go on the blink and the resultant experience is neither harmless nor happy:

> Is this then a touch? quivering me to a new identity,
> Flames and ether making a rush for my veins,
> Treacherous tip of me reaching and crowding to help them,
> My flesh and blood playing out lightning to strike what is hardly
>   different from myself,
> On all sides prurient provokers stiffening my limbs,
> Straining the udder of my heart for its withheld drip,
> Behaving licentious toward me, taking no denial,
> Depriving me of my best as for a purpose,
> Unbuttoning my clothes, holding me by the bare waist,
> Deluding my confusion with the calm of the sunlight and pasture fields,
> Immodestly sliding the fellow-senses away,
> They bribed to swap off with touch and go and graze at the edges of me,
> No consideration, no regard for my draining strength or my anger,
> Fetching the rest of the herd around to enjoy them a while,
> Then all uniting to stand on a headland and worry me.
>
> The sentries desert every other part of me,
> They have left me helpless to a red marauder,
> They all come to the headland to witness and assist against me.

I am given up by traitors,
I talk wildly, I have lost my wits, I and nobody else am the greatest
      traitor,
I went myself first to the headland, my own hands carried me there.

You villain touch! what are you doing? my breath is tight in its throat,
Unclench your floodgates, you are too much for me.   (pp. 45–46)

This passage presents an intense but mysterious erotic experience. Whitman makes a prudent confession; the self-revelation is muffled by the most opaque and ambiguous language and the oddest mixing of metaphors (the most immediate parallel I can think of is Rimbaud's "Bateau Ivre") to be found anywhere in "Song of Myself." The primary metaphor in the passage is of a cow being gang-milked. But this metaphor, weird though it be, is really more complicated, for the poet metamorphoses from cow back into poet back into cow, then splits into a whole herd. This process can be most clearly indicated in a diagram:

On all sides prurient provokers . . .

The poet is assailed by mysterious enemies, who succeed in arousing him.

Straining the udder of my heart . . .
Unbuttoning my clothes . . .
Deluding my confusion with the calm of the sunlight and pasture fields,
Immodestly sliding the fellow-senses away,
They bribed to swap off with touch and go and graze at the edges of me,

Poet into cow
Cow into poet
Back to the cow and the pasture

Now the senses other than touch become a herd of cattle. The poet becomes a pasture at the edges of which they graze. Touch, with which the other senses have swapped off, is usually located at the edges of the body; but now it has taken center stage. All awareness has become painfully tactile. The poet, either human again or an outcast cow, is in a field faced by a herd of cattle which huddles together, watching with the stupid, menacing, baleful suspiciousness that a herd of cows shows toward a strange human. These cattle represent the poet's own senses; thus, dissociated elements of his self are ganging up on him in an alliance between the senses and the prurient provokers.

No consideration, no regard for my draining strength or my anger,
Fetching the rest of the herd around to enjoy them a while,
Then all uniting to stand on a headland and worry me.

The subsequent images are less pyrotechnical. The metaphor changes to a frontier outpost deserted by its sentries and left helpless to Indian invaders. Indeed the sentries join in the plot, witnessing against the lone defender. But, in the midst of a hysterical denunciation of the traitors, the poet suddenly drops his masks. He is the greatest traitor, as indeed he would have to be—for he has been the lone actor in this entire complicated scene. Perhaps it is the admission of guilt which triggers sexual release, for in the last five lines of section 28 the rhythm speeds up, becomes actually frantic, then attains climax ("Unclench your floodgates"), and finally calms down.

In section 29 there are two lines of quite controlled retrospective summation:

> Blind loving wrestling touch, sheath'd hooded sharp tooth'd touch
> Did it make you ache so, leaving me? (p. 46)

The ache previously caused by a dissociated touch now oddly affects the touch which is leaving the speaker. Touch is characterized in two phrases, divided by commas and with quite different connotations. In the first phrase touch is blind. The immersion of the persona into the close, dense world of touch has blotted out the other senses. Everything is focused on the most smothering and intense, the least differentiated and individualized, of the senses. In the course of the previous passage the poet submerged himself in a world mysterious and transcendent (especially in the sense that it allows multiple identities) but also degrading, shameful, and dangerous. This last aspect is reinforced by the second "touch" phrase, in which touch exerts upon the speaker the paralyzing, fatal charm of the cobra over its victim. The whole section constitutes an astounding and radical metaphor of the simultaneous discovery, enfranchisement, enslavement, and degradation implicit in the persona's auto-erotic experience, an experience which combines in the most extreme terms the spiritual and the physical.[48]

It is all part of Whitman's making good his declaration:

> Through me forbidden voices,
> Voices of sexes and lusts, voices veil'd and I remove the veil,
> Voices indecent by me clarified and transfigured. (p. 42)

Whitman works through rather than around solipsism to a new ground of relationship. It is in the most private, least communicated realm of the American nineteenth-century self, the realm of sexual experience, that Whitman locates the ground for a new form of communion. This new form was precisely what the prevailing sexual ethos blocked and it could be articulated only by dissolving the self circumscribed by that ethos into the processual flow of sexual pathos. Community could then be regrounded in terms of a common deep structure of libidinal and kinesthetic rhythms, a structure which transcended the divisions built into a society committed to ethos, to moral and social hierarchy. But Whitman only discerned these rhythms through his seemingly solipsistic plunge into private, even illicit (in terms of the social ethos), sexual fantasy. Whitman's very deflection of mimesis can be seen as an illustration of John Dewey's classical pragmatic statement that the function of intelligence is not to copy objects but to enrich and extend our relations with them.[49]

Community is also reestablished through the poet's complex relationship with at least one separate, though rather problematic, character who runs (indeed is pursued) through the course of "Song of Myself": that is, the reader. The reader *is* a character in the poem, frequently addressed as "you," a character whom the poet takes it on himself to prod, scold, warn, soothe, enlighten, and undercut—"have you felt so proud to get at the meaning of poems?" (p. 26). Whitman attempts to cajole, bludgeon, or joke this reader into recognizing his deep-structure relation with the poet and all others. In section 7 Whitman announces to his putative reader:

> Undrape! you are not guilty to me, nor stale nor discarded,
> I see through the broadcloth and gingham whether or no,
> And am around, tenacious, acquisitive, tireless, and cannot be shaken
> away.   (p. 29)

This is a joke on the genteel Victorian reader. It is passages like these (rather than section 28, whose sexual imagery was probably too outrageous to be even perceived) that made Whitman so controversial to his contemporary American audience. Emily Dickinson once demurely commented, "You speak of Mr. Whitman—I never read his Book—but was told that he was disgraceful." (In fact, Dickinson almost certainly *did* read some of Whitman's poetry, if not his "book," *Leaves of Grass,* and may not have thought him so disgraceful as she had been "told.")[50]

But to other Victorian ladies the apparition of a gentleman who could believe "there is that lot of me and all so luscious" (p. 42) might have been unsettling—especially if the lady were undraped, though even gingham offers no protection from the poet's supervoyeuristic gaze. In this context Whitman's tenaciousness seems anything but reassuring, not to mention that the Victorian "good reader" might not feel inclined to admit he[51] is guilty, stale, and discarded. But if the passage functions satirically, much in the manner of the 1960s' "gross out," for the reader who would maintain the façade of respectability, it is a serious encouragement to the reader willing to explore the furtive inner life of sexual impulse. Much, then, depends on the putative identity offered to the reader and on the reader's response to it, matters of great concern to Whitman's critics and to Whitman himself.

There is certainly truth to the critical suspicion that the reader in *Leaves* exists only insofar as he is incorporated into the persona's solipsistic world, as a *substitute* for flesh-and-blood social relation: "Only with the creatures of his fancy, with an imagined 'you' (sometimes conceived as a lost lover; sometimes as the perfect 'camerado,' God; sometimes as an indiscriminate Everyman; often as the reader; most often as a second self, 'the real Me') could he enter into an orgasmic unity."[52] Richard Chase argues that:

> The emergence of Whitman's genius may be understood as the conse-

quence of his having failed because of neurotic disturbances to make
terms with the world. In the early 1850's he found a compensatory way
of dealing with a world which threatened to defeat him. If he could not
subdue it on its own terms, he would do so by committing himself entirely to that rich fantasy life of which he felt himself increasingly
capable.[53]

Whitman's poetic relation to the reader is, in this view, the reflex of his social
alienation: "This alienation, impelling Whitman to resort to symbolic and
ideal forms of reattachment, is one of the major sources of his art."[54] No
wonder that some readers emphatically reject this writer-reader, I-thou fictional contract in which "the second-person must necessarily be at the loving
mercy of the first."[55]

Is it necessary to point out, however, that all the critiques cited above are
grounded in the concept of social identity that Whitman quite deliberately
(for whatever pathological or, who knows, even artistic reasons) deconstructs?[56] Martin Green's approach to Whitman is unequivocally based on a
belief in identity-as-ethos:

> The 'I' of *Song of Myself* is first of all Walt Whitman, later all Ameri-
> cans, later the Unconscious or World Spirit; and though there is some
> humorous interplay of differentness between those selves, there is also
> a more remarkable indeterminate sliding from one into another. *The
> selfresponsible personality disappears. The crucial distinction, between
> what the poet felt, and what he might have felt if he had been some-
> body else, is fatally blurred*; and this blurring extends to his tone as
> well as to his vision. He is not speaking *to* any more than *as* a person.
> . . . There are no satisfactory persons in Whitman's poetic world, nei-
> ther the 'I' nor the 'You,' and consequently there is no satisfaction in it
> for the reader.[57]

There is certainly no satisfaction for the reader who worries about maintaining ethical responsibility even (or, rather, especially) when reading a fiction,
who is concerned with maintaining his own fiction of an uncompromisably
integral identity.

The disputants in Santayana's wonderful dialogue on Whitman precisely
define the ethical and the free-play responses to Whitman's invitation:

> McStout: . . . it is immoral to *treat life as a masquerade, as a magic
> pantomime in which acts have no consequences* and happiness and
> misery don't exist.
> Van Tender: Ah, but Whitman is nothing if not a spectator, a cos-
> mic poet to whom the whole world is a play.[58]

It is precisely personal identity which Whitman invites the reader to put into
play, and the absence of moral judgment which Green and Santayana-as-
McStout so condemn provides exactly the reassurance necessary for such a
dare: "We shall cease shamming and be what we really are. . . . The interior

American republic shall also be declared free and independent."[59] It is the masquerading which allows such freedom; the mask is donned so that we can cease shamming.

Moreover, the reader is not, in fact, altogether at the mercy of the persona. In the free play between two "essentially fluid" (the characteristic oxymoron of *Leaves*) characters, the fictive persona and the fictive reader, the dramatic intrigue absent from the other relationships in *Leaves* becomes constitutive:

> Whoever you are holding me now in hand
> Without one thing all will be useless
> I give you fair warning before you attempt me further,
> I am not what you supposed but far different.
>
> . . . .
>
> But these leaves conning you con at peril,
> For these leaves and me you will not understand
> They will elude you at first and still more afterward, I will certainly
>   elude you,
> Even while you should think you had unquestionably caught me,
>   behold!
> Already you see I have escaped from you.
>
> For it is not for what I have put into it that I have written this book,
> Nor is it by reading it you will acquire it,
> Nor do those know me best who admire me and vauntingly praise me,
> Nor will the candidates for my love (unless at most a very few) prove
>   victorious,
> Nor will my poems do good only, they will do just as much evil,
>   perhaps more,
> For all is useless without that which you may guess at many times and
>   not hit, that which I hinted at;
> Therefore release me and depart on your way.[60]

The persona flirts with the reader, provokes him, but evades the reader's attempt to vamp him spiritually.

Conceivably it is not Whitman's flirtatiousness but his refusal to stay in place, to be essentially comprehended, that alienates many readers. To be sure, there are themes in *Leaves of Grass*, but they are expressed under the sign of suggestiveness: "The word I myself put primarily for the description of them [the themes] as they stand at last is Suggestiveness. I round and finish little, if anything; and could not, consistently with my scheme. The reader will always have his or her part to do, just as much as I have had mine."[61] The reader is not lulled to passive acceptance but lured into strenuous and indeterminate activity:

> Books are to be call'd for and supplied [in the ideal American republic], on the assumption that the process of reading is not a half-sleep, but, in the highest sense, an exercise, a gymnast's struggle; that the

reader is to do something for himself, must be on the alert, must himself or herself construct indeed the poem, argument, history, metaphysical essay—the text furnishing the hints, the clue, the start or framework.[62]

The pleasure of Whitman's text is to be found not so much in any set idea or doctrine as in the "curious chess-game of a poem."[63]

It is just Whitman's masquerading, fluidity, and indirection that allow for his extraordinary imaginative breakthrough in section 11 of "Song of Myself":

Twenty-eight young men bathe by the shore,
Twenty-eight young men and all so friendly;
Twenty-eight years of womanly life and all so lonesome.

She owns the fine house by the rise of the bank,
She hides handsome and richly drest aft the blinds of the window.

Which of the young men does she like the best?
Ah, the homeliest of them is beautiful to her.

Where are you off to, lady? for I see you,
You splash in the water there, yet stay stock still in your room.

Dancing and laughing along the beach came the twenty-ninth bather,
The rest did not see her, but she saw them and loved them.

The beards of the young men glisten'd with wet, it ran from their long
    hair
Little streams passed all over their bodies.

An unseen hand also pass'd over their bodies,
It descended tremblingly from their temples and ribs.

The young men float on their back, their white bellies bulge to the sun,
    they do not ask who seizes fast to them,
They do not know who puffs and declines with pendant and bending
    arch,
They do not think whom they souse with spray.   (pp. 31-32)

Some major themes of "Song of Myself" are beautifully developed in this poem within a poem: the projection of the phantom self, the clarification and transfiguration of the forbidden voices of sex and lust, the spiritualization of the natural, and the naturalization of the spiritual. There are two projections in the poem. The first is the lady's projection of her phantom self onto the beach, where she engages in amorous play leading to sexual climax. Literally, what happens is that she incorporates the real bathers into her voyeuristic, auto-erotic fantasy. The process is analogous to the manner in which Whitman incorporates people into his fantasy world in "Song of Myself"—as, of course, he is doing in this very passage.

Indeed the second projection is that Whitman, to some degree, identifies with the lady. I emphasize "to some degree," since it would be all too easy to reduce the passage to merely a transparent disguise for the poet's supposed homoerotic longings. The passage may be a homoerotic fantasy on Whitman's part, but it is also (and more importantly, I think) many other things. For if this lady originated as a self-projection of the author she becomes a thoroughly "realized," separate character within the passage. The passage could not have worked without this separation, as its tone depends on a tricky series of relationships: the poet watches the lady who, unaware of the poet, watches the bathers who are unaware of her. (And, of course, the reader is watching the poet, who is very well aware of this additional voyeur.) The mutual unawarenesses give the poem an irony that complicates its pathos, while they are themselves part of the theme of the buried life of sexual yearning.

The situation in the poem is naturally pathetic, so much so that it could easily have slipped into bathos. Some readers, indeed, pity the lady, which is to miss the point. The poet deliberately avoids mawkishness, through the irony of the mutual unawarenesses and by maintaining toward the lady a tone compounded of patronizing tenderness and affectionate mockery—"Where are you off to, lady? for I see you, / You splash in the water there, yet stay stock still in your room." In fact, the poem is about the lady's triumph, not her tragedy. She has found an imaginative solution to the problem of her sexual yearnings: she projects her spiritual, phantasmal self into the sea where men, lady, and ocean, anima and animus, body and spirit, merge in a fantastic sexual culmination. The whole is comparable to something out of Ovid's *Metamorphoses*, or out of Pound's reworking of them:

> Twisted arms of the sea-god
> Lithe sinews of water, gripping her, cross-hold
> And the blue-gray glass of the wave tents them,
> Glare azure of water, cold-welter, close-cover.[64]

In section 11 of "Song of Myself" Whitman has taken an extreme dare, using an auto-erotic climax as a symbol of the spirit serving the body. The spiritual life, frequently so thin in post-romantic nineteenth-century poetry, has been naturalized here by being sexualized. Meanwhile sexuality is spiritualized, is recognized as one of the primary motions of the buried life. The putative reader of *Song of Myself* can "undrape" in the presence of the poet's imagination, thus to be incorporated into a kind of community of the subliminal.

Whitman's procedure in "Song of Myself" involves losses and gains. He creates an epic without a society. His hero is an Odysseus whose future readers are his only companions. There is a loss of the sense of the outlines, the limits of the self, of the relation of the self to others, to society. The hero's very body becomes phantasmal. And the sexual experiences the poem celebrates are not encounters of I and Thou but, rather, confused and shamefaced interminglings of Me, Myself, and I. But if Whitman's method entails a loss of the sense of overall coherence, of public reality, the method is essential to his dramatization of the self in process, of the self as continually generated and regenerated out of the rhythms of desire. If character-as-ethos is dissolved, character-as-pathos is envisioned as never before. Moreover, Whitman's pathos has none of the laxness, the easy appeal to the stock responses of sentimentality or self-pity, so frequent in nineteenth-century writing. His pathos breaks through preconceived molds to represent the dynamic rhythms of the self, rhythms that are transactions between the self and nature and that are expressed frequently in energetically kinesthetic images.

The dissociation of the self and of the poetic technique that expresses it allows the self to break free from old conditionings. The self can see its own strangeness in a series of proto-surrealistic images born out of the technique of dissociation. Finally, if the poet has deliberately abandoned certain public ways of relating himself to others (vide section 4 of "Song of Myself"), he has brilliantly elaborated various subliminal modes of relationship. Whitman's disintegration of the personality allowed him to reveal the rhythm of desire, the flow of psychobiological natural forces that make the whole world kin. Everyone breathes, everyone longs. Indeed the poem's sexual solipsism becomes part of this ground of relationship, for everyone also fantasizes.

It was, then, Whitman's dissociations that allowed him to outflank the sexual ethos of mid–nineteenth century America, as Henry Adams perceived:

> Adams began to ponder, asking himself whether he knew of any American artist who had ever insisted on the power of sex, as every classic had always done; but he could think only of Walt Whitman; Bret Harte, as far as the magazines would let him venture; and one or two painters for the fleshtones. All the rest had used sex for sentiment, never for force.[65]

If Adams overstates, we can qualify his comment by saying that Whitman was the first American to rediscover sexual pathos as a theme, without obscuring and complicating it with sentimental or gothic conventions. Whitman speaks not to the self as social actor but to the core of loneliness in each person. In this way, Whitman prepared the ground for such classic American studies of pathos and of the subliminal rhythms of the self as Stein's "Melanctha" and Dreiser's *Sister Carrie*. In these works,[66] though they include far more dialectical interplay with ethos and with the otherness of character than "Song of Myself," pathos displaces ethos, and desire, paradoxically portrayed as simultaneously frustrated and triumphant, is the subject.

3. *A Modern Instance*:
Pathos Subordinated to Ethos

That William Dean Howells never properly appreciated Walt Whitman's poetry is not inconsistent for a critic who was willing to leap to the defense of Ibsen and Stephen Crane. Howells was too sophisticated to attack literature for controversial content; it was, rather, the moral philosophy implicit in the work that he judged. The events depicted in *Ghosts* and *Maggie* might be shocking but the moralizing irony of each worked in an approvably homiletic fashion,[1] whereas Whitman's "method" was, in Howells' perspective, "unspeakably inartistic," "a failure."[2] Furthermore, Howells' disapproval of Whitman's poetry precisely keys in with his admiration for George Eliot's fiction. His rejection of Whitman's "method" in *Drum-Taps* and his fervent approval of Eliot's in *Romola* are two sides of the same coin: his responses evince his distrust of pathos and his need for ethical articulation. The strength and weakness of Howells' own fiction, as evidenced by his finest novel, *A Modern Instance*, result from his own method of subordinating pathos to ethos.

1. Whitman and Pathos, Eliot and Ethos

Whitman offers the reader a poetic exploration of the roots of emotion, of the primal rhythm of self dissociated from social articulation. Howells rejects this offer as explicitly as does Martin Green (see chapter 2, section 2):

> The method of talking to one's self in rhythmic and ecstatic prose is one that surprises at first, but, in the end, the talker can only have the devil for a listener, as happens in other cases when people address their own individualities; not, however, the devil of the proverb, but the devil of reasonless, hopeless, all-defying egotism. An ingenious French critic said very acutely of Mr. Whitman that he made you partner of the poetical enterprise, which is perfectly true; but no one wants to share the enterprise.[3]

The intangibility of Whitman's method is clearly perceived by Howells and as clearly rejected: "The trouble about it is that it does not give you sensation in a portable shape; the thought is as intangible as aroma; it is no more put up than the atmosphere."[4] This is just what I was demonstrating in the previous chapter; Howells differs not in perception but in evaluation.

Howells finely appreciates how the lull in Whitman's voice is a vehicle for a subtle form of magnetism, but he cannot accept the concomitant blurring of ethical articulation:

> No doubt the pathos of many of the poems gains something from the quaintness of the poet's speech. One is touched in reading them by the same inarticulate feeling as that which dwells in music; and is sensible that the poet conveys to the heart certain emotions which the brain cannot analyse, and only remotely perceives. This is especially true of his inspirations from nature; memories and yearnings come to you folded, mute, and motionless in his verse, as they come in a breath of a familiar perfume. They give a strange, shadowy sort of pleasure, but they do not satisfy, and you rise from the perusal of this man's book as you issue from the presence of one whose personal magnetism is very subtle and strong, but who has not added to this tacit attraction the charm of spoken ideas.[5]

The assumption behind all this is that "poetry, which is nobler than science, must concern itself with natural instincts only as they can be developed into the sentiments and ideas of the soul of man."[6] And Howells' conclusion is that "So long . . . as Mr. Whitman chooses to stop at *mere consciousness*, he cannot be called a true poet."[7] Clearly Howells fails to recognize Whitman's implicit moral grounding, which is evident enough throughout *Leaves of Grass* but also explicitly a "spoken idea" in the 1855 preface:

> The greatest poet does not moralize or make applications of morals . . . he knows the soul. The soul has that measureless pride which consists in never acknowledging any lessons but its own. But it has sympathy as measureless as its pride and the one balances the other and neither can stretch too far while it stretches in company with the other.[8]

But, then, Howells could never have accepted such a commendation of "measureless pride," however compounded it might be with sympathy.

For Howells, true art does not affirm pride but exposes egotism. The ethical purpose of realistic fiction

> is to make us . . . look to it . . . whether we are hypocrites, tyrants, pretenders, shams conscious or unconscious; whether our most unselfish motives are not really secret shapes of egotism; whether our convictions are not mere brute acceptations; whether we believe what we profess; whether when we force good to a logical end we are not doing evil. . . . If we find ourselves all right we can go ahead with a good conscience, but never quite so cocksure afterwards.[9]

Tolstoy's value is that he "has given many of his readers a bad conscience, and a bad conscience is the best thing a man can have."[10] Thus, Howells believes in the necessity to implicate the reader[11] —but always in an ethically directed fashion. The artist should shape morality into homily, not sermonizing:

> Where the artist and the moralist work together for righteousness, there is the true art; for it is the business of the moralist to feel and the business of the artist to portray. Otherwise you have a sermon, or you have a romance, and not the homily in which your own soul is mirrored in that of some fellow man.[12]

One should confront in the mirror not "measureless pride" but the "selfishness and conceit and falsehood" that Ibsen reveals.[13]

Romola is a touchstone for such homiletic artistry. Howells compares the moral failure of the hero of a Robert Herrick novel to that of Tito in *Romola*:

> As you look on with the wretched man, whose moral ruin has been so reasonable, so logical, you become one with him in your consciousness of like possibilities in yourself.* When a novelist can do this with a reader, he has taken himself out of the category of futile villain mongers and placed himself in the high, clear air where George Eliot discovered in our common human nature her immortal Tito.[14]

In *My Literary Passions* Howells declared that George Eliot's intellect "profoundly influenced me by its ethics."[15] This was especially true of *Romola*:

> I read it again and again with the sense of moral enlargement which the first fiction to conceive of the true nature of evil gave all of us who were young in that day. Tito Melema was not only a lesson, he was a revelation, and I trembled before him as in the presence of a warning and a message from the only veritable perdition. His life, in which so much that was good was mixed with so much that was bad, lighted up the whole domain of egotism with its glare, and made one feel how near the best and the worst were to each other, and how they sometimes touched without absolute division in texture and color.

Howells as a reader was powerfully implicated in the sense of being "full with horror for myself in Tito."[16] The influence was generative; Henry James wrote Howells that *A Modern Instance* was "the Yankee Romola!!"[17] Roswell Smith's letter to Howells spells out the resemblance, commenting that *A Modern Instance*

> reminds me of a certain quality in George Eliot's Romola. I used to throw the book from me, & say I would not finish it. The delineation of the naked selfishness of Romola's [sic] character & the keen analysis of motives was too painfully suggestive of the awful possibilities of wickedness one finds in one's own nature.[18]

---

*Cf. Howells' repudiation of "*mere* consciousness" in Whitman.

Howells' fascination with *Romola* was natural for a writer who, as much as any of the great Victorians, saw character *as* ethos and was interested in the self *as* Selfishness. Howells' Swedenborgian upbringing had instilled in him a powerful dread of selfishness.[19] As Edwin H. Cady notes, "a reading of George Eliot's *Romola* . . . revived in him the Swedenborgian conviction that egotism is the root of all true evil."[20] In *A Modern Instance*, the "Yankee Romola," the instance of divorce that gives the book its title is the central theme only insofar as it is a symptom of destructive self-centeredness—the pervading issue of the novel. All takes place under the sign of the Negative Self.

Howells reveals the negative self through a brilliant phenomenological analysis of its moods, reveries, and "tropisms" (see definition in section 4 below). The self is seen processually and almost totally in terms of the negative activity of self-deception. In this way Howells carries on the Victorian analysis of rationalization while simultaneously anticipating the insights into processual consciousness of James's *Principles of Psychology*—a work which, for that matter, Howells considered a handbook to ethics.[21] In the rest of this chapter I shall show how Howells contributed to the psychology of pathos through his development of Bartley's reveries and through his analysis of the stimuli and responses involved in marital warfare. But I shall also show how strictly subordinated to ethos is Howells' study of pathos and why this is an ultimate limitation of his technique.

2. Physical Signs as Ethical Signs

Bartley Hubbard has a weak chin. In literature, physical qualities are never insignificant; they are always signs. In Whitman physical signs (kinesthetic images) are used to evade social and ethical categories. In Howells, who organized everything in his novel around ethos, a physical sign is always an ethical clue. In the community ethos, weak chin = weak character; and everything subsequently revealed about Bartley builds from this initial cue. Toward the end of *A Modern Instance* Bartley's increasing fatness is emphasized. This fatness is a signifier which indicates his increasing self-indulgence and moral degeneracy. In terms of fictional logic (though not bio-logic) Bartley's fatness grows out of his weak chin.

Bartley's voice is also ethically significant: "The young fellow had a rich, caressing voice, and a securely winning manner which comes from the habit of easily pleasing; in this charming tone, and with this delightful insinuation, he often said things that hurt; but with such a humorous glance from his softly shaded eyes that people felt in some sort flattered at being taken into the joke, even while they winced under it."[22] One might say that Bartley's voice traces an interface between personal ethos and community ethos, since Howells implies throughout that the community ethos is at fault to indulge Bartley's self-indulgence. Though an orphan, Bartley is society's spoiled child; his superficial malice passes for smartness, a central community value.[23] Bartley's voice is a medium for imposition and he naturally finds his métier as a newspaper man, an occupation which rewards factitiousness. (In a modern American novel he would be in advertising or public relations.)

Finally, still on the level of physical signs, Bartley's actions are what one would expect of a man who is weak-chinned, destined to become fat, and possessed of a securely winning manner. Paradigmatic of Bartley's behavior is the mince-pie episode. Bartley returns his horse to its stable after an evening of courtship. (The mode of this courtship will be examined in the next section.) Feeling hungry after his strenuous spiritual posturing, he asks the stable boy to find him a snack. The boy serves him with mince pie and cheese which Bartley eats *without thinking of offering to share it*. This is the behavior of a selfish man. As if the action itself were not enough, obvious verbal cues direct our judgment of Bartley: he asks for food "in a pathetic tone of injury"; he asks for tea "while gazing thoughtfully at the pie"; he "reflected awhile" before realizing he could improve the cheese by toasting it.

Am I, or, for that matter, is Howells putting too much emphasis on a trivial and petty action, one which might almost seem below the dignity of fiction to record? No, for the pettiness of the action is the point. Selfishness exercised in grand designs is half-justified by the imagination. But someone who is thoughtful about a pie, who reflects over his digestive juices, lacks the afflatus of nobility. He is doubly condemned; morally for his weak-chinned selfishness and esthetically *as well as* morally for his pettiness. One cannot happily sympathize with concern over such a small self.

3. Community Ethos: Ideal Motivations

Bartley's voice is a role-playing device, an effective one since it gets him mince pie. Of course, a role player has to play either with or off of the ethos of his community. Bartley knows and even half believes in the ethical myths of his society. In a fine comic scene, we see how Bartley manipulates Marcia by invoking the community myth of sexual relations:

> Then he began to speak, soberly in a low voice. He spoke of himself; but in application of a lecture they had lately heard, so that he seemed to be speaking of the lecture. It was on the formation of character, and he told of the processes by which he had formed his own character. . . . When he came to speak of the influence of others upon him, she almost trembled with the intensity of her interest. "But of all the women I have known, Marcia," he said, "I believe you have had the strongest influence upon me. I believe you could make me do anything; but you have always influenced me for good; your influence upon me has been ennobling and elevating." (p. 10)

Howells is satirizing a central tenet of the genteel tradition: the sexual division of labor between Man, the practical, materialistic, meat- and money-gatherer, and Woman, the upholder of Culture, ideals, and ethics.[24] Woman's role is to uplift Man. Curiously enough, Marcia is quite sexually excited by Bartley's account of her spiritual influence ("she almost trembled with the intensity of her interest"—Henry Miller would say it differently but he was not writing in 1882). The myth is relevant to the actual situation of Bartley and Marcia only in that Bartley uses it to manipulate Marcia. In fact, it is he who influences her throughout—in this case by providing her with a culturally approved mask for her passion, i.e., by dressing up passion as ethos.

Howells, thus, inverts the myth. But Howells shows that Bartley not only partly believes in the myth but can fall back on it for self-justification:

> Now, he was here in the dark, with fifteen dollars in his pocket, and an unsalable horse on his hands; outcast, deserted, homeless, hopeless; and by whose fault? He owned even then that he had committed some follies, but in his sense of Marcia's all-giving love he had risen for once in his life to a conception of self-devotion, and in taking herself from him as she did, she had taken from him the highest incentive he had ever known, and had checked him in his first feeble impulse to do and be all in all for another. It was she who had ruined him.   (pp. 102-103)

Howells disliked the romanticism and idealism of his time because it set up a completely false model of motivations—that abstract ideal led to personal action. Thus it could function as a screen for blind passion (as with Marcia) or for unbridled egotism (as with Bartley).[25] Bartley's actual motivations are less grandiose: he proposes to Marcia because of the mince pie.

4. Tropisms: Real Motivations

The mince pie, it will be recalled, made its appearance early in the novel as an occasion for a show of selfishness by Bartley. Its long-range function is more important. The situation is this: the morning after Bartley's ethical courtship and late snack, he visits Marcia. The mince pie has given him indigestion and he seeks her sympathy. What he does not know is that Marcia has been shamed by her father's recognition of the unequal relationship between herself and Bartley. She withholds sympathy. This leads Bartley into an altogether unpremeditated declaration: "'Marcia, do you blame me for feeling hurt at your coldness when I came here to tell you—to tell you I—I love you?' With his nerves all unstrung, and his hunger for sympathy, he really believed that he had come to tell her this" (p. 30). So they become engaged, and, though only after a serious contretemps, they marry. And it all traces back to a mince pie's depressing influence upon Bartley.

The mince-pie episode implies something about "the processes by which [Bartley] had formed his own character." Evidently these processes do not correspond very well to such ideal abstractions as ennoblement, nor is Bartley as much in control of his character formation as he supposes. Howells is working in terms of a model of the self very close to that William James later advanced in his *Principles*. James there hypothesizes that *"our entire feeling of spiritual activity, or what commonly passes by that name, is really a feeling of bodily activities whose exact nature is by most men overlooked"* (*Principles*, I, 302-302).[26] What James has in mind is our vague awareness of such

"minimal reflexes" (p. 302) as the closing of the glottis and contraction of
the brows that go with "the acts of attending, assenting, negating, making an
effort" (p. 300). These adjustments are "unimportant and uninteresting except through their uses in furthering or inhibiting the presence of various
things, and actions before consciousness" (p. 302). But just this fact makes
them intensely interesting and important since

> They are reactions, and they are *primary* reactions. Everything arouses
> them; for objects which have no other effects will for a moment con-
> tract the brow and make the glottis close. It is as if all that visited the
> mind had to stand an entrance-examination, and just show its face so as
> to be approved or sent back. These primary reactions are like the open-
> ing or the closing of the door. In the midst of psychic change they are
> the permanent core of turnings-toward and turnings-from, of yieldings
> and arrests, which naturally seem central and interior in comparison
> with the foreign matters, *apropos* to which they occur, and hold a sort
> of arbitrating, decisive position, quite unlike that held by any of the
> other constituents of the Me. It would not be surprising, then, if we
> were to feel them as the birthplace of conclusions and the starting point
> of acts, or if they came to appear as what we called a while back the
> 'sanctuary within the citadel' of our own personal life.   (pp. 302–303)

A Modern Instance comes closer to examining these "primary reactions"
than any previous American fiction. These reactions resemble the "sub-
conversation" that Nathalie Sarraute found underlying the interior monologue:

> An immense profusion of sensations, images, sentiments, memories,
> impulses, little larval actions that no inner language can convey, that
> jostle one another on the threshold of consciousness, gather together
> in compact groups and loom up all of a sudden, then immediately fall
> apart, combine otherwise and reappear in new forms.[27]

Sarraute later called these phenomena "tropisms"; she sees Flaubert's *Madame Bovary* as constructed out of such tropisms.[28] "Tropism" can be defined, in a way quite consonant with Sarraute's use of the term, as the "turn-
ings-toward and turnings-from," the "yieldings and arrests" of the self toward
whatever is outside: other selves, objects, etc. Bartley's response to Marcia
has little to do with love, lust, and the usual apparatus of "very obvious, well-
known, frank motives," the "thick, perfectly visible wires" by which fictive
personalities had usually been moved.[29] It is more of a tropism.

5. Bartley's Reveries: The Ethical Structuring of Consciousness

Howells' fiction, then, is distinguished from previous American fiction by his
more analytical scrutiny of the processes of consciousness. Like Proust, he is
interested in "following the order of our perceptions rather than explaining
them first through their causes."[30] In effect, Howells gives us a process analy-

sis of Bartley's pathos. This focus on process is particularly apparent in Bartley's reveries.

In two passages, Howells' ethical condemnation of these reveries is explicit. The first passage catches Bartley on the borderland of sleep on the night of his engagement:

> He liked so well to think how fond of him Marcia was, that it did not occur to him then to question whether he were as fond of her. It is possible that as he drowsed, at last, there floated airily through the consciousness that was melting and dispersing itself before the approach of sleep, an intimation from somewhere to some one that perhaps the affair need not be considered too seriously. But in that mysterious limbo one cannot be sure of what is thought and what is dreamed; and Bartley always acquitted himself, and probably with justice, of any want of seriousness.   (p. 48)

This passage combines an extreme tentativeness about the exact status of these putative feelings of Bartley with unmistakable cues to the reader that these are indeed his feelings and that these feelings are to be judged adversely. Bartley's thoughts proceed from an area of the mind that is intrinsically ambiguous. Accordingly, the second sentence of the above quotation begins with an introductory conditional phrase ("It is possible that") and is qualified yet further with "perhaps." The third sentence professes doubt about even the conditionally qualified conclusions of the second. Eight years before *Principles of Psychology*, Howells was engaged in the process of "the reinstatement of the vague to its proper place in our mental life" (*Principles*, I, 254). But neither Howells nor James was vague about vagueness. The irony of "an intimation from somewhere to some one" can escape no reader and we are in no real doubt about what our response to Bartley should be.

The second passage reveals Howells' technique even more clearly. This passage describes a reverie (also discussed in section 8, below) wherein Bartley "generously" wishes Marcia well in a hypothetical second marriage:

> He even thought of her happy in a second marriage; and the thought did not enrage him; he generously wished Marcia well. He wished—he hardly knew what he wished. He wished nothing at all but to have his wife and child back again as soon as possible; and he put aside with a laugh the fancies which really found no such distinct formulation as I have given them; which were mere vague impulses [i.e., tropisms], arrested mental tendencies, scraps of undirected revery. Their recurrences had nothing to do with what he felt to be his sane and waking state. But they recurred, and he even amused himself in turning them over.
> (pp. 265-266)

Howells here reifies and structures the vague impulses, the arrested mental tendencies (we see Bartley arrest a tendency to "disappear" Marcia) of Bartley's consciousness. The principle underlying the technique is Howells' own (unarrested) moral tendency: his need to clarify ethical issues.[31] Howells' style, then, is designed to delineate ethos through pathos. In *A Modern Instance* character is revealed through moral choice—but choice is shown to be a complex process in which vague and not fully acknowledged impulses have a major role. Bartley slides gradually into certain feelings and his actions are a precipitate of this process of consciousness. But this does not exculpate him. Howells structures Bartley's reveries to reveal his weakness and selfishness. Character remains a process of choice, however vague and unacknowledged the choices are. Indeed, the major choice Bartley makes is to continue to entertain such dangerous thoughts. Other and better choices were possible.

6. Conscience as Inner Debate

Though William James emphasizes the horizontal flow of consciousness, he acknowledges the validity of the traditional vertical, hierarchical concept of it: "a tolerably unanimous opinion ranges the different selves of which a man may be 'seized and possessed', and the consequent different orders of his self-regard, in an *hierarchical scale, with the bodily self at the bottom, the spiritual self at the top, and the extracorporeal material selves and the various social selves between*" (*Principles*, I, 313). James does not believe in pure unselfishness, but he envisions a hierarchy which moves from concern for a narrow self to concern for a self circumscribed only by the claims of spirit:

> So it comes to pass that . . . men have arranged the various selves which they may seek in an hierarchical scale according to their worth. A certain amount of bodily selfishness is required as a basis for all the other selves. But too much sensuality is despised, or at best condoned on account of the other qualities of the individual. The wider material selves are regarded as higher than the immediate body. He is esteemed a poor creature who is unable to forego a little meat and drink and warmth and sleep for the sake of getting on in the world. The social self, as a whole, again ranks higher than the material self as a whole. We must care more for our honor, our friends, our human ties, than for a sound skin or wealth. And the spiritual self is so supremely precious that, rather than lose it, a man ought to be willing to give up friends and good fame, and property, and life itself.   (I, 314–315)

Bartley has barely got beyond stage 1 of this scheme (the narrower material self), although he has occasional glimpses of stage 3 (the social self). Of stage 4 he has hardly a clue. Still, his aspirations to stage 3 are important and Howells dramatizes them as a process in Bartley's consciousness. They take the primarily negative form of a series of not quite repressible objections by Bartley to the usual flow of his self-justifying rationalizations. The following passage analyzes Bartley's second thoughts about the disaster that his attentions to Hannah Morrison have brought about:

> He could rebel against the severity of the condemnation he had fallen under in the eyes of Marcia and her father; he could, in the light of ex-

ample and usage, laugh at the notion of harm in his behavior to Hannah Morrison; yet he found himself looking at it as a treachery to Marcia. Certainly, she had no right to question his conduct before his engagement. Yet, if he knew that Marcia loved him, and was waiting with life-and-death anxiety for some word of love from him, it was cruelly false to play with another at the passion which was such a tragedy to her. This was the point that, put aside however often, still presented itself, and its recurrence, if he could have known it, was mercy and reprieve from the only source out of which these could come.   (p. 67)

The psychological and narrative structure of this passage is not as simple as it might appear. Even Bartley's rationalizations imply his knowledge of their falsity, since rationalization is a mental operation grounded on bad faith. You can only rationalize what you inwardly know to be wrong. This secret knowledge belongs fully neither to the conscious nor the unconscious mind, but to the realm of the vague. But the inchoate motions of rationalization and the moral reality it attempts to evade are articulated here as an inner debate: he could . . . yet; certainly . . . yet. As James says, "What checks our impulses is the mere thinking of reasons to the contrary—it is their bare presence to the mind which gives the veto, and makes acts, otherwise seductive, impossible to perform" (*Principles*, II, 559).

The language of the last sentence in Howells' passage traces this process both logically and emotionally. The moral reality is a "point," implying a logical, argumentative structuring but it is a point that is "recurrent," which implies it is an element in a processual consciousness. Finally, Bartley tries to put it aside, which shows the falsity of his evasive consciousness. How is the "recurrence" of this "point" "mercy and reprieve from the only source out of which these could come"? The source is, in fact, consciousness itself.

The question is, then, how does proper volition (i.e., that high on the vertical scale) operate? In terms of Jamesian psychology "volition is primarily a relation, not between our Self and extra-mental matter . . . but between our Self and our own states of mind" (*Principles*, II, 567–568). Can we make ourselves responsible for these states of mind? Though not without difficulty, we can. The self chooses or evades a state largely by means of the name it assigns to it. Here, unfortunately, is where rationalization comes in:

in describing the 'reasonable type' of decision, it was said that it usually came when the right conception of the case was found. Where, however, the right conception is an anti-impulsive one, the whole intellectual ingenuity of the man usually goes to work to crowd it out of sight, and to find names for the emergency, by the help of which the dispositions of the moment may sound sanctified, and sloth or passion may reign unchecked.   (II, 565)

Contrariwise, "the effort by which he succeeds in keeping the right *name* unwaveringly present to his mind proves to be his saving moral act" (II, 565).

In both Howells and James, conscience is something of a nag, an irritating and unwelcoming presence in the consciousness. It can save only when *attended* to: "*The essential achievement of the will, in short, when it is most 'voluntary', is to ATTEND to a difficult object and hold it fast before the mind*" (II, 561). In sum, "the strong-willed man is the man who hears the still small voice unflinchingly" (II, 536). Such is not Bartley. To attain any lasting decency Bartley would have to negate his essentially negative self. At rare moments he feels such an impulse: "A curious feeling possessed him; sickness of himself as of some one else; a longing, consciously helpless, to be something different; a sense of captivity to habits and thoughts and hopes that centered in himself, and served him alone" (pp. 81–83). Here for once, Bartley ascends to stage 3 with even a look-in to stage 4. But Bartley's higher impulses are always abortive.

7. Negative Essence and False Consciousness

As we have seen, a mince pie causes Bartley's engagement—he is that kind of person. But the bitter quarrel over Hannah Morrison erupts between the engagement and the marriage. This quarrel is paradigmatic of the structure of Bartley's relationship to Marcia. Marcia makes wild accusations against Bartley, fired by her passionately jealous infatuation with him. But here is false consciousness compounded, for if Bartley is not in love with her, neither is he in love with anyone else. His occasional flirtations never go very far and yield him egoistic rather than any libidinal satisfaction. Marcia attacks Bartley in terms of her obsessional delusions while ignoring or indulging Bartley's very real failings of character. Bartley, thus, has the ultimate advantage in their marital warfare because Marcia, always fighting the wrong war, becomes abjectly repentant when she realizes her mistake. To put it another way, Bartley is always at fault, but it is never the fault that Marcia attacks. This pattern allows him to develop a quite unjustifiable sense of victimization. The mutual delusions of Bartley and Marcia provide the grounds for reconciliation and prepare the ground for new conflicts.

What Marcia never understands, her father immediately recognizes: "Don't you see that the trouble is in what the fellow is, and not in any particular thing that he's done? He's a scamp, through and through; and he's all the more a scamp when he doesn't know it. He hasn't got the first idea of anything but selfishness" (p. 77). Such a characterization could be very static. If Bartley's essence is so fixed, could it not be fictionally used up in a few tableaux such as the scene in the stable: the Egotist's Progress, as it were, in which there is temporal movement but no inner development? In a way, the novel does work out in this fashion: Bartley becomes more and more the same thing. Even Bartley's increasing fatness is a static property: a series of signs of self-indulgence lead to the final image of a fat-souled man. But what is more interesting in *A Modern Instance* is Howells' revelation of the complex inner action of being a selfish one (as Gertrude Stein might say): the shifty games "self" must play to maintain its fictions. It is through such transitive logic that Howells most tellingly exposes Bartley's essential nullity.

Howells thus unveils his character by tracking the process of reverie in Bartley, structuring the reveries according to the principles described in sections 5 and 6 above.

The first of these reveries comes as Bartley is sitting comfortably before the fire in the stable, after his selfish consumption of mince pie. (Although Howells is silent on this point it would be nice to suppose the reverie is partly inspired by Bartley's postprandial satisfaction, and thus counterpoints the later indigestion motive.)

> There were many things about his relations with Marcia Gaylord which were calculated to give Bartley satisfaction. She was, without question, the prettiest girl in the place, and she had more style than any other girl began to have. He liked to go into a room with Marcia Gaylord; it gave some pleasure. Marcia was a lady; she had a good education; she had been away two years at school; and when she came back at the end of the second winter he knew she had fallen in love with him at sight. He believed that he could time it to a second. He remembered how he had looked up at her as he passed, and she had reddened, and tried to turn away from the window as if she had not seen him. Bartley was still free as air; but if he could once make up his mind to settle down in a hole like Equity, he could have her by turning his hand. Of course, she had her drawbacks, like everybody. She was proud, and she would be jealous; but with all her pride and her distance, she had let him see that she liked him; and with not a word on his part that anyone could hold him to. (pp. 14–15)

The passage is a classic exposition of self-centeredness and self-complacency. Bartley responds not to Marcia directly but to other people's responses. Being seen with her is more satisfying than being with her. Her personal qualities, pride and jealousy, are noted as potentially troublesome but since Bartley is, happily, uncommitted, even these qualities simply reaffirm his self-esteem: this proud girl has chosen him! This is a heightened version of an I-it relationship. Lacking is the slightest hint not merely of love but even of sexual passion.

For Bartley, Marcia exists only as a reflection of his ego; he thinks of her entirely and cold-bloodedly in terms of his own self-enhancement. As the first sentence tells us, "there were many *things* about his relations" with her "which *were calculated*" to give him satisfaction. The relationship is in the passive case, it is materialistic but nonetheless less physical than mental. (The fact that Bartley relates Marcia to his wider material self rather than to his narrower, purely sexual one is *not* reassuring. In some situations the appetitive self ought to take precedence.) As they say these days, this relationship computes. Best of all, while self-enhancing for Bartley the relationship is not a commitment. He cannot be held to anything. Perhaps this self-protectiveness is the most disgusting thing about this almost null character. What lies behind the reader's disgust with Bartley will be examined in section 10 below.

8. Marital *Realpolitik* and the Stages of Degeneration

O. W. Firkins notes that *A Modern Instance* shows "a psychic process, a process of alienation between two persons . . . which ends in the bitterness of divorce."[32] Howells dramatizes this process through fine blow-by-blow accounts of particular quarrels and by tracing Bartley's progressive moral deterioration through his reveries. The quarrels begin to escalate about halfway through the book. In chapter 22 Marcia has one of her transports of jealousy, but Bartley chokes down his first impulse to make a savage response (pp. 182-183). Taken alone this incident has little significance, but as one step in a progression it is important. For, given Bartley's basic lack of any strong feeling for Marcia, and given her repeated hysterical assaults, he is bound to give way eventually to his savage impulses *and* to feel somewhat justified in doing so because of his previous forbearance. Thus the stage is set for a really major quarrel.

I shall quote at length Howells' account of one of the worst of the quarrels, interpolating commentary to explicate the tropistic movements (mostly turnings-from) within it. This quarrel takes the couple several steps further toward their final alienation. The passage which describes it is also notable as a brilliant study of the tactics of marital battle:

> "Miss Kingsbury treated you very well that night. She couldn't imagine your being jealous of her politeness to me."
>
> Marcia's temper fired at his treacherous recurrence to a grievance which he had once so sacredly and sweetly ignored. [The tropistic flare of Marcia's temper is set off by a fairly complex situation: she has given him mental credit for his previous forbearance so he is really cheating by using the incident now as grievance capital.] "If you wish to take up bygones, why don't you go back to Hannah Morrison at once? She treated you even better than Miss Kingsbury." [A tactical error by Marcia. It leaves her wide open by exposing her area of vulnerability.]
>
> "I should have been very willing to do that," said Bartley, "but I thought it might remind you of a disagreeable little episode in your own life, when you flung me away, and had to go down on your knees to pick me up again."
>
> These thrusts which they dealt each other in their quarrels, however blind and misdirected, always reached their hearts: it was the wicked will that hurt, rather than the words. [Howells is rarely quotable: he doesn't have that sort of style. But this aphorism about marital quarrels is devastating in its accuracy.] Marcia rose, bleeding inwardly, [her hysteria, always provoked by the inessential, has given way to trauma in the face of a real affront] and her husband felt the remorse of a man who gets the best of it in such an encounter. [Tropistically, Bartley has surged forward, but now he realizes he went too far and thus shrinks back, trying ineffectually to recall his last gibe, to rein in a situation which is rapidly getting beyond contol. Everything is happening too fast.]

"Oh, I'm sorry I said that, Marcia! I didn't mean it; indeed I—"
[Bartley's verbal rhythms are now tentative, conciliatory; could Marcia
only manage her emotions, she would have the advantage here.] She
disdained to heed him, as she swept out of the room, and up the stairs;
and his anger flared out again. [Marcia's typical tropism in a crisis is
a *noli me tangere* withdrawal. But, as we have seen, Bartley does not
particularly want to touch her. Thus Marcia's tactics are misapplied. She
appears to be doing everything she can to lose her momentary advantage—or so we might infer, though Howells does not really inquire
into her motivations. In section 10 of this chapter I will speculate on
why Howells shows us so little of Marcia's consciousness as opposed to
Bartley's.]

"I give you fair warning," he called after her, "not to try that trick
of locking the door, or I will smash it in." [Bartley has not been presented as capable of going quite that far, but the violence of his threat
releases the frustration and anger her refusal to even consider his peace
offer provoked. The curve of regret builds up and turns back on itself
into an anger fueled by guilt and resentment: guilt because Bartley
knows well enough he did go too far; resentment because Marcia will
not let him off the hook.]

Her answer was to turn the key in the door with a click he could not
fail to hear. [By turning the key Marcia is shutting herself off literally
as well as emotionally. We may take it that she finds a certain satisfaction in the action. But Marcia does not so much lock Bartley out as
lock herself into her own compulsions.]

The peace in which they had been living of late was very comfortable to Bartley; he liked it; he hated to have it broken; he was willing to
do what he could to restore it at once. If he had no better motive than
this, he still had this motive; [here a motive low on the hierarchical
scale almost proves a saving grace, showing that, in situational terms,
the hierarchical values can become equivocal. Spiritual torpor almost
holds Bartley's marriage together] and he choked down his wrath, and
followed Marcia softly upstairs. [More than ever, rhythm and timing
are crucial at this point. A choked-down wrath is volatile; it will erupt
all the more strongly if not resolved by mutual pacification signals.] He
intended to reason with her, and he began, "I say, Marsh," as he turned
the door-knob. But you cannot reason through a keyhole, and before
he knew he found himself saying, "Will you open this?" in a tone
whose quiet was deadly. [The closedness of the door, the quiet dead-
liness of the tone: in both Bartley and Marcia something is being
squeezed, closed up.] She did not answer; [how could she? She has put
them both into a structurally impossible situation where she must either lose dignity by reopening the door or wait for Bartley to beg. But
his strongest motivation is to avoid discomfort; he doesn't really *want*
Marcia. The easy way out would be for either of them to burst into
laughter at the absurdity of their situation and the posturing it involves.

Perhaps their fatal flaw is lack of a sense of humor.] he heard her stop in her movements about the room, and wait, as if she expected him to ask again. [This is clearly his cue but her timing is off; it is too late. Her attitude of reception, another tropism, is not rewarded.] He hesitated a moment whether to keep his threat of breaking the door in; but he turned away and went downstairs, and so into the street. [This is Alexander's solution to the puzzle of the Gordian knot.] Once outside, he experienced the sense of release that comes to a man from the violation of his better impulses; [William James offers a brilliant commentary on this emotional state: "Our self-feeling in this world depends entirely on what we *back* ourselves to be or do. It is determined by the ratio of our actualities to our supposed potentialities; a fraction of which our pretensions are the denominator and the numerator our success: thus, Self-esteem $= \frac{\text{Success}}{\text{Pretensions}}$. Such a fraction may be increased as well by diminishing the denominator as by increasing the numerator. To give up pretensions is as blessed a relief as to get them gratified. . . . There is the strangest lightness about the heart when one's nothingness in a particular line is once accepted in good faith. . . . Everything added to the Self is a burden as well as a pride" (*Principles*, I, 310-311)] but he did not know what to do or where to go. He walked rapidly away; but Marcia's eyes and voice seemed to follow him, and plead with him for his forbearance. But he answered his conscience, as if it had been some such presence, that he had forborne too much already, and that now he should not humble himself; that he was right and should stand upon his right. There was not much comfort in it, and he had to brace himself again and again with vindictive resolution. [In part, Bartley's anger is a consciously sustained emotion or even a self-directed performance: he has to keep pumping it up. There is an inner debate going on in which one part of his self must supply justifications to another part.]   (pp. 206-207)

Bartley proceeds to get drunk and, in the aftermath, is "not without a self-righteous sense of having given her a useful and necessary lesson" (p. 221).

The next stage comes with Marcia's discovery of how Bartley has cheated Kinney and allowed Ricker to be blamed for it. If she has overreacted in imagining Bartley unfaithful, she underreacts to this actual sign of moral nullity—perhaps because she knows it is real? In Bartley's mental negotiations with this dilemma we see his increasing tendency to let himself go. What is most alarming is the decrease in the quality of his rationalizations:

Once after a confidence of this kind [Bartley has *joked* about his dishonorable trick] at the club, where Ricker had refused to speak to him, he came away with a curious sense of moral decay. It did not pain him a great deal, but it certainly surprised him that now, with all these prosperous conditions, so favorable for cleaning up, he had so little disposition to clean up. He found himself quite willing to let the affair with Ricker go, and suspected that he had been needlessly virtuous in

his intentions concerning church-going and beer. As to Marcia, it
appeared to him that he could not treat a woman of her disposition
otherwise than as he did. At any rate, if he had not done everything he
could to make her happy, she seemed to be getting along well enough,
and was probably quite as happy as she deserved to be.   (p. 263)

The rationalization in the last two sentences is no longer even a self-
serving distortion of the moral norm; it is cold-bloodedly cynical marital
realpolitik. Bartley has turned the corner and is no longer even attempting
to live up to the norms. Later, when Marcia spends a summer in Equity, he
feels even more of the blessed relief that, James says, follows when we abandon our pretensions:

> There was no extravagance, and yet he seemed to live very much better
> after Marcia went. There is no doubt but he lived very much more at
> his ease. One little restriction after another fell away from him; he went
> and came with absolute freedom, not only without having to account
> for his movements, but without having a pang for not doing so. He had
> the sensation of stretching himself after a cramping posture; and he
> wrote Marcia the cheerfulest letters, charging her not to cut short her
> visit from anxiety on his account.   (p. 264)

Bartley more and more indulges in "ill-advised reveries" (p. 265) that do
much to destroy the threads of relationship tying him to Marcia.

It should be emphasized that Bartley's growing moral relaxation, his increasing indifference to Marcia, is ultimately more destructive than their
angriest quarrels—because habit is the strongest of the threads.[33] And Bartley
is semiconsciously preparing himself to break his Marcia-habit:

> In fact, he was still very fond of her; when he thought of little ways of
> hers, it filled him with tenderness. He did justice to her fine qualities,
> too: her generosity, her truthfulness, her entire loyalty to his best in-
> terests; he smiled to realize that he himself preferred his second-best in-
> terests; and in her absence he remembered that her virtues were tedious,
> and even painful at times. He had his doubts whether there was suf-
> ficient compensation in them. He sometimes questioned whether he
> had not made a great mistake to get married; he expected now to stick
> it through; but this doubt occurred to him. A moment came in which
> he asked himself, What if he had never come back to Marcia that night
> when she locked him out of her room? Might it not have been better
> for both of them? She would have reconciled herself to the irreparable;
> he even thought of her happy in a second marriage; and the thought
> did not enrage him; he generously wished Marcia well.   (p. 265)

This is much much worse than bad temper. It shows that Bartley is outside
the relationship, looking at it from a considerable emotional distance and
thinking of it in quasi-judicial, quasi-economic terms: he wants to "do justice" to Marcia, he worries that her virtues may not be "sufficient compensa-
tion." He is applying a self-serving version of Benthamite moral calculus.

Finally, Bartley's disinterested benevolence toward Marcia is disastrous, a sign that he has successfully externalized the relationship: it is something to do with Marcia, not with him. She has now become a merely intrusive and irrelevant object in his environment:

> Sometimes they sat a whole evening together, with almost nothing to say to each other, he reading and she sewing. After an evening of this sort, Bartley felt himself worse bored than if Marcia had spent it in taking him to task as she used to do. Once he looked at her over the top of his paper, and distinctly experienced that he was tired of the whole thing. (p. 271)

In their next major battle Marcia crumbles early but Bartley "had hardened his heart past all entreaty" (p. 275). It is the phenomenology of this heart-hardening that Howells has so carefully shown us.

What holds the marriage together is not the increasingly weak surges of Bartley's higher impulses but the rather more powerful force of habit. Habit almost brings Bartley back after the couple's most vicious, and, as it turns out, ultimate quarrel:

> Yet all the mute, obscure forces of habit, which are doubtless the strongest forces in human nature, were dragging him back to her. Because their lives had been united so long, it seemed impossible to sever them, though their union had been so full of misery and discord; the custom of marriage was so subtle and so pervasive that his heart demanded her sympathy for what he was suffering in abandoning her. (p. 277)

Only his discovery that he has lost Halleck's money confirms the finality of the break.

9. Chance, Timing, Rhythm

At this point chance enters—not as a *deus ex machina* but in a psychologically valid manner. We have seen how the corrosive effect of Bartley's reveries reduces his marriage to habit and then begins weakening the force of the habit itself. But the "set" of marriage is a very powerful one—as Howells ironically indicates in the last sentence of the quotation above—and, as with many conversionary and innovative as well as degenerative experiences of the self, one needs a push from outside oneself in order to break out of it. If we reverse the values and diminish the intensity (since Bartley is characteristically torpid) of the following description by St. Augustine of his soul's shrinking from grace, we can get a fair equivalent to Bartley's state just before the final rupture:

> Yet it [the soul] shrank back; it refused, though it had no excuse to offer. . . . I said within myself: "Come, let it be done now," and as I said it, I was on the point of the resolve. I all but did it, yet I did not

do it. And I made another effort, and almost succeeded, yet I did not reach it, and did not grasp it, hesitating to die to death, and live to life; and the evil to which I was so wonted held me more than the better life I had not tried.[34]

A chance event pushes Bartley over the line, but it could not have done so without the long process of "incubation"[35] that preceded it, as we have seen in Bartley's reveries. Bartley is now free to become a prisoner of disgrace.

Throughout the novel chance interacts in a complex fashion with tropistic responses and with higher and lower impulses. Howells emphasizes the importance of *timing* in both individual consciousness and personal relationships. The Hubbards' first major post-marital quarrel happens as a result of unfortunate timing. The sequence begins when Bartley sells his first freelance news story. He builds a satisfying and not implausible fantasy of how Marcia will respond:

> He did not stop to cash his order; he made boyish haste to show it to Marcia, as something more authentic than the money itself, and more sacred. As he hurried homeward he figured Marcia's ecstacy in his thought. He saw himself flying up the stairs to their attic three steps at a bound, and bursting into the room where she sat eager and anxious, and flinging the order into her lap; and then, when she had read it with rapture at the sum, and pride in the smartness with which he had managed the whole affair, he saw himself catching her up and dancing about the floor with her. He thought how fond of her he was, and he wondered that he could ever have been cold or lukewarm.   (p. 131)

Meanwhile Marcia's father has visited her and somewhat grudgingly announced he is reconciled to the marriage. She awaits Bartley with her own set of anticipations: "It seemed to her that, though her father had refused to see [Bartley], his visit was of happy augury for future kindness between them, and she was proudly eager to tell Bartley what good advice her father had given her" (p. 134). The two sets of rosy expectations collide disastrously—which is not surprising given that Bartley's surge of fondness for Marcia is all involved with his feeling of self-esteem and of impending triumph in her eyes, whereas she immediately confronts him with a reminder of the very man who has most grievously wounded his ego. Naturally enough Bartley flies into a rage and she locks her door.

In describing the aftermath of their reconciliation Howells emphasizes that they had lost forever a moment that could have bound them together:

> On the way to the restaurant she asked him of his adventure among the newspapers. He told her briefly, and when they sat down at their table he took out the precious order and showed it to her. But its magic was gone; it was only an order for twenty-five dollars, now; and two hours ago it had been success, rapture, a common hope and a common joy.
>
> (p. 134)

Chance, timing, and rhythm are crucial in this sequence: Bartley is brought so far down because he had flown so high on the wings of reverie.

That the sequence of events is more important than their particular content is confirmed by the fact that Howells structured the Hubbards' final marital quarrel identically to the first (though it is precipitated by opposite circumstances). After a frightening setback, Bartley comes home with a heart brimfull of sentiments of reform:

> After his frightful escape from losing half of it [a loan] on those bets, he had an intense longing to be rid of it, to give it back to Halleck, who would never ask him for it, and then to go home and tell Marcia everything, and throw himself on her mercy. Better poverty, better disgrace before Halleck and her, better her condemnation, than this life of temptation he had been leading. He saw how hideous it was in the retrospect, and he shuddered; his good instincts awoke, and put forth their strength such as it was; tears came into his eyes; he resolved to write to Kinney and exonerate Ricker, he resolved humbly to beg Ricker's pardon. [Throughout this sequence Howells undercuts Bartley ironically but he does not portray his consciousness as *totally* false. That is, with luck, Bartley might actually improve, and his impulse to do so is relatively a higher one. But, though not totally false, Bartley's consciousness is certainly touched with meretriciousness. Thus the ironic overformality of "resolved" shows Bartley thinking in stereotyped moral formulae.] He must leave Boston; but if Marcia would forgive him he would go back with her to Equity, and take up the study of the law in her father's office again, and fulfill all her wishes. He would have a hard time to overcome the old man's prejudices, but he deserved a hard time, and he knew he should finally succeed. It would be bitter, returning to that stupid little town, and he imagined the intrusive conjecture and sarcastic comment that would attend his return; but he believed that he could live this down, and he trusted himself to laugh it down. He already saw himself there, settled in the squire's office, reinstated in public opinion, a leading lawyer of the place, with Congress open before him whenever he chose to turn his face that way. [This is a marvelous sequence. In it there are six uses of the modal auxiliaries "would," "should," and "could." The sequence begins with a conditional dependence on Marcia's forgiveness but as it gains momentum, the modal auxiliaries indicate first possibilities then probabilities, then certainties. Difficulties are raised only to be overridden easily. Finally, in a stirring conclusion, the modal auxiliaries disappear altogether as Bartley's reverie carries him triumphantly into the halls of Congress.] He had thought of going first to Halleck, and returning the money, but he was willing to give himself the encouragement of Marcia's pleasure, of her forgiveness and her praise in an affair that had its difficulties and would require all his manfullness. [The pleasant thing about reverie is that one encounters no resistance in it. Desires can be realized without

any of those troublesome and irritating obstacles that real life awkwardly interposes. Bartley's reverie of reform *might* lead to better behavior
(if not to Congress), but it is precariously dependent on circumstance.
It is grounded not on principle but on the putative responses of others:
i.e., Marcia's pleasure, forgiveness, and praise. Morality is real to Bartley
only in terms of someone else's proper *appreciation* of his moral performance.] The maid met him at the door with little Flavia, and told
him that Marcia had gone out to the Hallecks', but had left word that
she would soon return, and that then they would have supper together.
Her absence dashed his warm impulse, but he recovered himself, and
took the little one from the maid. [Marcia is not found where his reverie placed her—an initial setback.] He lighted the gas in the parlor, and
had a frolic with Flavia in kindling a fire in the grate, and making the
room bright and cheerful. He played with the child and made her laugh;
he already felt the pleasure of a good conscience, though with a faint
nether ache in his heart which was perhaps only his wish to have the
disagreeable preliminaries to his better life over as soon as possible.
[Again, if everything were to go just right, Bartley might become a
relatively reformed man. But the irony of Bartley's inversion of ethical
time—his premature pleasure in good conscience, his dislike of the disagreeable preliminaries—like the other ironies in this sequence, all show
the vulnerability of "the frail structure of his good resolutions."]

(p. 274)

The next sequence begins with Marcia entering in a feverish transport of
jealousy, a monumental mischance of timing. It is after the ensuing battle
that Bartley leaves Marcia, loses Halleck's money, and fades out of the novel
until its concluding episodes.

10. Punitive Tragedy

William Gibson, in his brilliant introduction to the Riverside edition of *A
Modern Instance*, denies that Howells is writing "punitive tragedy" (p. xii).
But I have demonstrated, I feel, that Howells is doing just that. (I take it
Gibson would not have raised the issue had the possibility not worried him.)
Howells' tracking of Bartley's consciousness is a study in the pathology of pathos. In form, *A Modern Instance* is a clinical case history; Bartley is examined much as if he were the symptom of a dread disease.[36] Much of our pleasure in the novel derives from our participation in the rigorous making of this
case. To say this is only to restate what I have said earlier: that Howells structures Bartley's consciousness to reveal his negative ethos. At times we may
feel that the ultimate meaning of the novel is: whatever Bartley is, is wrong.

This raises an interesting problem: what is the reader's relation to such a
completely negated character? Unmistakably, Bartley is intended to be a
moral mirror, reflecting the reader's bad conscience. It seems to confirm our
experience of the novel to discover that Samuel Clemens only half-jokingly

suspected that he was the model for Bartley, and that Howells himself confessed Bartley was a self-portrait.[37] The rhetoric of the novel is designed to implicate any reader who is less than a saint in his domestic relations. The universality of the novel lies in its examination of not the content but the structure of marital quarrels, and yet more in its truly brilliant phenomenological analysis of the processes of rationalizing and justifying emotional failures and brutalities. This is where the novel is most alive: like Eliot's fiction, it is designed to stimulate the reader's ethical imagination. My interpolated comments on some of Howells' passages represent a response to Howells' implicit invitation. Through Bartley's characterization Howells achieves the traditional function of the novel: to increase our knowledge of the self. If the self we learn to know is a rather mean one—well, there is pleasure as well as pain in such self-unmasking. Exposing the wound to the open air can be therapeutic. Besides, as Aristotle says, there can be no learning unaccompanied by pain.

Perhaps, if anything, the novel is not painful enough. It is as fine a phenomenological analysis of ethos as can be found in American fiction, but the relentlessness of Howells' conversion of pathos into ethos leaves a sense of incompleteness, as if in some way the novel had nullified itself. I think it is no psycho-logical contradiction to state that the vital and the unsatisfying quality of the novel both stem from the same root: this close engagement with a negative self grounded in an ultimately stifling quotidien world. The ultimate message of *A Modern Instance* is a massive negation of consciousness. Consciousness has been so carefully, so beautifully tracked only in order to show it up, confound it, degrade it, disavow it. Certainly, Howells proves the need to disavow the selfish, essentially negative consciousness of which Bartley is the vehicle. Yet in doing so he runs into the same problem that T. S. Eliot saw in Irving Babbitt's ethics of the inner check: "And what, one asks, are all these millions, even these thousands, or the remnant of a few intelligent hundreds, going to control themselves *for?*"[38] The problem, then, is not the presence of a negative ethos but the absence of any moving passion.

In a sense, *A Modern Instance* presents a giant STOP sign to life's most vital forces. It seems to proclaim that "Consciousness will be ethical or it will be nothing at all."[39] This negativity appears not only in the ethical structuring of Bartley's consciousness but in Howells' outright refusal to track a consciousness which could *not* be relevantly structured in purely ethical terms. At the end of the novel, Howells tells us why he won't tell us how Marcia reacted to the news of Bartley's death:

> Marcia had been widowed so long before that this event could make no outward change in her. *What inner change, if any, it wrought is one of those facts which fiction must seek in vain to disclose.* But if love such as had been did not deny his end the pang of fresh grief, we may be sure that her sorrow was not unmixed with self-accusal as unavailing as it was passionate, and perhaps as unjust.   (p. 360; my italics)

The one notation we do get in fact makes a stab at ethical structuring, but

Marcia's perverse pathos cannot be reduced to these terms.

The impossibility of getting inside Marcia's passion is not, of course, a built-in defect of fiction, as Howells proclaims; he is merely projecting his own limits onto fiction in general.[40] That Howells found Marcia's inner life impossible to track is clear from the novel itself; it is one cause of the novel's esthetic imbalance. Certainly, we are given some signs of Marcia's character: she is prone to hot flushes, quivering lips, and bosom-heaving. Evidently she has a passionate nature: "At the door [Bartley] bent down his head and kissed her. 'Good night, dear—friend.' 'Good night,' she panted; and after the door had closed upon him she stooped and kissed the knob on which his hand had rested" (p. 10). This is almost as explicit as Casper Goodwood's orgiastic rocking of Isabel Archer's boat as they kiss, near the end of *Portrait of a Lady*. Moreover, as Kermit Vanderbilt convincingly argues, Howells antici- pated Jung in giving Marcia a full-blown Electra complex.[41] Still and all, we find out no more about Marcia than she shows through the external language of gesture. Our knowledge of Bartley would be commensurate if it stopped short with his weak chin and possessiveness toward mince pies.

Howells once thought of titling his novel *The New Medea*. Gibson points out:

> The germ for the novel came to him after he had witnessed a perfor-
> mance of *Medea* in Boston, probably in April, 1875. Howells had read
> Euripides in a German translation in Venice in 1862, and when he
> witnessed Francesca Janauschek's fiery re-creation on the stage of
> Medea's love for the self-centered Jason as it turned into hatred and
> engendered terrible acts of revenge, he said to himself, as he told an
> interviewer many years later: "This is an Indiana divorce case . . . and
> the novel was born."   (p. v)

One can *almost* see Bartley as a modernized Jason, minus the cold-blooded ambition; but Euripides' *Medea* was not an Indiana divorce case and Marcia is not Medea. Above all, she lacks the enabling of passion which is the essence of Euripides' character, a character who has things in common with the elemental forces of Nature. Howells is unwilling or unable to allow passion that much grace. (Medea, it should be remembered, is delivered from her enemies by a sun-chariot; Nature never did betray. . . .)[42]

Howells can hint at a pathology[43] in Marcia but her consciousness, unlike Bartley's, is too deeply irrational for convincing ethical structuring—which is why Howells shies away from it. In discussing the marital quarrel cited above, I noted that Marcia appears to work at losing her initial advantage, and that Howells only barely hints at her motivations. What lies behind her jealous delusions, which she herself recognizes as delusions once out of her trans- ports is left relatively unexplored—though the inferences Vanderbilt makes from the few hints Howells does provide seem plausible. Howells drops enough of these hints to give us the outline of a deeply perverse, even maso- chistic character. But he avoids filling in this outline, precisely because to do so would force him to depict a consciousness which is not reducible to his ethical terms. Thus Marcia is doubly reduced from Euripides' Medea: her passion is not enabled with power and, even in its powerlessness, it is not fully brought to light.

The limitations of Howells' technique are the limitations of moral sympathy.[44] That Howells was more than subliminally aware of these limitations shows up in his treatment of Atherton, whose problematic characterization is, I believe, Howells' tacit admission of the insufficient moral basis of the novel. Gibson summarizes the problem:

> As for Atherton (who figures almost entirely in that part of the novel written after Howells's illness),[45] there can be little doubt that Howells more than once puts into his mouth certain of his own ideas. . . . Nonetheless any careful reading of the closing debate between Atherton and his wife over the Hubbards' behavior and Ben's desire to marry the widowed Marcia will reveal a constant play of sharp dramatic irony between their eloquent moralizing and their luxurious surroundings. . . . In final effect, Atherton seems a respectable, hair-splitting snob, whose deepest failure lies in his judging and condemning others for thoughts and impulses which he cannot understand.
>
> That Howells wholly or consistently intended this impression is not clear. Atherton speaks for the good society of Howells's day; and yet Howells clearly undercuts a number of his character's most intense speeches.   (p. xiv)

The fuzziness of Howells' characterization of Atherton reflects his own moral uncertainties, which he was unable fully to transform into literature. In *A Modern Instance* Howells attacks those aspects of the community ethos which encourage the baser tendencies of a Bartley. Ultimately, though, Howells' judgment of Bartley depends merely on a refined version of that community ethos, an ethos which, on Howells' own showing,[46] no longer warrants conviction.

Howells has, with great skill and admirable intelligence, maneuvered himself into a blind alley, on both the technical and moral levels. He has pushed a nineteenth-century moral paradigm, the attack on the selfish self, to the point where it breaks down under the weight of its own negative data. The negative recommendation of the ethos—that is, the worthlessness of being a certain sort of self—is, in effect, overdetermined, while the counter-balancing aspects of the ethos (Dickens' "sentimentality," for example)[47] have been eliminated, as no longer credible. The result is a fiction subtle, even brilliant, in its ethical awareness but which ultimately lacks the density[48] and balance of Victorian fiction—or the very different density and balance of the fiction of Howells' contemporary and friend, Henry James.

4. Henry James:
An Ethics of Intensity

I. "The Beast in the Jungle"

1. "A Great Negative Adventure": Irony and Sympathy

Henry James's great admiration for George Eliot did not preclude reservations about the chilling effect of her ethical emphasis; by the same token, James unequivocally approved Balzac's participation in the intense life of even his most vicious characters.[1] James believed the flaw in his own *Roderick Hudson* was that Roderick's moral disintegration takes place too rapidly to sustain the reader's sympathy for him: "My mistake on Roderick's behalf—and not in the least of conception, but of composition and expression—is that, at the rate he falls to pieces, he seems to place himself beyond our understanding and our sympathy."[2] The flaw is not in conception—for James intended his book to be a critical analysis of Roderick's disintegration—but in composition and expression, since it was essential that the process of disintegration should engage the reader emotionally as well as ethically.

In his preface to "The Beast in the Jungle" James considers the problem of how to maintain tension in describing "a great negative adventure" (*A.N.*, p. 247), or, to put it another way, how to characterize a self-negating hero without negating the interest of the character and the sympathies of the reader. James takes up the problem at precisely the point where Howells' novels break down. At one point John Marcher reflects on May Bartram's choice of attitudes toward his obsessive fantasy: "If she didn't take the ironic view she clearly took the sympathetic."[3] James's contemporary readers and critics may have been justified in complaining that his early work overemphasized the analytic and ironic view,[4] but one of the unique qualities of his later fiction is precisely its blend of irony and sympathy.

James believed that merely negative irony, that criticizes without envisioning any alternatives, is artistically and ethically invalid. In his preface to "The Lesson of the Master" James explains his idea of genuinely "operative irony":

> I was able to plead that my postulates, my animating presences, were all, to their great enrichment, their intensification of values, ironic; the strength of applied irony being surely in the sincerities, the lucidities, the utilities that stand behind it. When it's not a campaign of a sort, on behalf of the something better (better than the obnoxious, the provoking object) that blessedly, as is assumed *might* be, it's not worth

> speaking of. But this is exactly what we mean by operative irony. It
> implies and projects the possible other case, the case rich and edifying
> where the actuality is pretentious and vain.   (*A.N.*, p. 222)

The "something better" might be suggested solely by nuances of style, in the
manner of Wolfgang Iser's "gap of indeterminacy" or of the "world elsewhere" that Richard Poirier glimpses in those white spaces between the lines
of American texts.[5]

But James also has in mind a more determinate imagining of "the honor-
able, the producible case":

> What better example than this of the high and helpful public and, as
> it were, civic use of the imagination—a faculty for the possible fine
> employments of which in the interest of morality my esteem grows
> every hour I live. How can one consent to make a picture of the pre-
> ponderant futilities and vulgarities and miseries of life without the
> impulse to exhibit as well from time to time, in its place, some fine
> example of the reaction, the opposition or escape?   (*A.N.*, p. 223)

Howells, characteristically, tries to solve this problem by bursts of rhetoric
as unconvincing to the reader as they are to the characters and the author
himself. But in his preface James seems to apologize for just such a rhetorical
imposition at the end of "The Beast in the Jungle":

> My picture leaves him [Marcher] overwhelmed—at last he understood;
> though in thus disengaging my treated theme for the reader's benefit I
> seem to acknowledge that this more detached witness may not success-
> fully have done so. I certainly grant that any felt merit in the thing
> must all depend on the clearness and charm with which the subject just
> noted expresses itself.   (*A.N.*, pp. 247-248)

In fact, the disengaged theme has been present in every line of the story, in
the mode of operative irony. The cunning reader will catch the clues to
Marcher's egoism immediately; the more credulous may need the disengaged
revelation—thus implicating themselves in Marcher's unawareness.[6]

James practices the sort of mystification in "The Beast in the Jungle" that
he had elsewhere noted as a charming effect:

> He [the artist] has consistently felt it (the appeal to wonder and terror
> and curiosity and pity and to the delight of fine recognitions, as well as
> to the joy, perhaps sharper still, of the mystified state) the very source
> of wise counsel and the very law of charming effect. He has revelled in
> the creation of alarm and suspense and surprise and relief, in all the
> arts that practice, with a scruple for nothing but any lapse of applica-
> tion, on the credulous soul of the candid or, immeasurably better, on
> the seasoned spirit of the cunning reader.   (*A.N.*, p. 253)

The mystifying device is point of view: so long as the reader treats Marcher's
point of view as a transparency through which the story is told—the story of

a mysterious beast—the reader misses the real subject of the story. The real subject, foregrounded in the demystifying ending, is Marcher's point of view. So "The Beast in the Jungle" is constructed around an epistemological *peripeteia* in which, traditionally, the protagonist discovers his tragic identity, and in which, less traditionally, subject and object in the story, figure and ground, reverse themselves. Marcher's point of view *is* the beast, and the ending is simply the culmination of the leap which has been in process throughout.

Unlike Roderick Hudson, Marcher falls to pieces over the course of the story and we, perhaps, along with him. The mystification, however, prevents a premature foreclosure of our sympathy, as in Marcher's response to May Bartram's allusion to their original meeting:

> He had forgotten, and he was even more surprised than ashamed. But the great thing was that he saw it was no vulgar reminder of any "sweet" speech. The vanity of women had long memories, but she was making no claim on him of a compliment or a mistake. With another woman, a totally different one, he might have feared the recall of possibly even some imbecile "offer." So, in having to say that he had indeed forgotten, he was conscious rather of a loss than of a gain. (p. 195)

On one level this passage appears to tell us some pleasant things about both May and Marcher: she is not vulgar and he is perceptive enough to recognize it. In fact both these propositions are true. It is only on later consideration that we recognize Marcher's exaggerated fear of claims being made upon him, his association of the conventions of romantic passion with vulgarity and imbecility, and his weighing of relationships in a scale of profit and loss.

In some respects, we can see in Marcher simply a late version of the Victorian villain of "self." As with Tito Melema and Bartley Hubbard, we are shown Marcher's consciousness busy in the continuous production of bad faith. Nowhere is this more evident than in his self-congratulating estimation of his unselfishness: "He had disturbed nobody with the queerness of having to know a haunted man. . . . This was why he had such good—though possibly such rather colourless—manners; this was why, above all, he could regard himself, in a greedy world, as decently—as, in fact, perhaps even a little sublimely —unselfish" (p. 203). This self-serving rationalization is far more visible when one isolates the passage by quoting it than when one reads it in context. The clues are there, clues of the same sort that alert us to the presence of "self" in a Victorian narrative, but James deliberately understates them.

It is not completely evident where the reader stands in relation to Marcher until the explicit ending. However, both the passages I have quoted hint at a flaw in Marcher that is comparable to that found in one variant of the Victorian villain of "self," albeit developed here in a uniquely extreme fashion. In the first passage, Marcher "in having to say that he had indeed forgotten . . . was conscious rather of a loss than of a gain"; in the second, "He had disturbed nobody with the queerness of having to know a haunted man." Both passages show a decidedly weird habit of thought in Marcher. The weirdness in the second passage, that of considering the avoidance of human relation as the height of virtue, is fairly obvious. But the first passage is likely to disturb the reader without its being immediately apparent why. On reflection, we can see that Marcher's typical mode of thought is perversely backwards; *on this occasion* he regrets forgetting—but generally forgetting, for him, is a gain and remembering a loss.

In both cases, Marcher reveals an extreme habit of negation: negation of relationship, negation of consciousness. The pity and terror of "The Beast in the Jungle" center in its dramatization of a "poor sensitive gentleman" (*A.N.*, p. 246) caught in a quietly violent, perfectly unknowing self-cancellation. By negating his world Marcher negates himself, and thus moves us from the Victorian paradigm of "self" to the modern paradigm of solipsism.

2. Marcher as Solipsist: The Ethics of Intensity

There is a sort of negativity built into the Victorian villain of "self." The larger he tries to become, through self-aggrandizement, the smaller he actually seems. The gap between his large claims and the petty self they are made for is illustrated afresh in each show of ego. (The exception would be characters like Quilp, whose demonic aspects savor more of the id than the ego.) If these exemplars of "self" grow smaller in their attempts at self-magnification, they nonetheless do make active claims—to money, sexual satisfaction, social status, or merely to privilege and comfort. They impinge on others, seeking mirrors to reflect their inflated ego-images (like Sir Willoughby Patterne) or victims over whom they can exercise power (like Grandcourt and Quilp). This holds for even the most shrunken of souls, such as Casaubon.

Marcher differs from all these; he has a quite genuine sensitivity and even perceptiveness. But his egoism is even more disturbingly negative, his existence even more qualified by non-being. The most disturbing thing about Marcher's egoism is that it makes no claims on the social world; to make such claims, however unjustified, at least establishes a relationship, acknowledges— in however left-handed a fashion—the necessity *of* relation. But Marcher seeks neither material goods nor social status; the status he claims is totally self-defined: it is a personal vision of his own spiritual self-sufficiency. Marcher is a man of imagination and perception, but he employs his highest qualities solely to escape any human claim upon them.

Leo Bersani's characterization of Merton Densher almost exactly fits Marcher: "The psychological and moral point of view . . . is that of a single isolated individual justifying and consecrating his alienation from everything except his inner vision of an ideal above and beyond the unacceptable real possibilities of life."[7] The equation is exact once we substitute an inner vision of a *dread* for that of an ideal, and, in fact, Marcher idealizes his sense of dread. He is a self-cherishing hero, who celebrates the unique *frissons* of his carefully nurtured *angst*. Marcher's diffidence is, of course, a social mask. His avoidance of social claim enables him to play, without fear of challenge, a grandiose role in the theater of his own consciousness. He is perfectly certain that his vision of the beast marks him out as special, unique; he assures himself that May Bartram's prospective death could not be the horrific event he awaits for "it had only the stamp of the common doom" (p. 228). But where else, if not within the sphere of the "common doom," do the possibilities for passionate response and special relations exist?

Marcher's failure is total: he fails in conception, perception, and emotion— all of which are acts of relationship. Marcher is what he does, which is nothing. May intentionally puns when she assures Marcher he will never "consciously" suffer and questions whether "nothing" is better:

> "Then tell me if I shall consciously suffer?"
> She promptly shook her head. "Never!"
> It confirmed the authority he imputed to her, and it produced on
> him an extraordinary effect. "Well, what's better than that? Do you
> call that the worst?"
> "You think nothing is better?" she asked.   (pp. 224–225)

The repeated, unaware choice of nothing sums up the all-negating process of Marcher's consciousness. James images this in a figure so cruel that we can accept it only because it is Marcher's own unconscious judgment on himself: "Such a feature in one's outlook [Marcher's beast] was really like a hump on one's back. The difference it made every minute of the day existed quite independently of discussion. One discussed, of course, *like* a hunchback, for there was always, if nothing else, the hunchback face" (p. 205).

Marcher's vainglory for having disturbed nobody with the queerness of having to know "a hunted man" is more than pride masquerading as humility; it is a perverse denial of a classical principle of identity. Though James did not specifically point the contrast, his story takes on fuller significance when seen in relation to this classical principle: Marcher is a counter-archetype. As George E. Dimock shows in his luminous article, "The Name of Odysseus," the meaning of Odysseus' name—"Trouble"—is emblematic of the identity of the archetypal hero of Western consciousness. Odysseus affirms his identity by causing as well as suffering pain: "The secret of life which Odysseus has come to the realms of the dead to discover is the necessity of pain and its value." The value of pain lies not, of course, in itself, but in its inextricable involvement with identity: "In exposing Odysseus to Poseidon, in allowing him to do and suffer, Zeus is odysseusing Odysseus, giving him his identity. In accepting the implications of his name, Trouble, Odysseus establishes his identity in harmony with the nature of things. In the ultimate sense he is Zeus-sprung, one whose existence is rooted in life itself."[8]

By the same token, Marcher is one of the first American versions of a modern archetype: the protagonist whose existence is characterized by the lack of roots, the avoidance of life. Himself anticipated by Hawthorne's Miles Coverdale,[9] Marcher anticipates a line of modern American anti-heroes: refusers and evaders of life. Since, traditionally, the true hero has risked trouble for and got trouble from women, the refusal or evasion of sexual relationships is the anti-hero's typical gesture. If Marcher never explicitly refuses May, it is only because he is culpably blind to her offer; Prufrock, whom Eliot partly based on Marcher,[10] refuses to disturb the universe by asking the overwhelming question—to invite a sexual involvement that would raise him from the dead; Hugh Selwyn Mauberley, like Marcher, misses the invitation;[11] Jack Burden's hesitation to seduce Anne Stanton leads to her choice of the more odyssean Willie Stark.[12] There could hardly be a more extreme inversion than this last example of one Victorian variant on the villain of "self": Steerforth, Alex D'Urberville, Arthur Donnithorne, and the other selfish seducers. Curiously, the *failure* to seduce has become a modern convention which signifies a protagonist's solipsistic withdrawal, his fear of doing or suffering. These modern characters are judged for their deficiency, rather than for their excess, of passion and self-will. Their self-ishness takes the form of a retreat from claims upon others as much as from others' claims upon them.

"The Beast in the Jungle," then, is one of the great modern dramas of affectlessness. It is not Marcher's desire that is at fault—but his lack of any. He receives his final revelation merely from seeing, at the graveyard, the face of a man whose sole designated quality is his acquaintance with passion:

> Marcher felt him on the spot as one of the deeply stricken—a perception so sharp that nothing else in the picture lived for it, neither his dress, his age, nor his presumable character and class; nothing lived but the deep ravage of the features that he showed. He *showed* them—that was the point. . . . What Marcher was at all events conscious of was, in the first place, that the image of scarred passion presented to him was conscious too—of something that profaned the air; and, in the second, that, roused, startled, shocked, he was yet at the next moment looking after it, as it went, with envy. . . . The stranger passed, but the raw glare of his grief remained, making our friend wonder in pity what wrong, what wound it expressed, what injury not to be healed. What had the man *had* to make him by loss of it, so bleed and yet live?
>
> (pp. 241-242)

The divestiture of the stranger's social attributes is as overt as anything in Whitman. What matters is not dress, nor age, nor even character—none of the attributes of ethos—but the intensity and authenticity of passion as proved by scars, ravage, rawness. To bleed is to live. James's story is intensely ethical but it champions the ethics of intensity, not those of restraint, renunciation, or abnegation. In "The Beast in the Jungle" to retreat from passion is a sign of an excess of "self."

That passion resides at the center of the ethics of James's late fiction may seem odd to those who accept certain critics' portrayal of him as a compulsive renouncer.[13] Certainly, renunciation is a recurrent theme in James's fiction; but in the later fiction it is always in a tense dialectic with passion and is not always the clearly valid alternative. Indeed, Marcher can be seen as a case history of the corruptibility of the renunciatory impulse.

In James's later critical writings the theme of passion is more recurrent and more forceful than the theme of renunciation. The valorization of passion is especially evident in his late essays on George Sand and Balzac. Frank Moore Colby's comic attack on the supposed licentiousness of the Sand essay is, of course, deliberately exaggerated: "here he is as bold as brass, telling women to go ahead and do and dare, and praising the fine old hearty goings-on at the court of Augustus the Strong, and showing how they can be brought back again if women will only try."[14] In fact, James's essay is constructed around his ambivalence toward Sand and he is careful to cite her as an anomaly as much as an example. James even shrinks somewhat from her vulgarity: "Vulgar somehow in spite of everything is the record of so much taking and tasting and leaving, so much publicity and palpability of 'heart,' so much experience reduced only to the terms of so many more or less greasy males."[15]

But Colby's half-serious objection to James's supposed licentiousness comes closer to the mark than W. C. Brownell's dismissal of him as a writer who evoked "a picture of human life without reference to the passions."[16] What James finally values in George Sand is a passionateness that is triumphant despite the deficiencies of the objects on which it is bestowed: "What greater *tour de force* than to have bequeathed in such mixed elements, to have principally made up of them, the affirmation of an unprecedented intensity of life? For though this intensity was one that broke down, in each proposed exhibition, the general example remains, incongruously, almost the best we can cite."[17] The objects of Sand's passion are less important than the force of her passion—as, in "The Beast in the Jungle," we learn nothing of the cause, object, or occasion of the stranger's intensity.

James's famous essay on Balzac, "The Lesson of Balzac" (1905), presses the case for passion with less equivocation. He does not condemn Balzac's world for its un-Jamesian jumble, its near-insane proliferation of persons, places, things, relationships:

> The relations of parts to each other are at moments multiplied almost to madness—which is at the same time just why they give us the measure of his hallucination, make up the greatness of his intellectual adventure. His plan was to handle, primarily, not a world of ideas, animated by figures representing these ideas; but the packed and constituted, the palpable, provable world before him by the study of which ideas would inevitably find themselves thrown up. If the happy fate is accordingly to *partake* of life, actively, assertively, not passively, narrowly, in mere sensibility and sufferance, the happiness has been greatest when the faculty employed has been largest.[18]

Balzac's is a fictive world justified by its intensity: "What it comes back to, in other words, is the intensity with which we live—and his intensity is recorded for us on every page of his work."[19] If intensity is the criterion, it is clear why Balzac "aime sa Valérie": she is so *intensely* vicious.

John Marcher is not intensely anything, but he has his chance—in May's repeated offer of not an intellectual relationship, which they already have, but of a passionate one. She cannot make this verbally, not merely because of genteel social convention but because what she offers is not a thing nor an idea which can be named substantively, but a current of relationship, a force of feeling that belongs to the realm of the tacit. May becomes, in effect, an embodiment of *l'esprit de finesse* desperately trying to overcome the limitations of Marcher's rigid *esprit de géométrie*. The appropriate language for this task is body language, kinesics; May must radiate rather than speak her appeal. She must try to educate Marcher to emotional sublimity by sending subliminal signals of a totally generous, unwithholding self.

Already suffering from an illness essentially caused by Marcher's physical and emotional neglect of her, May rises from her chair to assure him she will not abandon him: " 'No, no!' she repeated. 'I'm with you—don't you see?—still.' And as if to make it more vivid to him she rose from her chair—a movement she seldom made in these days—and showed herself, all draped and all soft, in her fairness and slimness. 'I haven't forsaken you' " (p. 224). Marcher takes this to mean she will chat on to the end of time about his egoistic obsession. But May's movement is not adverbial, an intensifier of the commitment to verbal reassurances, but a kinesic sign of the need to move beyond words and toward each other. Only so can she save Marcher and Marcher save her:

> She waited once again, always with her cold, sweet eyes on him. "It's never too late." She had, with her gliding step, diminished the distance between them, and she stood nearer to him, close to him, a minute, as if still full of the unspoken. Her movement might have been for some finer emphasis of what she was at once hesitating and deciding to say.
> (p. 226)

Marcher, aware only of the "unspoken," misses the noble eloquence and "finer emphasis" of May's kinesthetic discourse.

The following passage dramatizes May's noblest speech, though there is not a spoken line in it:

> It had become suddenly, from her movement and attitude, beautiful and vivid to him that she had something more to give him; her wasted face delicately shone with it, and it glittered, almost as with the white lustre of silver, in her expression. She was right, incontestably, for what he saw in her face was the truth, and strangely, without consequence, while their talk of it as dreadful was still in the air, she appeared to present it as inordinately soft. This, prompting bewilderment, made him but gape the more gratefully for her revelation, so that they continued for some minutes silent, her face shining at him, her contact imponderably pressing, and his stare all kind, but all expectant. The end, none the less, was that what he had expected failed to sound. Something else took place instead, which seemed to consist at first in the mere closing of her eyes. She gave way at the same instant to a

slow, fine shudder, and though he remained staring—though he stared, in fact, but the harder—she turned off and regained her chair.

(pp. 226-227)

May's presentation is through movement and attitude; she radiates meanings at Marcher, "shining" her revelation at him, imponderably "pressing" toward him—and he, in return, gapes, all kind but all expectant. The result of so much energy failing to complete its circuit is inevitable: May collapses. Marcher meets May's tacit eloquence with the expectation that she will solve the riddle of his irrational anxiety with its cube root.[20] The true answer—akin to that of the riddle of the Sphinx,[21] the answer of humanity—is not within his logic. Marcher fails a life-test graded on the ethics of intensity.

II. *The Wings of the Dove*

1. Self and Other

Michael Shriber's excellent study of James's late style concludes that it "implies an essentially empiricist view of cognition—i.e., a view that relationships between and among things are inherent in experience."[22] William James foreshadowed, though he did not overtly define, this concept, the keystone of his radical empiricism,[23] in his famous chapter on "The Stream of Thought" in *Principles of Psychology*. James argued that "our mental reaction on every given thing is really a resultant of our experience of the world up to that date" (*Principles*, I, 234). Thus:

> When the identical fact recurs, we *must* think of it in a fresh manner, see it under a somewhat different angle, apprehend it in different relations from those in which it last appeared. And the thought by which we cognize it is the thought of it-in-those-relations, a thought suffused with the consciousness of all that dim context.   (I, 233)

To apprehend such contextuality requires an emphasis on the "transitive" as opposed to the "substantive" parts of the stream of thought. It is this emphasis which makes William's *Principles*, his subsequent *Essays in Radical Empiricism*, and Henry's "third manner" in fiction similarly extraordinary breakthroughs into new modes of awareness and which justified Henry's claim that, like Monsieur Jourdain, he had always unconsciously pragmatized.[24] That Henry James meant this, and that he was right, has been elegantly demonstrated by Richard Hocks.[25] Anyone familiar with *Principles of Psychology* and *Essays in Radical Empiricism* must note the obvious parallels between William James's theory and Henry James's practice. R. W. Short notes, for instance, that the antecedent in the late James is typically "not a word, phrase, or sentence, but more generally what has been going on for some time past,"[26] which represents in literary style the "dim context" William James analyzed. The center of the Jamesian sentence is frequently relational rather than substantive: "The relating expressions extend in every direction like the arms connecting the chemical elements in diagrams of molecules. In these . . . the antecedents are indistinct; the referents tend to include all of the complex consciousness of a character or situation achieved up to the present moment."[27]

William's half-admiring protest against Henry's late style is, ironically enough, aimed at the most radically empiricist qualities of that style:

> You know how opposed your whole 'third manner' of execution is to the literary ideals which animate my crude . . . breast, mine being to say a thing in one sentence as straight and explicit as it can be made, and then to drop it forever; yours being to avoid naming it straight, but by dint of breathing and sighing all round and round it, to arouse in the reader who may have had a similar perception already (Heaven help him if he hasn't!) the illusion of a solid object, made . . . wholly out of impalpable materials, air, and the prismatic interferences of light, ingeniously focused by mirrors upon empty space. But you *do* it, that's the queerness! And the complication of innuendo and associative reference on the enormous scale to which you give way to it does so *build out* the matter for the reader that the result is to solidify, by the mere bulk of the process, the like perception from which he has to start. As air, by dint of its volume, will weigh like a corporeal body; so his own poor little initial perception, swathed in this gigantic envelope of suggestive atmosphere, grows like a germ into something vastly bigger and more substantial.[28]

How else but with such a method could one convey a vision of consciousness equivalent to William's: "There is not a conjunction or a preposition, and hardly an adverbial phrase, syntactic form, or inflection of voice, in human speech, that does not express some shading or other of relation which we at some moment actually feel to exist between the larger objects of our thoughts" (I, 245)? No writer comes closer than Henry James to meeting William James's challenge that "We ought to say a feeling of *and*, a feeling of *if*, a feeling of *but*, and a feeling of *by*, quite as readily as we say a feeling of *blue* or a feeling of *cold*" (I, 245-246). Henry, as we shall see, added a few categories—such as a feeling of "almost as if."

In one respect, Henry carries the radical empiricist emphasis on relation further than William, into the realm of social psychology.[29] If Henry James's fiction parallels William James's psychology, it anticipates G. H. Mead's social definition of the self. To Henry James the experience of the self was, by definition, social: "Experience, as I see it, is our apprehension and our measure of what happens to us as social creatures—any intelligent report of which has to be based on that apprehension" (*A.N.*, pp. 64-66). Certainly this is the measure of Marcher, a self defined by its non-relation.

More than "The Beast in the Jungle," in which there are only two main actors, *The Wings of the Dove* works out the experience of social situations. The Jamesian "situation" can be defined as a force field of interpersonal relationships, wherein any change in any part of the field affects the whole field. Or, to put it another way, what a James character mostly thinks about is another James character—frequently to speculate on what that character is thinking about him: "If he had an idea at the back of his head she had also one in a recess as deep, and for a time, while they sat together, there was an extraordinary mute passage between her vision of this vision of his, his vision of her vision, and her vision of his vision of her vision."[30]

James's fiction anticipates Mead's definition of mind and intelligence as the reflex of social experience on the individual, and of the personal self as a sort of eddy in the social process. "The self," Mead says, "is not something that exists first and then enters into a relationship with others, but it is, so to speak, an eddy in the social current and so still a part of the current. It is a process in which the individual is constantly adjusting himself in advance to the situation to which he belongs, and reacting back on it."[31] Compare this with the James passage above. We see over and over in James's fiction dramatizations of the idea that consciousness consists of "the taking of the attitude of the other toward one's own behavior."[32] James not only anticipated Mead's idea but worked it out in a far more complex, not to mention sinister, fashion.

We first see Kate Croy trapped in the situation created by the sponsorship of her aunt, Maud Lowder. Kate herself, though with ironic reservations, is willing to play the roles others assign to her: "It wouldn't be the first time she had seen herself obliged to accept with smothered irony other people's interpretation of her conduct. She often ended by giving up to them—it seemed really the way to live—the version that met their convenience."[33] Milly Theale, from the moment she appears on the London scene, finds herself "in a current determined . . . by others" (I, 299); this current itself is partly determined by "the truth of truths that the girl couldn't get away from her wealth" (I, 135). At a banquet the relative appearance of Mrs. Lowder and Susan Stringham qualify their identities for Milly: "Mrs. Lowder grew somehow more stout and more instituted and Susie, at her distance and in comparison, more thinly improvised and more different" (I, 177). Even—or, I should say, especially—her idea of her own identity is socially derived: "It was a fact . . . that Milly actually began to borrow from the handsome girl a sort of view of her state" (I, 193). (That is, Milly's idea of herself derives from her impression of Kate's impression of her.) Finally, when Milly discovers that Kate and Merton Densher know one another, Kate begins looking "other" to Milly (I, 232) because Milly now sees Kate as she imagines Merton sees her. It is equally logical that for Merton, seeing Milly for Kate's purposes, Kate becomes a ghostly intruder: "it was almost as if the other party to their [Kate and Merton's] remarkable understanding had been with them [Merton and Milly] as they talked, had been hovering about, had dropped in, to look after her work" (II, 83). Mead conceived of no such lurid variations on the theme of self and other.

All social relations are constructions, and all constructions are fictions; but some fictions are true and some are false. Milly's construction of Aunt

Maud's English, institutionalized quality, as defined against Susan Stringham's American, improvised quality, is, for instance, a true construction. But the tacit, constructed, fictive nature of social relations allows a wide margin for deceit. Kate's ghost, hovering over Milly and Merton, is sinister because it presides over a deliberately falsified social construction. Even at best, social relations are roles in a drama, and conflict is intrinsic to drama. Thus Kate, in the process of social survival, must be both an actress playing a prescribed, traditional role, and a "faultless soldier on parade" (II, 38).

The very prevalence of social role-playing gives a special intensity to moments in which the masks could be dropped, as in the early stage of Kate and Merton's relationship:

> It had come to be definite between them at a primary stage that, if they could have no other straight way, the realm of thought at least was open to them. They could think whatever they liked about whatever they would—or, in other words, they could say it. Saying it for each other, for each other alone, only of course added to the taste. The implication was thereby constant that what they said when not together had no taste for them at all, and nothing could have served more to launch them, at special hours, on their small floating island than such an assumption that they were only making believe everywhere else.
>
> (I, 74)

Yet even their relationship is a "particular performance" (I, 60); it cannot exist without enactment, a continually renewed engagement, and is only as good as the best they bring to it. The difference, then, is not between performing and not performing, but between true and false performances. It is really a question of the quality of play.

2. Social Construction: Pseudo-Selves

Some performances seem peculiarly lacking in reality. Since these performances must function as foils for the "more real" ones, defining realness by negating it, James dramatizes them with an extraordinary precision. This precision is created not only by the usual method of "breathing and sighing" but by a fairly forthright demonstration of how the characters themselves are little more than the product of the "breathing and sighing" of a generalized social voice. In particular, the remarkable description of Lionel Croy creates a character who seems almost a kind of anti-matter, a walking void, the breath of negation. As we see Croy from Kate's perspective at the beginning of the novel, in a declining state of fortune, he is a sort of human pseudo-event who is in the process of losing the plausibility that previously constituted him. Kate comments on "the silence that surrounds him, the silence that, for the world, has washed him out. He doesn't exist for people" (I, 76).

But Croy's existence for people is all there is to him; his stock in trade is his perfect, and perfectly meretricious, representation of a social type:

> His perfect look, which had floated him so long, was practically perfect

> still. . . . He looked exactly as much as usual—all pink and silver as to
> skin and hair, all straitness and starch as to figure and dress—the man in
> the world least connected with anything unpleasant. He was so partic-
> ularly the English gentleman and the fortunate, settled, normal person.
> Seen at a foreign *table d'hôte,* he suggested but one thing: "In what
> perfection England produces them!"   (I, 8-9)

The curious reversals of substance and attribute in this passage focus the manner in which society deludes itself into seeing a solid object—what could be
more solid than the stereotypical English gentleman Croy evokes?—in an illusion constructed wholly out of impalpable materials, air, and the prismatic in-
terferences of light, ingeniously focused by mirrors upon empty space.

For Croy, there is no doubt that *esse est percipi*; his figure, skin, and hair
become attributes of their straightness, pinkness, and silverness; his dress becomes an attribute of its starchiness. His substance is the sum of his social
appearances:

> It was so respectable a show that she felt afresh, and with the memory
> of their old despair, the despair at home, how little his appearance ever
> by any chance told about him. His plausibility had been the heaviest of
> her mother's crosses; inevitably so much more present to the world
> than whatever it was that was horrid—thank God they didn't really
> know!—that he had done. He had positively been, in his way, by the
> force of his particular type, a terrible husband not to live with; his type
> reflecting so invidiously on the woman who had found him distasteful.
>   (I, 12)

In the passage above it is Croy's negations that act, that "positively" *are*
something, for what it comes down to is that "there was no truth in him"
(I, 7).[34] He is characterized as a null entity: "The inconvenience—as always
happens in such cases—was not that you minded what was false, but that you
missed what was true" (I, 7-8). He is too positively not there to fit even
esthetic categories:

> She had, however, by this time, quite ceased to challenge him; not only,
> face to face with him, vain irritation dropped, but he breathed upon the
> tragic consciousness in such a way that after a moment nothing of it
> was left. The difficulty was not less that he breathed in the same way
> upon the comic: she almost believed that with this latter she might still
> have found a foothold for clinging to him. He had ceased to be amus-
> ing—he was really too inhuman.   (I, 8)

In response to Croy's almost cheerful claim of being unable to get on, Kate
perceives in the emanations of his flat a nothingness that altogether glows
with reality:

> His daughter took in the place again, and it might well have seemed odd
> that in so little to meet the eye there should be so much to show. What
> showed was the ugliness—so positive and palpable that it was somehow

sustaining. It was a medium, a setting, and to that extent, after all, a
dreadful sign of life; so that it fairly put a point into her answer. "Oh,
I beg your pardon. You flourish."   (I, 14)

The more the description of Croy is displaced to his room the closer we come
to his essence; it is perhaps located most palpably in "the armchair upholstered
in a glazed cloth that gave at once—she had tried it—the sense of the slippery
and of the sticky" (I, 3). The last we hear of Croy is when Kate, at the end of
the novel, tells Merton of the effect of Croy's final divestiture of social plausibility:

> "He looked as wonderful as ever. But he was—well, in terror."
> "In terror of what?"
> "I don't know. Of somebody—of something. He wants, he says, to
> be quiet. But his quietness is awful."
> She suffered but he couldn't not question. "What does he do?"
> It made Kate herself hesitate. "He cries."   (II, 416)

In the preface to *The Wings of the Dove* James regrets having insufficiently
characterized Croy. Yet the characterization of Croy, which begins by describing his slipperiness for others and ends by describing his dread of others,
is as powerful a portrayal of personal nullity as can be found in James's fiction. It represents one extreme pole of James's vision of the relation of self to
society: the opportunities open to but the dread attendant upon a completely
meretricious self, a self constituted only by its social appearances.

The characterization of Lord Mark further develops, though in a less extreme fashion, the idea of the intrinsic limitations of the socially defined self:

> What they best knew [Lord Mark] by at Lancaster Gate was a thing
> difficult to explain. One knew people in general by something they had
> to show, something that, either for them or against, could be touched
> or named or proved; and she could think of no other case of a value
> taken as so great and yet flourishing [Kate's word for Lionel Croy as
> well] untested. His value was his future, which had somehow got itself
> as accepted by Aunt Maud as if it had been his good cook or his steam-
> launch. [The comparisons begin to reify Lord Mark's "value."] She,
> Kate, didn't mean she thought him a humbug; he might do great things
> —but they were all, as yet, so to speak [the array of qualifying clauses
> here is of the essence], he had done. On the other hand it was of course
> something of an achievement, and not open to every one, to have got
> one's self taken so seriously by Aunt Maud. [Lord Mark's most positive
> "achievement" is in the passive case and absolutely conditional on the
> point of view of a social other.] The best thing about him, doubtless
> [doubtless!] on the whole, was that Aunt Maud believed in him. She
> was often fantastic, but she knew a humbug, and—no, Lord Mark
> wasn't that. [He *does* differ from Lionel Croy—not in what he is so
> much as in what he isn't.] He had been a short time in the House, on
> the Tory side, but had lost his seat on the first opportunity, and this

was all that he had to point to. However, he pointed to nothing; which was very possibly just a sign of his real [real!] cleverness, one of those that the really clever had in common with the really void. Even Aunt Maud had frequently admitted that there was a good deal, for her view of him, to come up in the rear.   (I, 196–197)

Lord Mark, then, is a character who, though not a humbug (we should trust Aunt Maud's shrewdness that far), differs from the "really void" only in the construction put upon him by a social other. As he is depicted in *The Wings of the Dove*, he cannot be defined as anything other than a field created by other people's points of view. He exists at two removes from reality: first, because we see him only in terms of what he shows to others; and, second, because this show is purely of an as-yet unmanifested quality. Yet it is logical that this character precipitates the central action in the novel, destroying Milly by his reconstruction for her of Merton and Kate's relationship. Milly is, in effect, destroyed by an emptiness at the center of the social construction of reality. Nothing could be more true than Kate's observation that Lord Mark "has somehow an effect without his being in any traceable way a cause" (II, 67).

3. Social Construction: The "Original Fun of Mistakes"

The inference to be drawn from the characterizations of Lionel Croy and Lord Mark in *The Wings of the Dove*, and from that of John Marcher in "The Beast in the Jungle," is that the self defined purely in terms of social construction and the self defined purely in terms of social alienation end up in much the same place: in a wasteland of palpable negation. Where then, if anywhere, can a true self be found? Can such a self, in fact, exist in so compromised a world? The answer James gives, in the whole pattern of his fiction, is that a true self can indeed exist, but that it cannot escape compromise.

But to understand the inevitability of compromise we must first understand the nature of personal genuineness. This quality is defined most clearly, logically enough, in the response of the novel's truest character to its most false. Milly Theale, at her first great English reception, challenges Lord Mark's construction of the people there, whom she sees as glamorous, as mercenary:

"... you all, here, know each other—I see that—so far as you know anything. You know what you're used to, and it's your being used to it—that, and that only—that makes you. [As good a definition of sociological reality as can be found anywhere.] But there are things you don't know."

He took it in as if it might fairly, to do him justice, be a point. "Things that *I* don't—with all the pains I take and the way I've run about the world to leave nothing unlearned?"

Milly thought, and it was perhaps the very truth of his claim—its not being negligible—that sharpened her impatience and thereby her wit. "You're blasé, but you're not enlightened. You're familiar with everything, but conscious, really of nothing. What I mean is that you've no imagination."   (I, 179–180)

In Milly's definition, to be "conscious" implies engagement, engagement implies discovery, discovery implies wonder. Lord Mark's human failure is his inability to envision the "possible other case," the new reality-script which one can make true only by performing it. It is the kind of truth where, as William James said, *"faith in a fact can help create the fact."*[35]

If, as C. S. Peirce pronounced and William James argued, beliefs are rules for action,[36] Lord Mark's cynicism could be not merely an accurate recognition of the state of society but a sustaining element in that state. His ideas, like everyone's, have consequences, but only in the sense that they add one more minus to a deep negation. William James's pragmatism refuses to separate ideas from what they lead to: " 'Grant an idea or a belief to be true,' [Pragmatism] says, 'what concrete difference will its being true make in any one's actual life? How will the truth be realized? What experiences will be different from those which would obtain if the belief were false? What, in short, is the truth's cash-value in experiential terms?' "[37] The answer in Lord Mark's case is: none. Things will go on as before.

In G. H. Mead's terms, Lord Mark is a "me" without an "I." Although Mead believes that "all selves are constituted by or in terms of the social process,"[38] he differentiates the "me" which is totally submerged in the community experience from the "I" which critically, consciously, reflectively reacts upon that experience. Though the "I" cannot exist without a "me"— since the "I" constitutes itself by reacting upon its internalized social experience—there can be people who are all "me," who are little more than mirror images of the social system:

> We speak of a person as a conventional individual; his ideas are exactly the same as those of his neighbors; he is hardly more than a "me" under the circumstances; his adjustments are only the slight adjustments that take place, as we say, unconsciously. Over against that there is the person who has a definite personality, who replies to the organized in a way which makes a significant difference. With such a person it is the "I" that is the more important phase of the experience.[39]

Social change and evolution are dependent on the "I," the individual, reacting potential of the self. Indeed, without this potential we would have, as William James argues, a dead world: "What really *exists* is not things made, but things in the making. Once made they are dead."[40] Lord Mark's world is essentially inert, his relation to it altogether passive. (The paradox that he "runs about" is a rhetorical reinforcement. It is in spiritual activity that he is null.) Lord Mark is "familiar with everything" in a world where reality can be enlivened only by defamiliarization.[41] Milly doubts whether Lord Mark is "adequately human" (II, 161).

Milly's reality is defined in oppposition to Lord Mark's void; she is familiar with nothing but attempts to be conscious, really, of everything. But there is one problem. About actual personal relationships, the realm that matters most to Milly, Lord Mark is almost always right and Milly is almost always wrong. Implicit in the "operative irony" by which James projects "the possible other case" are some grim possibilities. The generous faith of the superior consciousness collides with the mean facts of the social system. William James broke philosophical precedent in declaring that "In truths dependent on our personal action . . . faith based on desire is certainly a lawful and possibly an indispensable thing."[42] But this leaves a wide margin for a kind of rationalization almost directly opposite to that characteristic of the egoistic protagonists of Victorian fiction, a rationalization based on generous rather than mean assumptions about others.

It is typically Henry James's most valuable characters, his highest representatives of consciousness, who misperceive in this fashion. Lord Mark and the Pococks (of *The Ambassadors*) clearly perceive relations that the supposedly superior consciousnesses of Milly Theale and Lambert Strether discern only at the cost of considerable personal suffering and after innumerable blunders. Yet what reader so perverse as to deny the superiority of the latter figures? *The Wings of the Dove* is an extended demonstration of the truth that to be Milly Theale and wrong is better than to be Lord Mark and right. Error, even disastrous error, is, in fact, the risk contingent upon all genuine experience. In both Milly's and Lambert's cases the moral risk was worth taking and their value is defined by their willingness to take it. They venture all and gain nothing—but they have added their own new possibilities to the scale and the *reader's* gain may be immense.

It is almost as if Milly and Lambert represent the unaware products of an evolutionary leap,[43] as if their errors were all the result of supposing that the primitives they live among share in the civilization which does not yet exist externally, but which their own superior consciousnesses gloriously, if prematurely, project. And the game is worth the candle. In William James's words: "Not a victory is gained, not a deed of faithfulness or courage is done, except upon a maybe; not a service, not a sally of generosity, not a scientific exploration or experiment or texture, that may not be a mistake. It is only by risking our persons from one hour to another that we live at all."[44] Or, in Merton Densher's words: "There would never be mistakes but for the original fun of mistakes" (I, 90). The authentic James characters condemn themselves by their susceptibility to original fun.

4. Performance

In James, then, one validates oneself through a relation to experience which is original and, therefore, risky. An equally important form of validation is the character's relation to biological imperatives. The passion of the stranger at the cemetery devalues, by contrast, John Marcher's dispassion, his emotional inadequacy in face of the ultimate biological imperatives, love and death. But this encounter itself is a relationship. Marcher realizes a truth of self only through a mediation, however unintended, of an other. The biologi-

cal imperative can affect human experience only in terms of social media-
tions. Human passion is not an entity but, always, a performance, a transaction, a negotiation. Negotiations, however, can be transacted with quite
varying degrees of good or bad faith. An excess of bad faith can vitiate the
worth of the negotiation, cheapen the performance, transform energy into
ugliness.

Kate and Merton's performance of their passion begins in high good faith.
If "they were only making believe everywhere else" it is because the generalized society does not sustain high performances. (The kind of performances
this society *does* sustain are those of Lionel Croy and Lord Mark.) In its
early stages, their passion evinces a quite refined ethical scrupulousness. They
avoid embarrassing questions, it is true, but they have scrupled not to lie
directly. Part of their very desire is to do the best by others as well as themselves. "I shall sacrifice nobody and nothing," Kate says, "and that's just my
situation, that I want and that I shall try for everything" (I, 82). The irony of
this becomes clear as the plot against Milly develops, a plot that corrupts the
relation from within. James dramatizes most subtly how this plot effects the
negotiation of Merton's passion (in the sense of his physical desire) for Kate.

Initially, the negotiation is heavily qualified by Merton's considerate recognition of the relationship's difficulty for Kate. His ethical sense constrains
him to avoid any overly selfish claim:

> Life might prove difficult—was evidently going to; but meanwhile they
> had each other, and that was everything. That was her reasoning, but
> meanwhile, for *him*, each other was what they didn't have, and it was
> just the point. Repeatedly, however, it was a point that, in the face of
> strange and special things, he judged it rather awkwardly gross to urge.
>
> (I, 69-70)

As James notes later, "the verbal terms of intercourse" have a "vulgar sound"
(II, 7); this is part of the reason why James employed euphemism and *double
entendre* when describing his characters' sexual negotiations.[45] Whether "the
point" that Merton judges "rather awkwardly gross to urge" is intentionally
a *double entendre* may be questionable. But phallic imagery is relatively explicit in the passage in which Merton, who has returned from America with a
heightened physical desire for Kate, reflects on the difficulty of asking her to
his flat:

> He was aware later on that there were questions his impatience had
> shirked; whereby it actually rather smote him, for want of preparation
> and assurance, that he had nowhere to "take" his love. He had taken it
> thus, at Euston—and on Kate's own suggestion—into the place where
> people had beer and buns, and had ordered tea at a small table in the
> corner; which, no doubt, as they were lost in the crowd, did well
> enough for a stopgap. It perhaps did as well as her simply driving with
> him to the door of his lodging, which had to figure as the sole device of
> his own wit. [Even the most passionate sexual affairs cannot avoid the
> practical questions of logistics—of where and when. Merton has these

questions much on his mind but, even more, he feels a frustrating sense of sexual non-fulfillment.] That wit, the truth was, had broken down a little at the sharp prevision that once at his door they would have to hang back. She would have to stop there, wouldn't come in with him, couldn't possibly; and he shouldn't be able to ask her, would feel that he couldn't without betraying a deficiency of what would be called, even at their advanced stage, respect for her: that again was all that was clear except the further fact that it was maddening. Compressed and concentrated, confined to a single sharp pang or two, but none the less in wait for him there on the Euston platform and lifting its head as that of a snake in the garden, was the disconcerting sense that "respect," in their game, seemed somehow—he scarce knew what to call it—a fifth wheel to the coach.   (II, 5-6)

Passion, biologically grounded and theologically disreputable (disturbing the Edenic quality of their relationship), comes into direct conflict here with social ethos. It sets the two lovers, defined in James's preface in terms of "their intimate affinity and congruity, the reciprocity of their desire" (*A.N.*, p. 303), in opposition: "If Kate had consented to drive away with him and alight at his house, there would probably enough have occurred for them, at the foot of his steps, one of those strange instants between man and woman that blow upon the red spark, the spark of conflict, ever latent in the depths of passion" (II, 6). This conflict obviously qualifies the reciprocity of the desire between Merton and Kate, but increases, in some respects, its intensity. Merton, as attacking self, and Kate, as resisting self, act out a kind of sexual *adagio*.

But fulfillment is also displaced as the sole end of sexual desire. Kate's resistance is not only a reaction to the prevailing social ethos but a means of control. If she is trying to escape being used as a commodity by Aunt Maud, she uses herself as a commodity to gain power over Merton. Kate plans to make Merton's fortune somehow. Meanwhile she attracts him and holds him off, maintaining him in a state of suspension in order to keep him at her disposition for some future scheme:

His absence from her for so many weeks had such an effect upon him that his demands, his desires had grown; and only the night before, as his ship steamed, beneath summer stars, in sight of the Irish coast, he had felt all the force of his particular necessity. [Kate stands in relation to this sexual force as an engineer to a natural force: she is going to run a project with it.] He had not in other words at any point, doubted he was on his way to say to her that really their mistake must end. Their mistake was to believe that they *could* hold out—hold out, that is, not against Aunt Maud, but against an impatience that, prolonged, made a man ill. He had known more than ever, on their separating in the court of the station, how ill a man, and even a woman, could be with it; but he struck himself as also knowing that he had already suffered Kate to begin finely to manipulate it.   (II, 7)

Merton increasingly resents the skill with which Kate avoids even minor dangers, such as sharing a hansom cab with him: "A small matter, however, doubtless—since when it came to that they didn't depend on cabs, good or bad, for the sense of union: its importance was less from the particular loss than as a kind of irritating mark of her expertness" (II, 13). (In the 1950s the cigarette was used as a defensive weapon in much the same fashion.) Discussing Kate's efforts to find opportunities for them to talk, Merton ruefully admits to her, with obvious sexual innuendo: "You keep the key of the cupboard, and I foresee that when we're married you'll dole me out my sugar by lumps" (II, 18).

So far Merton is slightly ridiculous—begging Kate for her kisses does not put him in the most structurally dignified position—but James's treatment is not unsympathetic. Merton's passion seems at least honest, as opposed to Kate's rather cold-blooded management of it. But there is a kind of emotional ratio in literature, whereby the sorrier a character feels for himself, the less the reader sympathizes. Merton's "impatience of desire" (II, 192), his fear of being in "bondage" (II, 20) to Kate, are legitimate enough responses in themselves, but they gradually lead to a state of consciousness more deeply corrupt than Kate's manipulativeness. Kate does not exercise power for power's sake; she means to use Merton for what she conceives as his own good. This motive, an example of "the high brutality of good intentions,"[46] is corrupt enough. But for something far more devious, we should consult another passage. Merton, seeing the "little white papers" that announce his former lodgings in Venice are vacant, begins to get a notion of how he might prove, to himself, by means of a sexual assertion, that he is not overly passive in his relation to Kate:

> The proof of a decent reaction [we are always suspicious of a character who sets out to prove anything to himself, especially if it is his decency] in him against so much passivity was, with no great richness, that he at least knew—knew, that is, how he was, and how little he liked it as a thing accepted in mere helplessness. . . . His question . . . was the interesting question of whether he had really no will left. How could he know—that was the point—without putting the matter to the test? It had been right to be *bon prince*, and the joy, something of the pride, of having lived, in spirit, handsomely was even now compatible with the impulse to look into their account; [so says Merton. But it is not compatible with a supposedly spontaneous spiritual generosity retrospectively to check the balance of the books. Merton begins more and more to reveal himself as John Marcher's alter ego] but he held his breath a little as it came home to him with supreme sharpness that, whereas he had done absolutely everything that Kate had wanted, she had done nothing whatever that he had. So it was, in fine, that his idea of the test by which he must try that possibility kept referring itself, in the warm, early dusk, the approach of the southern night . . . to the glimmer, more and more ghostly as the light failed, of the little white papers on [the] old green shutters.   (II, 193-194)

It is clear that Merton intends to rent the room in order to ask Kate there to give him *his* rent. In so doing, he will not only satisfy for once his sexual desire, but will balance his books with Kate and receive a payment, on account, for acting the lover's role toward Milly that Kate has so carefully stage-managed. From a relationship exemplifying the "reciprocity of desire" we have moved to a relation where Merton uses Kate as an element in a test designed to prove something to himself. In wanting to prove this something to himself, Merton is really appealing to an imaginary audience of others. In terms of the then-prevailing notions of sexual roles, Merton's role in Venice of servitor to Aunt Maud, Kate, Susan Stringham, and Milly, his passive *disponibilité*, is shamefully unmanly: "He was glad there was no male witness; it was a circle of petticoats; he shouldn't have liked a man to see him" (II, 229).

Merton's relationship with Kate begins as a high two-person performance that contrasts with the emptiness of the generalized performances of society. The relation ends in sexual culmination, heavily compromised by the presence in Merton's mind of a generalized other, a convocation of anonymous men summoned to witness his "proof" of sexual mastery. From Kate and Merton's original conception of their relationship as the perfect game which both sides win, it has become this: "He had never, he then knew, tasted, in all his relation with her, of anything so sharp—too sharp for mere sweetness—as the vividness with which he saw himself master in the conflict" (II, 252–253). Sexual desire has come full circle from biological imperative to a mere mock-demonstration of role competency. In the process, the performance of desire has been drained of genuineness, reciprocity, and good faith. Merton's relationship to Kate, their mutually sustained performance, has become less important to him than how others might judge their relationship. The internalized audience has become more important than the actress, and Merton's performance has become increasingly solipsized: it is to himself and for himself, no longer an act of engagement but of involuted self-justification. Merton is now the hero and sole spectator of his own closet drama.

5. The Biological Imperative

In Milly's case, the biological imperative is illness and death. If there is a non-negotiable demand, death would appear to be it. Yet all humans must form some relation to their impending death; death is the ultimate other. And the relation one chooses to death affects all other relations. (This is especially true for those who avoid all thought of death: the avoidance is the relation.)[47] "Death is the mother of Beauty" in the sense that it intensifies things, concentrates the consciousness, motivates it toward seriousness:

> Why had one to look so straight in the face and so closely cross-question that idea of making one's protagonist "sick"?—as if to be menaced with death or danger hadn't been from time immemorial, for heroine or hero, the very shortest of all cuts to the interesting state. Why should a

figure be disqualified for the central position by the particular circumstance that might most quicken, that might crown with a fine intensity, its liability to many accidents, its consciousness of all relations? This circumstance, true enough, might disqualify it for many activities—even though we should have imputed to it the unsurpassable activity of passionate, of inspired resistance. This last fact was the real issue, for the way grew straight from the moment one recognized that the poet essentially *can't* be concerned with the act of dying. Let him deal with the sickest of the sick, it is still by the act of living that they appeal to him, and appeal the more as the conditions plot against them and prescribe the battle. The process of life gives way fighting, and often may so shine out on the lost ground as in no other connection.

(*A.N.*, 289–290)

For Milly, "It was queerly a question of the short run and the consciousness proportionately crowded" (I, 177).

It is in the great scene at Matcham, standing before her "pale sister" (I, 243) in the Bronzino portrait, that Milly begins to form a vision, even an apotheosis, of her mortality:

Perhaps it was her tears that made it just then so strange and fair—as wonderful as he [Lord Mark] had said: the face of a young woman, all magnificently drawn, down to the hands, and magnificently dressed; a face almost livid in hue, yet handsome in sadness and crowned with a mass of hair rolled back and high, that must, before fading with time, have had a family resemblance to her own. The lady in question, at all events, with her slightly Michelangelesque squareness, her eyes of other days, her full lips, her long neck, her recorded jewels, her brocaded and wasted reds, was a very great personage—only unaccompanied by a joy. And she was dead, dead, dead. Milly recognized her exactly in words that had nothing to do with her. "I shall never be better than this."

(I, 242)

The passage associates sorrow, death, art, nobility, and social play-acting. The lady is seen in a double artistic frame: first, obviously, is the portrait; second is the elegant artifice her historical setting required of a "personage." Milly sees as part of the lady's pathos that she is forced to play a historical role, Milly is conscious, really, of everything in the portrait, because it reminds her both of her own mortality and of the necessity for her to adopt a role, to become a "personage."

Milly's choice of role must correspond to her sense of doom, for this is the atmosphere she moves in: "The air, for Milly Theale, was, from the very nature of the case, destined never to rid itself of a considerable chill" (I, 261–262). The role must also unite several paradoxes implicit in Milly's response to her situation: her dual sense of herself as doomed aristocrat and charter member of the democracy of death, as isolated and socially enmeshed, as special and ordinary. Milly works out these complications walking in Regent's

Park after Dr. Luke, through his attitude rather than any statement, has confirmed the seriousness of her illness:

> Wanting to know more about a patient than how a patient was constructed or deranged couldn't be, even on the part of the greatest of doctors, anything but some form or other of the desire to let the patient down easily. When that was the case the reason, in turn, could only be, too manifestly, pity; and when pity held up its tell-tale face like a head on a pike, in a French revolution, bobbing before a window, what was the inference but that the patient was bad?   (I, 163)

Milly's courage is revealed simply in her ability to imagine and contemplate such a ferocious *memento mori*. Her relation with starkness validates her.

Milly is unaware, of course, of the dramatic irony of her own image: that as the intended victim of a plot motivated by her privileged possession of great wealth, she is also isolated and doomed by her aristocratic distinction. She is perfectly aware, however, that her illness isolates her. That is why, with conscious symbolism, she chooses to visit Dr. Luke alone, knowing that in the face of death she will be "really alone," that "Nobody can really help" (I, 262). Yet she is all the more in a relation to people—that is, to people in general: "She literally felt, in this first flush, that her only company must be the human race at large, present all round her, but inspiringly impersonal, and that her only field must be, then and there, the grey immensity of London" (I, 270). In her deliberate momentary self-isolation from her social circle, she is inspired to a vision of the anonymous fellowship constituted by the common doom:

> She had come out, she presently saw, at the Regent's Park, round which, on two or three occasions with Kate Croy, her public chariot had solemnly rolled. But she went into it further now; this was the real thing; the real thing was to be quite away from the pompous roads, well within the centre and on the stretches of shabby grass. Here were benches and smutty sheep; here were idle lads at games of ball, with their cries mild in the thick air; here were wanderers, anxious and tired like herself; here doubtless were hundreds of others just in the same box. Their box, their great common anxiety, what was it, in this grim breathing-space, but the practical question of life? They could live if they would; that is, like herself, they had been told so; she saw them all about her, on seats, digesting the information, feeling it altered, assimilated, recognising it again as something, in a slightly different shape, familiar enough, the blessed old truth that they would live if they could. All she thus shared with them made her wish to sit in their company; which she so far did that she looked for a bench that was empty, eschewing a still emptier chair that she saw hard by and for which she would have paid, with superiority, a fee.   (I, 273-274)

The "real thing," Milly's fronting of the existential limit, is, in effect, a reduction, an impoverishment:

its operation [Dr. Luke's compassion] for herself was as directly divest-
ing, denuding, exposing. It reduced her to her ultimate state, which was
that of a poor girl—with her rent to pay for example—staring before her
in a great city. Milly had her rent to pay, her rent for her future; everything else but how to meet it fell away from her in pieces, in tatters.

(I, 277)

Milly's ultimate fate must be the background for any projected version of her
self, but she must also adjust to the expectations and desires of others: she
has her rent to pay. Yet, if her role is limited, she can still *choose* it (as John
Marcher fails to do), become responsible to it, adopt a military discipline in
relation to it, use it as a means of discovery:

The beauty of the bloom had gone from the small old sense of safety—
that was distinct: she had left it behind her there forever. But the beauty of the idea of a great adventure, a big dim experiment or struggle in
which she might, more responsibly than ever before, take a hand, had
been offered her instead. [The offer only exists, it should be emphasized, as her imaginative construction, as an act of consciousness—which
all the more validates it and her.] It was as if she had had to pluck off
her breast, to throw away, some friendly ornament, a familiar flower, a
little old jewel, that was part of her daily dress; and to take up and
shoulder as a substitute some queer defensive weapon, a musket, a
spear, a battleaxe—conducive possibly in a higher degree to a striking
appearance, but demanding all the effort of the military posture.

(I, 271–272)

It is at this point that Milly begins to move toward the conscious adoption of
two roles that are offered her: the princess and the dove. These roles are, in
part, a "defensive weapon"—but a weapon Milly needs because of her conscious decision to risk "taking full in the face the whole assault of life" (I,
140).

"Life" is what Milly is after and life consists of human relationships felt
intensely: so Milly defined it to Lord Mark in their first encounter. It is, appropriately, Lord Mark who again serves as the foil for Milly's intensified
need of life, an intensity grounded on her relation with death, when he comes
to Venice to propose to her. His motives are mercenary but not malicious; he
knows she is fatally ill, wants her money, has no passion for her, but, com-
placently enough, believes that he can "look after" her. He feels he proved
this in the Bronzino episode: "I wanted you to take it from me that I should
perhaps be able to look after you—well, rather better. Rather better, of
course, than certain other persons in particular" (II, 168-169). But what that
incident proved to Milly was her need for the "real thing," for emotional
depth; and Lord Mark is no more than a well-polished social surface. He cannot make his proposal even moderately convincing: "As a suggestion to her of
a healing and uplifting passion it *was* in truth deficient; it wouldn't do as the
communication of a force that should sweep them both away" (II, 173).

Lord Mark has never previously imagined the possibility of a relation based on uncompromising reality:

> Born to float in a sustaining air, this would be his first encounter with a judgment formed in the sinister light of tragedy. The gathering dusk of *her* personal world presented itself to him, in her eyes, as an element in which it was vain for him to pretend he could find himself at home, since it was charged with depressions and with dooms, with the chill of the losing game. Almost without her needing to speak, and simply by the fact that there could be, in such a case, no decent substitute for a felt intensity, he had to take it from her that practically he was afraid— whether afraid to protest falsely enough, or only afraid of what might be eventually disagreeable in a compromised alliance, being a minor question. She believed she made out besides, wonderful girl, that he had never quite expected to have to protest, about anything, beyond his natural convenience—more, in fine, than his disposition and habits, his personal *moyens* in short, permitted. His predicament was therefore one he couldn't like, and also one she willingly would have spared him had he not brought it on himself. No man, she was quite aware, could enjoy thus having it from her that he was not good enough for what she would have called her reality.   (II, 173-174)

Lord Mark's identity *is*, as we have seen, a social convention. Milly, on this occasion, simply refuses to sustain the convention, and Lord Mark all but disappears before her very eyes. In contrast, this passage makes the novel's most persuasive claim to Milly's validity. "What she would have called her reality" is here nobly enacted. She has attained authority through a superior exercise of consciousness. She is a personage.

6. The Construction of a Personage

Milly's awareness of her mortality leads her to become a personage. She adopts roles in order to play the social game—which is for her the life game— and asks only that the other performances, like her own, be backed by realities. Any social role, however, has a peculiar duality of passivity and activity. One can choose a role, but not in isolation, as any role involves a negotiation with the images others hold of one. Lord Mark offers Milly the Bronzino portrait as a role model and she accepts it because it sorts well with her emerging sense of herself as a doomed aristocrat and with the role of Byzantine princess being thrust upon her by Susan Stringham. With these she combines the role of dove offered her by Kate. Milly finds her roles, then, partly from passive acquiescence to others' images and expectations. But she plays her roles with certain reservations, quite deliberately allowing others to read her performance in a way that differs from her own interpretation of it. Her conscious choice of roles is primarily enabling; it allows her to choose a part in the social drama and to mediate her sense of reality, based on an active, daring consciousness and an intense sense of doom, to society. It allows her also to defend herself and others from the terror inherent in her situation. But this defense, a major motivation of which is her deeply scrupulous consideration for others, becomes a great convenience to the others in their schemes against her.

With Lord Mark, partly because Milly has less consideration for him, she momentarily drops the mask. She thus not only makes things temporarily inconvenient for him, but positively threatens his sense of identity:

> It wouldn't have taken much more to enable her positively to make out in him that he was virtually capable of hinting—had his innermost feeling spoken—at the propriety rather, in his interest, of some cutting down, some dressing up, of the offensive real. He would meet that halfway, but the real must also meet *him*. Milly's sense of it for herself, which was so conspicuously, so financially supported, couldn't, or wouldn't, so accommodate him, and the perception of that fairly showed in his face, after a moment, like the smart of a blow.　(II, 174)

With Susan Stringham, Milly goes more than halfway. Suspecting that Milly is seriously ill but not realizing that she knows how ill she is, Susan tries to protect Milly's sensibility by casting her as an unapproachable Byzantine princess. Actually it is her own sensibility that Susan is protecting. Milly, understanding all this, protects Susan by indulging her in her fantasy, a fantasy that helps give Susan an identity. Milly, then, quite consciously allows herself to be transcendentalized, though she feels intensely the gap between image and reality:

> If one *could* only be Byzantine!—wasn't *that* what she insidiously led one on to sigh? Milly tried to oblige her—for it really placed Susan herself so handsomely to be Byzantine now. The great ladies of that race— it would be somewhere in Gibbon—weren't, apparently, questioned about their mysteries. But oh, poor Milly and hers! Susan at all events proved scarce more inquisitive than if she had been a mosaic at Ravenna. Susan was a porcelain monument to the odd moral that consideration might, like cynicism, have abysses.　(I, 279–280)

How abysmal consideration can become, and how indistinguishable it can be from cynicism, is shown by Kate and Merton Densher's estheticizing of Milly. It makes them feel somehow justified in their scheme to defraud her. Kate reassures Merton by pointing out how perfectly Milly fits into the scene in which they have framed her:

> "But she's *too* nice," Kate returned with appreciation. [She adopts a connoisseur's perspective.] "Everything suits her so—especially her pearls. They go so with her old lace. I'll trouble you really to look at them." Densher, though aware he had seen them before, had perhaps not "really" looked at them, and had thus not done justice to the embodied poetry—his mind, for Milly's aspects, kept coming back to that— which owed them part of its style.　(II, 238)

Certain sinister advantages of contextual thought and social construction here
come to the fore—the scheme against Milly is part of the "everything" that
suits her. Merton manages to assuage his moral qualms by contemplating
Milly's pictorial perfection.

Milly's idealization is a joint construction of Milly herself, Lord Mark,
Susan Stringham, and Merton. The construction begins with Milly's conception of her Venetian palace as a fortress and Lord Mark's conversion of it to
a Veronese painting:

> The romance for her, yet once more, would be to sit there for ever,
> through all her time, as in a fortress; and the idea became an image of
> never going down, of remaining aloft in the divine, dustless air, where
> she would hear but the plash of water against stone. The great floor on
> which they moved was at an altitude, and this prompted the rueful
> fancy. "Oh, not to go down—never, never to go down!" she strangely
> sighed to her friend.
>
> "But why shouldn't you," he asked, "with that tremendous old
> staircase in your court? There ought of course always to be people at
> top and bottom, in Veronese costumes, to watch you do it."   (II, 162)

Milly almost explicitly states that for her the palace is a retreat from life, but
Lord Mark, uncomprehending, puts her back in the social picture. Thus he en-
hances both her esthetic glory and his convenience (since he is about to propose to her). Susan Stringham, quite independently of Lord Mark, further
composes the Veronese, partly to play her own favored role—"It's a Veronese
picture, as near as can be—with me as the inevitable dwarf, the small blacka-
moor, put into the corner of the foreground for effect"—but mainly in order
to put Merton "in the picture": "You'll be the grand young man who sur-
passes the others and holds up his head and the wine-cup" (II, 225-226).

The perfection of the picture somehow, in Merton's mind, "nobly dis-
owns" the sordidness of his sexual bargaining with Kate.

> The effect of the place, the beauty of the scene, had probably much to
> do with it; the golden grace of the high rooms, chambers of art in them-
> selves, took care, as an influence, of the general manner, and made
> people bland without making them solemn. They were only people, as
> Mrs. Stringham had said, staying for the week or two at the inns, people
> who during the day had fingered their Baedekers, gaped at their fres-
> coes and differed, over fractions of francs, with their gondoliers. But
> Milly let loose among them in a wonderful white dress, brought them
> somehow into relation with something that made them more finely
> genial; so that if the Veronese picture of which he had talked with Mrs.
> Stringham was not quite constituted, the comparative prose of the pre-
> vious hours, the traces of insensibility qualified by "beating down"
> [Merton half-consciously assimilates his bargain with Kate to haggling
> with gondoliers], were at last almost nobly disowned.   (II, 233)

The true valve of this estheticizing fog-bank is revealed by its contrast to

"the clearance of the air" in the face of the "intense" "facts of physical suffering, of incurable pain, of the chance grimly narrowed" (II, 326). Merton
resents such clarity, realizing that the function of everyone's pictorial compositions of Milly has been to avoid "the outrage even to taste involved in
one's having to *see*" (II, 325). With intense irony James shows how the ugly
specifics of reality spoil Merton's esthetic construction:

> He had not only never been near the facts of her condition—which had
> been such a blessing for him; he had not only, with all the world,
> hovered outside an impenetrable ring fence, within which there reigned
> a kind of expensive vagueness, made up of smiles and silences and beau-
> tiful fictions and priceless arrangements, all strained to breaking; but he
> had also, with everyone else, as he now felt, actively fostered suppres-
> sions which were in the direct interest of everyone's good manner,
> everyone's pity, everyone's really quite generous ideal. [The abysses of
> consideration!] It was a conspiracy of silence, as the cliché went, to
> which no one had made an exception, the great smudge of mortality
> across the picture, the shadow of pain and horror, finding in no quarter
> a surface of spirit or of speech that consented to reflect it.   (II, 325)

Merton almost recognizes the terror of Milly's reality and the courage of
her response to it—but only to reject it as an affront to his esthetic sense. Her
reality, inseparable from the great smudge of mortality across the picture
everyone has conspired to frame her inside, is too much for Merton, as it had
been for Lord Mark. By the time he reaches London, however, he has safely
estheticized Milly's pathos into a sentimental drama which he can even perform for Aunt Maud:

> His nearest approach to success was thus in being good for something to
> Aunt Maud, in default of any one better; her company eased his nerves
> even while they pretended together that they had seen their tragedy
> out. They spoke of the dying girl in the past tense; they said no worse
> of her than that she had *been* stupendous. . . . It was almost as if she
> herself [Aunt Maud] enjoyed the perfection of the pathos; she sat there
> before the scene, as he couldn't help giving it out to her, very much as a
> stout citizen's wife might have sat, during a play that made people cry,
> in the pit or the family-circle.   (II, 369)

Thus the estheticizing of Milly, the fitting of her into the social picture, the
assignment to her of a part in the social drama, terminates in an extraordinary
display of bad taste. All along this estheticizing of Milly has been a "considerate" form of violating her; so long as she could be envisioned as a personage,
one didn't have to respond to her as a person.

7. The Larger Self

As it turns out, Milly is less the "heiress of all the ages" than a prisoner in the
palace of art. She is a "pale sister" not only to the lady of the Bronzino

portrait but to the Lady of Shallott. (Early in the Venetian scene Milly imagines Kate looking at her "from the far side of the moat she had dug round her tower" [II, 133].) When reality—in the form of Lord Mark's revelations—breaks in, she dies; or, as some critics imply, James kills her. Two of the most striking interpretations of *The Wings of the Dove*, those of Leon Edel and Leo Bersani, identify Densher with James and see the novel as acting out James's own compulsion to substitute art for life, to renounce passionate involvement in favor of esthetic stasis.

Edel and Bersani believe that James saw the construction of art as a justifiable refuge from the demands of passion. Thus the Jamesian hero can fall in love with the Jamesian heroine only after she is safely dead and transformed into an icon to be worshipped. This, on Edel's showing, is the essential theme of "The Beast in the Jungle" as of *The Wings of the Dove*.[48] Edel feels that James condemns John Marcher's failure of passion in "The Beast in the Jungle," but both he and Bersani feel that James endorses Merton Densher's justifications of his renunciation of Kate and his belated worship of an iconicized Milly. In fact, James depicts Merton's estheticizing of Milly with intense irony; he strictly parallels it to the attempts of all the major characters to reduce Milly to an element in their social and imaginative constructions. If she takes center stage in Merton's reconstruction, so does she in some of the others' as well; the characters are well content to benefit from the richness of Milly's Veronese composition. Moreover, Merton's solipsizing of Milly also parallels his solipsizing of Kate as he moves from perfect reciprocity with her to using her to demonstrate his sexual competency to an imaginary audience. Thus, *The Wings of the Dove* is not a solipsistic novel, but a novel in which solipsism is a major theme, rendered by James with excruciating irony. If James drew on his own compulsions he did so with a critical awareness and ironic tension.

The energy of the novel comes from its tensions, only a few of which I have explored.[49] The structurally central tension, which infects all the others, is between the "me" and the "I"—that is, between the self that is no more than the sum of its social conditions and the personally spontaneous self. The "I," by its very existence, redefines social possibilities; it cannot make itself good in solipsistic isolation. Indeed, as Mead argues, it cannot even come to be except through others: "Selves can exist only in definite relationships to other selves. No hard-and-fast line can be drawn between our own selves and the selves of others, since our own selves exist and enter as such into our experience only in so far as the selves of others exist and enter as such into our experience also."[50] Milly instinctively perceives that she can only grow in consciousness by engaging in the risks of social performance. These risks are considerable, since many of the other performers play negative roles, whether they are falsified through duplicity, like Lionel Croy's, or nullified through emptiness like Lord Mark's. These are selves that have gone dead, selves no longer in a process of constructing their world, but parasitically dependent on a completed construction.

The characterization of Milly is in direct contrast, for she has derived from Minny Temple the quality of "moral spontaneity."[51] She has a pragmatically open consciousness, a desire to project herself into unpredictable situations where she will affect others and be affected by them. Milly's self is further validated by the intensity of her response to the biological imperative represented by her fatal illness—an intensity that takes the form of further projecting herself into dangerous social relations. Milly must play a social role, but the nobility of her performance is guaranteed by her moral spontaneity and her consciousness of the "common doom." What finally destroys Milly is that her society cannot live up to the generosity with which she has constructed it.

Society's constructions of Milly, on the other hand, both enable her energy and tend to freeze her into place in an esthetic composition. Milly, as the Lady of Shallott, is destroyed by seeing the reality of her Lancelot, by departing from her tower—but outside the tower is where life, as she herself defined it, is to be found. That she is finally turned into an image, an esthetic icon, is, *within the terms of the story*, clearly a defeat rather than a triumph. The story says this all the more if James in fact knew the temptation to estheticize others from having sometimes indulged it. The art Merton makes of Milly is bad art, spiritually vicious art, and James shows it as such.

James's novels maintain a balance between ethos and pathos. The arena in which emotional intensity finds expression must be social. Roles are a way of playing out emotional intensity, a form for it, but the intensity is what gives the roles their reality. Social performances not validated by emotional intensity are empty, factitious, and self-negating. And when society sustains and supports only such negative roles, James not only condemns it by the operative irony of his "possible other case" but projects the vision of a superior society in which the "something better" might find its home. In *The Wings of the Dove* and "The Beast in the Jungle" James moves toward an ethics of intensity; he judges his characters on the intensity and quality of their responses. In the last analysis all the characters are judged by the extent to which they have widened or narrowed their own and other characters' possibilities of selfhood.

This ethic, perhaps less an idea than an instinct on James's part, has more than slight affinities with the pragmatic social ethic formulated by G. H. Mead. Mead argued that impulses are bad if "the results which they bring are narrowing, depressing, and deprive us of social relations."[52] He claims:

> If we look at the individual from the point of view of his impulses, we can see that those desires which reinforce themselves, or continue on in their expression, and which awaken other impulses, will be good; whereas those which do not reinforce themselves lead to undesirable results, and those which weaken the other impulses are in themselves evil. If we look now toward the end of the action, rather than toward the impulse itself, we find that those ends are good which lead to the realization of the self as a social being.[53]

Mead defines selfishness, like William James in his *Principles*, as the choice of the narrow self over the larger self:

> We are definitely identified with our own interests. One is constituted out of his own interests; and when those interests are frustrated, what is called for then is in some sense a sacrifice of this narrow self. This should lead to the development of a larger self which can be identified with the interests of others. I think all of us must be ready to recognize the interests of others even when they run counter to our own, but that the person who does that does not really sacrifice himself but becomes a larger self.[54]

This ethical position is more consonant with *The Wings of the Dove* than the interpretation that sees the novel as the triumph of art and renunciation over life and social engagement. James clearly shows that Merton's conversion of Milly into art is narrowing, depressing, depriving, and ultimately tragic for himself, Kate, and Milly. Merton's impulse to narrow and freeze, revealed as much in his relationship with Kate as with Milly, shows his kinship not only to John Marcher but to Lord Mark and Lionel Croy, those models of self-negation. Against it we should set Milly's impulse toward self-expansion, the fact that she responds to her intense realization of doom by, first, recognizing her spiritual kinship with "the great common anxiety" and, second, throwing herself into a complex and unpredictable set of relationships.

The critics' problems in evaluating James's evaluations are extreme but not really surprising. For it is of the essence of James's late style to implicate us in crucial moral dilemmas without providing any clear, determinate answers to them. The reader must unconsciously pragmatize his way across extended gaps of indeterminacy. When the reader is a critic, and obliged to respond determinately, he is likely to attack James with some exasperation, as not being properly passionate or properly ethical or properly modern or properly Victorian or as being *too* properly any of the above. In doing so the critic ceases to unconsciously pragmatize; teased out of his shell of moral anonymity he reveals as much about his own ethical and passional predilections as about those of James.

Thus one critic attacks Milly for turning her face to the wall and leaving Merton to Kate, while another attacks her for stealing Merton from Kate by dying in so irresistibly romantic a fashion (the Camille maneuver). And while Milly and Lambert Strether are told, a bit retrospectively, that they ought *not* to renounce, Maggie Verver is condemned *for* not renouncing.[55] The critics rush about on the ground from one pole to the other, while James enacts his dazzling moral performance on the wire overhead. James's true moral "position" can be found not at either pole but, in a radically empirical way, in the force field between them. More modernist than Victorian in both moral vision and technical practice, James was most of all pragmatist and radical empiricist. He did not so much renounce (as the critics might say) Victorianism for modernism as reconcile the modernist emphasis on the necessity of passion for full human be-ing with the Victorian ethical sensitivity to the full reality, the necessary claims, of others. Like subject and object in radical empiricism, ethics and passion are, in Henry James, not substantive objects but terms definable only by their interaction.

5. Dreiser:
Pathos as Ethos

1. Dreiser's Barbaric Naturalism: The Ethical Attack

In 1915 Stuart Sherman wrote his notorious assault on Theodore Dreiser, "The Naturalism of Mr. Dreiser" (later republished under the more piquant title, "The Barbaric Naturalism of Theodore Dreiser"). Sherman's article survives, in anthologies and critical commentary, mostly as a horrible example of obtuse and prejudiced literary judgment. Yet, as wrong-headed as Sherman's evaluation is, it raises some crucial questions about Dreiser's philosophy and its operation in his fiction. Sherman understood rather well what Dreiser was up to.

The premise of Sherman's article seems unexceptionable: he claims that to defend Dreiser as a "realist" begs the question, since all good writing, whether Dreiser's or John Bunyan's, attempts to represent reality: "The real distinction between one generation and another is in the thing which each takes for its master truth—in the thing which each recognizes as the essential reality for it. The difference between Bunyan and Dreiser is in the order of facts which each reports."[1] Any novel, no matter how "realistic," emerges from a process of selection and patterning: "In the case of any specified novelist, the facts chosen and the pattern assumed by them are determined by his central theory or 'philosophy of life', and this is precisely criticism's justification for inquiring into the adequacy of any novelist's general ideas."[2]

Aside from his naïve assumption that bad philosophy leads to bad art, Sherman is on firm critical ground here. There is nothing unreasonable in his insistence that we

> dismiss Mr. Dreiser's untenable claims to superior courage and veracity of intention, the photographic transcript, and the unbiased service of truth; and let us seek for his definition in his general theory of life, in the order of facts which he records, and in the pattern of his representations.[3]

To Dreiser's theory and his representation of it, Sherman was sharply antagonistic; given Sherman's new humanist perspective, with its valorization of ethos and denigration of pathos, he was bound to reject Dreiser and all his ways.

The "nature" in Dreiser's "barbaric naturalism" was the naturalism of a
primitivistic romantic (realism "is simply . . . romanticism going on all
fours").[4] It was exactly the sort of romanticism which Irving Babbitt had de-
nounced:

> for the classicist, nature and reason are synonymous. The primitivist, on
> the other hand, means by nature the spontaneous play of impulse and
> temperament, and inasmuch as this liberty is hindered rather than
> helped by reason, he inclines to look on reason, not as the equivalent
> but as the opposite of nature.   (Babbitt, p. 44)

The primitivistic definition of "nature" leads into the "transformation of
conscience from an inner check to an expansive emotion" that occurs in
Shaftesbury's philosophy (p. 48). And "once accept Shaftesbury's transformation of conscience and one is led almost inevitably to look on everything
that restricts expansion as conventional or artificial" (p. 49). Intensity becomes not a concomitant of a value but a value in itself: "The romanticist indeed bases . . . on the very intensity of his longing his claims to be an idealist
and even a mystic" (p. 126). Intensity is a matter of temperament more than
of reason, as the romanticist by his corruption of conscience "made it possible to identify character with temperament" (p. 263).

Dreiser is a horrible example of all these fallacies; he had, Babbitt asserted,
no standard beyond temperament.[5] But the definitive new humanist attack
was Sherman's earlier article, which is itself simply applied Babbitt. Sherman
attacks the Dreiser hero as all pathos, no ethos:

> He acquires naught from his experience but sensations. In the sum of
> his experiences there is nothing of the impressive mass and coherence of
> activities bound together by principles and integrated in character, for
> all his days have been but as isolated beads loosely strung on the thread
> of his desire.[6]

Though the specific reference is to Eugene Witla and Frank Cowperwood, this
excellent phenomenological description could look back to Sister Carrie and
forward to Clyde Griffiths. But, of course, Sherman intends this as denunciation rather than description. By centering on such characters Dreiser has

> deliberately rejected the novelist's supreme task—understanding and
> presenting the development of character; he has chosen only to illus-
> trate the unrestricted flow of temperament. He has evaded the enter-
> prise of representing human conduct; he has confined himself to a
> representation of animal behavior.[7]

Thus, naturalism is unrealistic:

> a realistic novel is a representation based upon a theory of human con-
> duct. If the theory of human conduct is adequate, representation con-
> stitutes an addition to literature and to social history. A naturalistic
> novel is a representation based upon a theory of animal behavior. Since
> a theory of animal behavior can never be an adequate basis for a repre-

sentation of the life of man in contemporary society, such a representation is an artistic blunder.[8]

The last part of Sherman's argument is the most interesting and the most
vulnerable. Sherman drastically misreads Dreiser by failing to see that Dreiser's major subject is, precisely, what happens when the flow of temperament
is restricted. The tension in Dreiser's fiction is between the flow of desire and
the restrictions of circumstance and convention. Dreiser himself noted that
Sherman's distinction between (1) a "theory of human conduct" and (2) "a
theory of animal behavior" was the weakest point in the attack. In the margins of his copy of the *Nation* Dreiser responded "Rot" and "Good conduct,
of course" to (1) and "animal behavior being evil of course" to (2).[9] These
crude responses go to the heart of the matter. No one now takes Sherman's
attack seriously, precisely because his "theory of conduct" is so obviously
limited to a particular and not universally defensible ethical code—i.e., the
official code of conduct (not the actual behavior) of upper middle–class
American Protestants in 1915. This is what Dreiser meant by "Good conduct,
of course."

As an evolutionary thinker, Dreiser was ready both to attack the current
status quo as an inadequate facsimile of the eternal measure of man and to
defend the biological inheritance of "animal behavior." The relation between
human conduct and animal behavior was problematic rather than axiomatic
for him. On the other hand, Dreiser does not deny his fascination with desire
and temperament nor his relative indifference to "principles." In a sense, it is
even true that Dreiser does not develop characters in the traditional sense but,
rather, represents the flow (though not the unrestricted flow) of their temperaments. But his best characters do not thereby lose coherence; they cohere
not in the integration of their principles but in the rhythms, the ebb as well as
the flow, of their moods and temperaments.

2. Pathos as Ethos

Dreiser's rejection of the Victorian ethos, a thinned-out and provincialized
version of which stands behind Sherman's attack, was central to his fiction.
Dreiser was, in this rejection, "a characteristic product of our revolt against
the nineteenth century."[10] He wrote in 1918, "I have absolutely no place in
my philosophy for a religious or one-sided, so-called ethical interpretation of
life."[11] One of Dreiser's few citations of William James notes his approval of
James's attack on the scholastic absolutizing of truth and morality.[12] Some
of Dreiser's early reviewers praised the very quality of his writing that Sherman most condemned: a 1907 review of *Sister Carrie* approvingly commented, "There is no attempt to complicate the facts as they are with notions
of things as they should be morally, or as they might be sentimentally or
aesthetically."[13] Another reviewer, expressing a basically pragmatic viewpoint, noted that Carrie's conduct "will be instantly condemned by those
who carry a stock of adhesive labels ready for instant application to the con-

duct of others."[14] In fact, Dreiser's avoidance of such labels puzzled a *Dial* reviewer: "It offers one of those special instances, which seem to defy the application of all the general principles of conventional morality, and which puzzle the mind that would base its sympathies upon a clean-cut distinction between what is right and what is wrong."[15] Floyd Dell's review of *Jennie Gerhardt* understood that Dreiser was deliberately avoiding ethical messages: "He does not point to a mistake in Jennie's life or in Lester Kane's, and say that the trouble lay there; that if they had done the right thing, everything would have gone well. There is no right thing to do."[16] Sherman might have felt he had answered such approbations by showing that Dreiser deliberately patterned his fiction so that moral judgments appear to disappear. Sherman did note, accurately, how often Dreiser "comments 'editorially' " against conventional ethical notions.[17] Dreiser's early lack of popular success certainly had something to do with his rejection of the Victorian ethos. But defenders of Dreiser may have partly misconstrued the situation when they attributed his unpopularity almost solely to his violation of sexual tabus.[18] There was, of course, some controversy about *The "Genius"* but the treatment of sexuality in that book, though it hardly deserved censorship, is, in fact, offensive in its simple-minded fatuousness.

Most reviewers of *Sister Carrie* were either unconcerned about or even mildly approved its heroine's sexual unconventionality; however, a number of them *were* disturbed by a more direct threat to the Victorian ethos: Carrie's "hard cold selfishness," her "abysmal selfishness."[19] One reviewer acutely summed her up from this point of view: "She is good natured and kind-hearted, but at the same time perfectly selfish. She is unemotional but relentless."[20] "Selfish" was one adhesive label that seems to have stuck, perhaps because one of the first things Dreiser tells us about Carrie is that "self-interest in her was high, but not strong. It was, nevertheless, her guiding characteristic."[21] If Jennie Gerhardt, Dreiser's next heroine, was the soul of unselfishness, Dreiser went on to create in Frank Cowperwood a hero of "unparalleled selfishness."[22] As if in deliberate antithesis to the mainstream Victorian novel, Dreiser created heroines and heroes of "self," and his evident (though not unironic) sympathy with such egoists may have upset readers as much as or more than any sexual subversiveness.

Sister Carrie, in a quite calculated fashion, depreciates ethos and valorizes desire. Randolph Bourne's early assessment identified the central theme: "The insistent theme of Mr. Dreiser's work is desire, perennial, unquenchable." In Dreiser sex is subsumed under desire, thus outflanking the usual American defenses against the complications and extensions of sexual desire: "As it is currently used, sex has a subtly derogatory sense. What it really means is 'We have no intention of making primary the values and implications which cluster around desire.' " The true hero of Dreiser's fiction is the force of desire:

> His hero is really not Sister Carrie or the Titan or the Genius, but that
> desire within us that pounds in multifold guise against the inner walls of

experience. Sister Carrie was a mass of undifferentiated desire, craving finery and warmth and light and sympathy quite as much as satisfied sex.

Unlike Sherman, Bourne realized that Dreiser built his fiction not only around desire but around all that resisted, constrained, and distorted it; Dreiser is

> significant as the American novelist who has most felt this subterranean current of life. Many novelists have seen this current as a mere abyss of sin from which the soul is to be dragged to the high ground of moral purpose and redemption but this will not quite do. The great interpreters see life as a struggle between this desire and the organized machinery of existence, but they are not eager, as we are, to cover up and belittle the desire.[23]

Perhaps Bourne was thinking of Howells as one of the "many novelists" he contrasts to Dreiser. A reviewer of *Sister Carrie* drew the contrast explicitly: "Its realism lies deeper than that of any story of Mr. Howells for the reason that it deals not alone with the pettiness of human nature, but with its more elemental passions as well."[24] Though Howells' fiction goes well beyond the pettiness of human nature, he does, as we have seen, treat passion as pathological and does structure consciousness in ethical terms. For Dreiser, ethos merely confuses and distorts desire, and consciousness is most authentic when it is least articulate, closest to the nonverbal rhythms of desire and repulsion.

Both Bourne and Sherman saw, from their opposite points of view, that Dreiser's philosophy implied a radical departure from the traditional view of character. Gordon O. Taylor notes: "In *Uncle Tom's Cabin* and in the early fiction of James and Howells, mental process *is* moral reflex. In *Sister Carrie*, moral analysis has become altogether a matter of psychological analysis." In *Sister Carrie* mental/moral problems arise after the fact "of essentially instinctive responses to and accommodations with environmental stimuli and circumstances."[25] Dreiser thus developed an analytic of consciousness designed to bypass the traditional view of "character" by breaking the self down into its tropistic responses and denying the relevance of ethical judgment.

Dreiser's process analysis never ethically unmasks, as Howells typically does; rather it embodies the force beyond good and evil that Dreiser celebrates in *Notes on Life*:

> *Process* is more real than bodies. The life process or Creative Energy (the electro-magnetic theory of matter and radiation) or Deity must be considered to be a part of the process or *The* Process rather than an external creator. In that sense, all that is good and evil, as you choose— good and evil or contrast become necessary factors of the creative process or electro-magnetism or Deity.   (*Notes*, p. 16)

Donald Pizer shows that Dreiser continually dramatizes "the same essential ethical reality—that conscious decision-making has little to do with the most important moments in our moral lives."[26] Carrie's drift into a sexual relationship with Drouet is dramatized not as a crucial moral decision but as a tropistic turn away from cold and toward warmth:

> The 'Counsel of Winter' ... replaces the counsel of a just and sapient conscience; the 'voice of want'—of physical needs and emotional desires—replaces the voice of a moral guide. This new, or newly dominant, voice within her answers the questions posed by environment rather than those posed by conventional morality, and it does so without her conscious agency.[27]

As Ellen Moers analyzes Dreiser's distinction between will and volition, volition is "the minute cerebral-neural-muscular acts, like the yank on a pulley or the discrimination of a color, that separately, and in a definite order, make up the accomplishment of an act of will." Dreiser's interest is in volition: "The large intellectual, moral, and social problems of the will Dreiser left oddly open and vague, somewhere in the realm of the Spencerian inscrutable. But the minute and special problems of volition he attacked with all the vigor and imagination of which he was capable."[28]

Dreiser didn't come across Jacques Loeb's work on tropism until after *Sister Carrie*, [29] but tropism, as Dreiser uses it, is simply a synonym for volition. In *Notes on Life* he describes mental as well as physical life as tropistic. Dreiser asserts that the associative processes in the mind which select and arrange stimuli are

> due to existing chemical and physical attractions and repulsions, or affinities and oppositions, which characterize the various elements—their varying electrons, atoms, molecules, which automatically arrange themselves according to not only such environing influences as hold at the time but their past experience and tensile as well as (possibly) emotional pull affinities.   (*Notes*, p. 65)

One of Dreiser's letters describes *Sister Carrie* as "a story which deals with the firm insistence of law, the elements of chance, and sub-conscious direction."[30]

"Character," then, is not a matter of choice, nor a reflection of ethos—not for a novelist who, as a reviewer said, "adores temperament in all its phrases"[31] and who himself declared in *The "Genius"* that human nature "is not so much governed by rules of ethics and conditions of understanding as a thing of moods and temperaments."[32] All this, of course, is exactly what upset Sherman. Even Floyd Dell, who had favorably reviewed *Jennie Gerhardt*, thought *The "Genius"* went awry in concentrating on the realm of impulse: "In the world of action there is good and evil; but not in the hidden world of impulse. Over the entrance to that obscure world, as over the gate of Dante's hell, might be an inscription: 'Abandon judgment, ye who enter here.'"[33] Dreiser's hero does so repeatedly, as did Dreiser in writing the novel. But what *The "Genius"* discredits is not Dreiser's attempt to develop a new analytic of mood and temperament, to articulate the inarticulate, but rather his attempt to create a credible articulate hero as an advocate of his doctrine. *The "Genius"* fails for the same reason that the quasi-intellectual Ames is the dimmest and least credible character in *Sister Carrie*: Dreiser's difficulty with the task that was second-nature for the traditional novelist—creating a character convincingly motivated by conscious choices.[34]

What Dreiser does do with finesse is create characters moved by volition and tropism. H. L. Mencken wrote of *The Financier* that it evokes "that higher sympathy that grows out of a thorough understanding of motives and processes of mind."[35] But most readers feel such sympathy more for Carrie, Hurstwood, and, later, Clyde Griffiths than for the relatively more conscious and articulate Frank Cowperwood. A 1901 review of *Sister Carrie* cited Dreiser's "ability to suggest those delicate mental conditions in which the thought, or sentiment of one person reacts silently upon that of another."[36] Dreiser is at his best in his rendering of such silent, tropistic reactions—reactions not only of characters on each other but of things on characters.

But these effects work only with characters distinguished by their lack of distinction. This is consistent with Dreiser's belief that life is a mechanism through which an impersonal force expresses itself: "Life is not a substance, but a mechanical phenomenon; it is a dynamic and kinetic transference of energy determined by physico-chemical reactions and their mode of association and succession—their harmony, in fact—which constitutes life" (*Notes*, p. 14). Thus, when Drouet "seduces" Carrie, his "character" has nothing to do with it: "The purse, the shiny tan shoes, the smart new suit, and the air with which he did things, built up for her a dim world of fortune, of which he was the centre."[37] And: "As he cut the meat his rings almost spoke. His new suit creaked as he stretched to reach the plates, break the bread and pour the coffee. He helped Carrie to a rousing plateful and contributed the warmth of his spirit to her body until she was a new girl" (p. 65).

Everything speaks, speaks eloquently, except the people: Drouet, for Carrie, is a semiotic cluster which advertises warmth and competence, the two qualities that, at this moment, she most feels the lack of. His animal warmth helps revive Carrie's sinking spirits.[38] When they do talk, as Ellen Moers has shown,[39] the very inarticulateness of the discourse—"'Well,' he said, as he took her arm—and there was an exuberance of good fellowship in the word which fairly warmed the cockles of her heart" (p. 63)—turns words into something like kinetic vectors. Dreiser editorializes on this point:

> How true it is that words are but the vague shadows of the volumes we mean. Little audible links, they are, chaining together great inaudible feelings and purposes. Here were these two, bandying little phrases, drawing purses, looking at cards, and both unconscious of how inarticulate their real feelings were. Neither was wise enough to be sure of the working of the mind of the other. He could not tell how his luring succeeded. She could not realize that she was drifting, until he secured her address. Now she felt that she had yielded something—he, that he had

> gained a victory. Already he took control in directing the conver-
> sation.   (pp. 15-16)

In this passage, which depreciates words, the key words are: "links," "feelings," "luring," "drifting," "secured," "yielded," and "gained." Feelings are
linked, a struggle for mastery is enacted and, in effect, consummated. The last
sentence, which asserts Drouet's masculine assertiveness, is about as overtly
erotic as Dreiser gets in this novel—but need he say more? And the whole
thing is described in a way that makes it impossible to get any sort of ethical
hold on it. Which vector is right, which wrong? Yet this is a "seduction"
scene.

Dreiser does not lack moral purpose; rather he inverts the paradigm, valorizing his characters for the intensity of their pathos rather than for the clarity
of their ethos. Pathos becomes ethos. For the vertical world of ethos—rise and
fall, heaven and hell, higher self and lower self—Dreiser substitutes the horizontal world of pathos—expansion and contraction, broadening and narrowing, fulfillment and constraint. In her relationship with Drouet, Carrie's is "a
fall upwards," as a 1901 review observed.[40] That is, her horizons broaden,
life opens up for her. What Drouet counteracts is the narrowness of life at the
Hansons: "She felt the drag of a lean and narrow life" (p. 19). Dreiser makes
the reader feel too, feel kinesthetically, the leaden weight of "how unrecep-
tive these two people were," how "it was like meeting with opposition at
every turn to find no one here to call forth or respond to her feelings" (p.
57).

A little vignette, with a minimum of action, conveys the drag of Hanson's
presence on Carrie. The only pleasure she can afford is to watch the life on
the streets go by:

> The first floor of the building, of which Hanson's flat was the third,
> was occupied by a bakery, and to this, while she was standing there,
> Hanson came down to buy a loaf of bread. She was not aware of his
> presence until he was quite near her.
> "I'm after bread," was all he said as he passed.
> The contagion of thought here demonstrated itself. While Hanson
> really came for bread, the thought dwelt with him that now he would
> see what Carrie was doing. No sooner did he draw near her with that in
> mind than she felt it. Of course, she had no understanding of what put
> it into her head, but, nevertheless, it aroused in her the first shade of
> real antipathy to him. She knew now that she did not like him. (p. 58)

"All he said" is, of course, irrelevant, except for the heavy, dull tread of the
four syllables—it is a damp, doughy sentence. It is Hanson's presence that
Carrie becomes aware of. Compare to this her first awareness of Drouet: "The
train was just pulling out of Waukesha. For some time she had been conscious
of a man behind. She felt him observing her maze of hair" (p. 11).

Both Drouet and Hanson impinge on Carrie by way of a kinesthetic force
wave, the one positive, the other negative. She reacts tropistically in both

cases, pulling toward Drouet and away from Hanson. The passive syntax of "the thought dwelt with him" accurately reveals Hanson as the carrier of a negative force. Minnie Hanson, in adapting to her husband's negativity, has gone from narrow to narrower: "She was now a thin, though rugged, woman of twenty-seven, with ideas of life coloured by her husband's, and fast hardening into narrower conceptions of pleasure and duty than had ever been hers in a thoroughly circumscribed youth" (p. 21).

Dreiser perfectly exemplifies Babbitt's Rousseauistic romantic, looking on everything that is expansive as natural or vital and on everything that restricts expansion as conventional or artificial, valuing intensity for its own sake. Worse yet, from a new humanist point of view, Dreiser embodies these moral views so that the reader himself *feels* the dead weight of convention, feels the suffocation of a narrow and circumscribed life.

How different is, say, Howells' treatment of the quarrel between Mr. and Mrs. March in the opening section of *A Hazard of New Fortunes*. There is certainly some irrationality in this quarrel, some mutual manipulation, but the closest Howells comes to capturing the subliminal forces at work in their relationship is merely to assert: "March had seen some pretty feminine inconsistencies and trepidations, which once charmed him in his wife, hardening into traits of middle age, which were very like those of less interesting elder women. The sight moved him with a kind of pathos, but he felt the result hindering and vexatious."[41] This is all Howells can do to make the reader feel the effect of these two articulate—shallowly articulate—people on each other. The result is that they never quite matter enough, they never become weighty enough to carry the story, which is seen primarily through Basil March's eyes. The characters do not sufficiently impinge on each other or on the reader. They are capable of ethical distinctions beyond the range of any Dreiser character—but their observations float somewhere in midair, they never touch ground. This is why *A Hazard of New Fortunes* is so much less intense a novel than *A Modern Instance*, which does powerfully represent impingement, however ethically controlled. *Sister Carrie*, of course, removes the ethical controls.

Dreiser, then, imposes his moral inversion by rendering it so thoroughly and convincingly. But he also, as Sherman claimed, does a considerable amount of special pleading. For instance, when Carrie, before Drouet rescues her, is working in a shop Dreiser attempts to argue her superiority to the other shop-girls:

> The machine girls impressed her even less favorably. They seemed satisfied with their lot, and were in a sense "common." Carrie had more imagination than they. She was not used to slang. Her instinct in the matter of dress was naturally better. She disliked to listen to the girl next to her, who was rather hardened by experience.   (p. 59)

And:

> In the shop next day she heard the highly coloured reports which girls give of their trivial amusements. They had been happy. . . . All that

evening she sat alone in the front room looking out upon the street, where the lights were reflected on the wet pavements, thinking. She had imagination enough to be moody.   (p. 61)

Both passages "grade" Carrie against the shop-girls on the basis of her superior pathos, but neither convinces us of the fairness of the standards. In the first, Carrie's I.Q.—her Imagination Quotient— is merely asserted, not dramatized. So far as Dreiser specifies, Carrie seems merely more genteel. In the second, her superiority seems based less on divine discontent than on solipsistic isolation. In both passages, moodiness is rather too easily identified with imaginative superiority. The difficulties are, perhaps, intrinsic: any "grading" must be based on distinction, which depends upon articulation, which implies an ethos.[42] Dreiser convincingly shows Carrie's tropistic responses and convincingly nullifies the conventional moral notions about how she ought to respond. But his prose cracks under the strain of trying to prove that she is especially sensitive: "Now Carrie was affected by music. Her nervous composition responded to certain strains, much as certain strings of a harp vibrate when a corresponding key of a piano is struck. She was delicately moulded in sentiment, and answered with vague ruminations to certain wistful chords" (p. 106). The rhetorically forcing "Now" and the attempt to convince us of the excellence of what is so purely passive and responsive simply don't work to raise Carrie's status. We might more logically congratulate her maker, as we would the harp's.

At such moments Dreiser comes close to displaying Carrie as a proletarian des Esseintes (or, at least, as a middlebrow esthete).* What makes *The "Genius"* so wretched a book is its several hundred pages of such philosophically shabby special pleading. The "Genius," Eugene Witla, is, as Randolph Bourne said in 1915, "only a second-rate personality," and no one, then or now, could stay involved with his rhapsodic celebrations of his unextraordinary feelings. Bourne went on to say of Dreiser that "his real hero, anyway, is not his second-rate personality, but the desire of life. For this, much shall be forgiven him."[43] To forgive *The "Genius"* is excessive, but *Sister Carrie* and *An American Tragedy* need no forgiveness; in them desire finds effective form.

3. Dreiser's Platonism: "When I Read Spencer I Could Only Sigh"

William James, though he disapproved of the tone of George Santayana's philosophical writings, saw that "his naturalism, materialism, Platonism, and atheism form a combination of which the centre of gravity is, I think, very deep."[44] Dreiser, though allied to the Whitmanesque poetry of barbarism that Santayana so elegantly deplored, has a philosophy which almost exactly matches what James describes in Santayana. Admittedly, to speak of Dreiser

---

*See section 4 on how Dreiser's depiction of Carrie's career involves a similar special pleading.

as a philosopher smacks of paradox. He was relatively inept as a speculative
thinker and, when he attempts to write about abstractions, his prose generally
becomes either unreadably glutinous or banally apostrophic. Nevertheless, the
philosophy Dreiser patched together out of personal observation and propen-
sity, reinforced by highly selective reading, has a great deal to do with the
best as well as the worst of his fiction. If it led to such disasters as *Hey Rub a
Dub Dub* and *The "Genius,"* it also enabled *Sister Carrie* and *An American
Tragedy*.

Dreiser derived his philosophy primarily from Herbert Spencer, so far as its
sources were intellectual rather than experiential. What is interesting about
Spencer's effect on Dreiser is how it helped him as an enablement of his
fiction:

> At this time I had the fortune to discover Huxley and Tyndall and
> Herbert Spencer, whose introductory volume to his *Synthetic Philoso-
> phy (First Principles)* quite blew me, intellectually, to bits. Hitherto,
> until I had read Huxley, I had some lingering filaments of Catholicism
> trailing about me, faith in the existence of Christ, the soundness of his
> moral and sociologic deductions, the brotherhood of man. But on read-
> ing *Science and Hebrew Tradition* and *Science and Christian Tradition*,
> and finding both the Old and New Testaments to be not compendiums
> of revealed truth but mere records of religious experiences, and very
> erroneous ones at that, and then taking up *First Principles* and discover-
> ing that all I deemed substantial—man's place in nature, his importance
> in the universe, this too, too solid earth, man's very identity save as an
> infinitesimal speck of energy or a "suspended equation" drawn or
> blown here and there by larger forces in which he moved quite uncon-
> sciously as an atom—all questioned and dissolved into other and less
> understandable things, I was completely thrown down via my concep-
> tions or non-conceptions of life.

From his reading of Spencer Dreiser drew deterministic, mechanistic conclusions:

> Of one's ideals, struggles, deprivations, sorrows and joys, it could only
> be said that they were chemic compulsions, something which for some
> inexplicable but unimportant reason responded to and resulted from
> the hope of pleasure and the fear of pain. Man was a mechanism, unde-
> vised and uncreated, and a badly and carelessly driven one at that.

It all fitted in with the social injustice and the callous indifference it received, to which he was daily exposed as a newspaperman:

> Also before my eyes were always those regions of indescribable poverty
> and indescribable wealth previously mentioned, which were always
> carefully kept separate by the local papers, all the favors and compli-
> ments and commercial and social aids going to those who had, all the
> sniffs and indifferences and slights going to those who had not; and

when I read Spencer I could only sigh. All I could think of was that since nature would not or could not do anything for man, he must, if he could, do something for himself; and of this I saw no prospect, he being a product of these self-same accidental, indifferent and bitterly cruel forces.[45]

What should be emphasized, however, is not the self-evident naturalism, materialism, and atheism in this response, but how it led Dreiser into a vision of insubstantiality and metamorphosis. Man's place in nature, his importance in the universe, the very ground he stands on, his essential identity—all dissolve into a "suspended equation." It is this vision of the immateriality of matter which Dreiser derived from his reading of Spencer that stands behind his best writing.

Dreiser was a materialist who believed that the universe is composed "of solidified or partly solidified matter-energy forms. And they are the result of primal energy materialized" (*Notes*, p. 141). Material forms are not fixed but responsive to "the endless push of creative energy which has no fixed place of abode unless in the eternal changing of form and knowledge" (p. 139). Moreover, "universal energy may be universal mind" (p. 101). On the social level, the value of all material possessions is relative and socially conditioned. The "value" of a dollar depends on demand, which is relative, so that money value is "in the realm of the Mythical." In fact, "the real value of anything is . . . no more substantial than the mood or desire of the so-called possessor" (pp. 127–131).

Dreiser was, then, the most idealistic of materialists—a fact that was apparent to some of his contemporaries, if not to Stuart Sherman. In his 1915 article Randolph Bourne commented that "Of sordid realists Mr. Dreiser is certainly the most idealistic. You cannot disillusion him. He still believes in, and still gives, a sense of the invincible virginity of the world."[46] The world of flux described above would, of course, be ever renewing itself. H. L. Mencken, in 1916, noted a strain of philosophical idealism in Dreiser which recalled Berkeley and Fichte: "He would interpret the whole phenomenon of life as no more than an appearance, a nightmare of some unseen sleeper or of men themselves."[47] In *The "Genius"* Dreiser speculates that the world might be "a state of mind, and as such, so easily dissolvable."[48] (From Sherman's point of view this notion would be, of course, *worse* than materialism, since it reduces all of nature to mood and temperament.)

Dreiser described buildings, fashions of clothing, etc.—all that critics have attacked as the apparatus of an earth-bound "naturalist"—so specifically precisely because he was fascinated by their shimmering temporality:

> And the time seems certain to come—the mysterious processes of nature and change and disillusionment being what they are—when there will be no least record in any essence anywhere of either of you, neither as to this joint stage appearance or in any other way. And more, it is not only entirely possible, but plausible that in the endlessly changing welter and play of forces, the society in which you thought you were

entities, plus the period of time in which this appearance of you both was made, will merge and be effaced, leaving no trace of all that was so dramatically enacted. Like a letter or a word at one time drawn in water, they will not be.   (*Notes*, p. 272)

Nature is a masquerade since it "has the power to assume endless . . . disguises and at the same time the power to end them and be that which can be something else when it chooses" (p. 209). The human equivalent of this is that "Nature has invented a game of hide-and-seek in which *all*, whether they choose to be or not, by their ignorance thrust upon them and the appetites and hungers they did not invent, are compelled to participate" (p. 215).

Not only are individuals, willy-nilly, part of a cosmic drama, but their very personae are merely the temporary masks of the life force. J. C. Powys in 1915 compared Dreiser to Whitman, seeing in them both "the same subordination of the individual to the cosmic tide." Dreiser is concerned not with characters but with the "life tide."[49] A modern critic describes Dreiser's affinities with Emersonian transcendentalism; Dreiser's characters are vehicles of the oversoul:

> As to the characters—at least the major ones—they are essentially forces which move forward and come into conflict with other forces, but they have no idiosyncracies, no minor traits. They are never sharply individualized. They remind the reader of Majakovksy's "Clouds in trousers," for their clothes are carefully described, but, though they have bodies full of appetites and desires, they have no faces. Dreiser's point of view is not psychological, but social and metaphysical. He is not interested in his characters as individuals, but as social types *and* as manifestations of the central life force which flows through all things, as parts of the 'oversoul.'[50]

It is not that Dreiser never treats characters in terms of their social roles. But he either discredits these roles as dead conventions or ironically counterpoints them to underlying, more ontologically authentic, movements of desire. For example, Donald Pizer notes how Dreiser portrays Lillian Cowperwood and Edward Butler in *The Financier* as mistaking role for real: "Both . . . think of life in terms of social roles—those of the faithful husband and pure daughter—which disregard the emotional (or in Dreiser's terms, the chemical) reality of the individuals involved."[51] It was just these conventional ethical roles that Dreiser's reading of Spencer put into suspension.

Dreiser's irony appears in the extended scene in which Carrie plays the part of Laura, the self-sacrificing heroine of Augustin Daly's drama, *Under the Gaslight*. Ellen Moers shows how Carrie, by, literally, playing the role of a self-abnegating exemplar of the Victorian ethos, sets up a dynamic sexual interplay among herself, Hurstwood, and Drouet. Her dramatic role is in direct ironic opposition to the backstage action.[52] The role provides a means for her to negotiate her desire: Carrie, by becoming an actress, enters a world of greater possibility. But roles—indeed character and personality—are all mere epiphenomena of the underlying force of desire.

Thus, Dreiser is not only an idealist but a monist. One could even call him a pietist,[53] since he felt religious emotions toward the basic energy which courses through and vitalizes all phenomena: "One can, without religious or dogmatic illusions, experience awe, reverence, gratitude, and more, love for so wondrous a process or spirit, whichever one chooses to emphasize" (*Notes*, p. 279). Just such an attitude toward the cosmic Unknowable in Dreiser's mentor, Herbert Spencer, had outraged William James: "Mere existence commands no reverence whatever, or any other emotion, until its quality is specified. Neither does mere cosmic 'power,' unless it 'make for' something which can claim kinship from our sympathies. . . . As well might you speak of being irreverent to Space or disrespectful of the Equator."[54] James demanded a God of ethos, not one of mere pathos and power. At any rate, James believed that an idealistic monist could not, logically, be a moralist, as he wrote to Shadworth Hodgson, who was trying to be both:

> What I care for is that my moral reactions should find a real outward application. All those who, like you, hold that the world is a system of "uniform law" which repels all variation as so much 'chaos,' oblige, it seems to me, the world to be judged integrally. Now the *only* integral emotional reaction which can be called forth by such a world as this of our experience, is that of dramatic or melodramatic interest— romanticism—which is *the* emotional reaction upon it of all intellects who are neither religious nor moral.[55]

Dreiser is the consistent monist whom James imagines. He saw life as a game, a play, a drama—even if it took on "the look at times of a very badly played melodrama."[56] More than once Dreiser qualified his radical political sympathies by expressing not only a feeling of the inevitability but of the dramatic qualities of injustice. In 1920 he wrote:

> In too many cases the individual is accidentally favored beyond his deserts, in others too horribly denied, and these extremes will never be wholly overcome by social law, or if they were, life would become so tame and tasteless that it would cease. For it is only change and difference and so contrasts that make it worth while.[57]

In the midst of the Great Depression Dreiser explained that, from his perspective, no social order could be perfect "because I look on life as a progressive* game that is being played for some purpose, probably for self-entertainment." There is no evidence that the rules are changing so the game "has and will have continuously tragic, comic elements which can never be escaped."[58] History is merely a dramatic cycle staged by the life force:

*"Progressive" here is a synonym for "processive." It has no political connotations.

> Human history is a series of spectacles and has nothing to teach man except that man is a creature of attitudes. . . . His resolutions, celebrations, hero worship, wars, morals, religions, renunciations, self-glorifications are all attitudes or attitudinizings—the natural posings of the Great Impresario called Nature; God, Matter-Energy, Mechanism.
>
> (*Notes*, p. 16)

If life is a game, what matters is not right and wrong, but winning and losing. If it is a drama, what matters is how the parts are played. Dreiser finds as much interest in imagining himself into the loser's role as the winner's. And frequently the losers gain our sympathy by the unexpected dignity of their suffering. Many reviews of *Sister Carrie* thought Hurstwood declining overshadowed Carrie, rising. William Marion Reedy, in his 1901 review, catches the force of Dreiser's processual representation of Hurstwood's decline:

> The slow slackening of will, the subtle growth of indecision and self-abandonment, the loosening of manly fibre, the crumbling, rotting of character in a kind of narcotic procrastination touched with fitful gleams of paretic, puling pride, until he comes to beggary on the streets, and final rest in a fifteen-cent room with the gas out but turned on—all this is shown with a power which no endeavor to keep awake a critical attitude can resist. The terrible slowness of the ruin of a man, the descent marked by the clever, casual bringing to light of little, obscure symptoms, is hideously oppressive.[59]

Dreiser's sympathy with Hurstwood's decline, as much as with Carrie's rise, is implied in his awe before the life process: "I am thrilled by life's endless grandeur and genius as it presents itself in space and time."[60] Reedy was obviously touched, not at all comfortably, by the grandeur not of Hurstwood's character but of the process of his decline. What enables Dreiser to bring this off is his double perspective: "Both in and out of the game and watching and wondering at it."

Dreiser can authenticate Hurstwood's drift into oblivion because he has been there; he can resist sentimentalizing it because it is all part of the game. Dreiser's power comes from his double vision of the inescapable centrality and the fundamental illusoriness of all objects of desire. This is why he is so good on cities. He gives full value to the glitter of the city while he simultaneously sees it as a nexus of illusions, a communal phantasm. Above all, he shows the city as a force field of energy and desire, a focus of that life force which is always the true hero of his novels. Dreiser captures the vibrations of vitality that William James eloquently responded to in New York City of 1907: "The courage, the heaven-scaling audacity of it all, and the lightness withal, as if there were nothing that was not easy, and the great pulses and bounds of progress, so many in directions all simultaneous that the coordination is indefinitely future, give a kind of *drumming background* of life that I've never felt before." To sketch New York City "Balzac ought to come to life again. His Rastignac imagination sketched the possibility of it long ago."[61]

Dreiser too had "the Rastignac imagination." Balzac was, in fact, the main literary influence on Dreiser[62] and, as a 1913 reviewer commented, "Both his merits and his faults suggest Balzac."[63] Another reviewer saw Sister Carrie as an American equivalent of Rastignac, and, except for Jennie Gerhardt and Solon Barnes, almost all Dreiser's protagonists have a family resemblance either to Balzac's Rastignac or to his more passive Lucien de Rubempré. *An American Tragedy* replays many of the motifs of *Illusions Perdues*, though in a deliberately lower-key—Clyde is a slower learner than Lucien. Even Jennie Gerhardt is a cousin, once removed, of Eugénie Grandet. Like Balzac, Dreiser was fascinated with all that radiated desire—whether suppressed or fulfilled—and energy.

Dreiser wrote to Mencken that "Sister Carrie . . . gets over with those who love the shine and tingle of Broadway and the Metropolitan atmosphere generally."[64] In *Notes on Life* he argues that this shine and tingle causes a tropistic reaction and in his portrayal of Sister Carrie especially he has caught "the sense of magic which comes with the fresh and inexperienced contact of one large city—one's *first* large city" (*Notes*, p. 142).[65] But, of course, the city is where Hurstwood dies, alone, and is buried, nameless, in Potter's Field. The city's energy is morally neutral; to those who cannot flow with it, the force of the city may prove fatal. And like all other materializations, the grandeur of the city, its promise of ultimate fulfillment of desire, is illusory. Many of Dreiser's critics have analyzed the artistry with which he presents his dual vision of the appeal and the ultimate meretriciousness of the objects of his characters' desire. The objects range from the "truly swell saloon" to "a peculiar little tan jacket with large mother-of-pearl buttons which was all the rage that fall" to the ineffable Sondra Finchley. They are all versions of what Dreiser "always noticed about American cities and missed abroad . . . a crude sweet illusion about the importance of all things material."[66] Robert Penn Warren describes the value of Dreiser's representation exactly: "Part of the wisdom of the unillusioned man is to recognize that even more redemptive than illusion is the pity for illusion."[67] Dreiser shows the subjective beauty of the objectively tawdry.

Dreiser's protagonists, especially Carrie and Clyde Griffiths, suffer from Bovaryism. What they desire is always, always must be, over the rainbow. They suffer, following Irving Babbitt's definition, from the prototypical malignancy of the romantic imagination, an imagination diseased with anticipation and nostalgia:

> The essence of the mood is always the straining of the imagination away from the here and now, from an actuality that seems paltry and faded compared to the radiant hues of one's dream. The classicist, according to A. W. Schlegel, is for making the most of the present, whereas the romanticist hovers between recollection and hope. In Shelleyan phrase he 'looks before and after and pines for what is not.'

Rousseau's "indeterminate longing" typifies the romantic: "I was burning with desire," says Rousseau, "without any definite object" (cited in Babbitt,

p. 83). Albert Thibaudet, discussing Emma Bovary, sees the disjunction in a more compassionate light:

> Emma, like Don Quixote, doesn't place her desire and the things she desires on the same plane. Emma's sensuous desire, like Don Quixote's generous fantasies, are in themselves magnificent realities in which Flaubert and Cervantes project the best part of themselves. They admire desire and abandonment, but they have contempt for the things desired, the miserable bottle that comes out of a ridiculous pharmacy. Neither have any illusions about the value of the object desired by the imagination, and one half of their artistic nature—the realist half— mercilessly paints these mediocre and derisive objects.

Moreover, "Apart from her sensuous desire, everything else about Emma is mediocre."[68] So with Dreiser's heroine, whose greatest, perhaps only, distinction is that she is "strong in feeling" (p. 70).

Romantic idealism is Platonism with a truncated ladder. Objects are shadows on the wall of the cave, but the Platonic Idea has been transformed into something like Spencer's Unknowable. And even objects have lost some of their glamour. Emma Bovary's dreams, inspired by popular romances, seem almost sophisticated in contrast to the mass-produced fantasies offered Carrie and Clyde Griffiths in "the markets of delight" (p. 35). The real poignancy of the inarticulate desire for inadequate objects is caught beautifully in the passage in which Carrie returns to Drouet's apartment after a drive past the "elegant mansions" of North Shore Drive:

> When she came to her own rooms, Carrie saw their comparative insignificance. She was not so dull but that she could perceive they were but three small rooms in a moderately well-furnished boarding-house. She was not contrasting it now with what she had had, but what she had so recently seen. The glow of the palatial doors was still in her eye, the roll of cushioned carriages still in her ears. What, after all, was Drouet? What was she? At her window, she thought it over, rocking to and fro, and gazing out across the lamp-lit park toward the lamp-lit houses on Warren and Ashland Avenue. She was too wrought up to care to go down to eat, too pensive to do ought but rock and sing. Some old tunes crept to her lips, and, as she sang them, her heart sank. She longed and longed and longed. It was now for the old cottage room in Columbia City, now the mansion upon Shore Drive, now the fine dress of some lady, now the elegance of some scene. She was sad beyond measure, and yet uncertain, wishing, fancying. Finally, it seemed as if all her state was one of loneliness and forsakenness, and she could scarce refrain from trembling at the lip. She hummed and hummed as the moments went by, sitting in the shadow by the window, and was therein as happy, though she did not perceive it, as she ever would be.   (p. 119)

The surface structure of Carrie's longings—mansions and carriages—may be pure Horatio Alger but the deep structure is the Platonic ladder—except that it leads, ultimately, nowhere. Carrie rocks, a movement expressive of a rhythm with process but no progress, and she sings. "Music," as Babbitt disapprovingly pointed out, "is exalted by the romanticists above all arts because it is most nostalgic, the art that is most suggestive of the hopeless gap between the 'ideal' and the 'real'" (Babbitt, p. 84). What "old tunes" does Carrie sing? Emma Bovary was entranced by *Lucia di Lammermoor*, but Carrie is hardly at that level. If it were not that it was written eight years after the fictional time of *Sister Carrie*, one might suspect she sang Paul Dresser's "On the Banks of the Wabash," which Theodore Dreiser inspired and wrote part of. The song has most of the ingredients of Carrie's reverie: nostalgia, loneliness, the old home place. It is itself in the form of reverie:

> Round my Indiana homestead waves the cornfield,
>   In the distance looms the woodland clear and cool;
> Often times my thoughts revert to scenes of childhood
>   Where I first received my lessons, Nature's school;
>
> But one thing there is missing in this picture—
>   Without her face it seems so incomplete—
> I long to see my mother in the doorway,
>   As she stood there years ago her boy to greet.
>
> Oh, the moonlight's fair tonight along the Wabash,
>   From the fields there comes the breath of new mown hay,
> Through the sycamores the candle lights are gleaming,
>   On the banks of the Wabash far away.[69]

Carrie's reverie and Dreiser and Dresser's song are both expressions of a quite fascinating and underinvestigated phenomenon: the mediation of standard romantic motifs and emotions through popular culture. Reverie and song are Platonism without an Idea, pop romanticism. Or, looking forward, they are pop anticipations of existentialism; Carrie suffers, in her reverie, the same "modern" disease that Sainte-Beuve attributed to Madame Bovary: "At last, she is seized by a kind of disease; they call it a nervous condition, but it is like a nostalgia, a homesickness for an *unknown country*."[70] Though Madame Bovary herself is, in fact, trapped in a village, Bovaryism, particularly of the pop sort, is very much an urban emotion. Carrie is affected by the sad tunes, and remembers, for one of the very few times in the novel, her home town. But all this is mixed up with mansions on Shore Drive, and neither mansions nor Columbia City are anything more than completely inadequate, indeed factitious, objective correlatives for Carrie's desire.

Though she is not so self-possessed, and nowhere near so self-conscious, Carrie's nostalgia resembles that of the speaker in T. S. Eliot's "Portrait of a Lady":

> You will see me any morning in the park
> Reading the comics and the sporting page.

Particularly I remark
An English countess goes upon the stage.
A Greek was murdered at a Polish dance,
Another bank defaulter has confessed.
I keep my countenance,
I remain self-possessed
Except when a street piano, mechanical and tired
Reiterates some worn-out common song
With the smell of hyacinths across the garden
Recalling things that other people have desired.
Are these ideas right or wrong?[71]

Could Eliot be punning on Platonic "ideas"? It would fit the passage. The title of "Portrait of a Lady" draws on Henry James, not Dreiser, but this passage explicates the forms of Sister Carrie's desire. The very inadequacy of the worn-out common song—its mechanical quality—is part of the pathos, as is the displacement, the second-hand quality of desire.

For Carrie, the dreams of the mansion on Shore Drive, of the fine dress of some lady, fade in significance in direct ratio to the possibility of their fulfillment. They have a glamour for her as part of the communal, mass desire. T. S. Powys' review of *An American Tragedy* clarifies the meaning of mass desire in Dreiser's best work: Americans throw off "a cloud of invisible eidola, airy images of their grosser desires; and these are the filmy bricks of which Dreiser builds his impregnable dream-world." Powys notes that "It seems a strange use of the word 'realistic' to apply it to this stupendous objectification of the phantasmal life-dreams of so many tin-tack automatons of a bastard modernity." And Powys indicates the historical valence of Dreiser's pop images of paradise: "*An American Tragedy* is the other side of the shield of that 'plain democratic world' whereof Walt Whitman chanted his dithyrambic acceptance."[72]

Whitman's world of fluid desire must, in Dreiser, be mediated through the mass culture. The passages quoted above from Dreiser and Eliot represent a significant progression along this route. Further stages can be found in *The Great Gatsby* (recall Gatsby's beautiful shirts), *Paterson*, and Joyce Carol Oates's "Where Are You Going, Where Have You Been?" (which carries on the musical motif). The correlative objects become increasingly trivial at each step of the progression (or degeneration).

In giving the feeling its full emotional value while recognizing the illusoriness of the object, these writers attain a peculiarly contemporary mode of pathos.[73] George Levine notes that one of the essential differences between modern fiction and Victorian realistic fiction is that the Victorian realists tried to deal with "things as they are" whereas "there developed a recognition, which we can see in Hardy, Conrad, Virginia Woolf, and others around the turn of the century, that things as they are are themselves a convention, and that the convention was a peculiarly painful one."[74] I believe that *all* the major Victorian novelists show more than a glimmer of such recognition; but the point at issue is that Dreiser's realism focused on the force things as they are exert while fully recognizing "that things as they are are themselves a convention." This is what Dreiser had learned from Spencer's explosion of the world of convention.

4. Carrie's Face: The Natural Expression of Longing

Warwick Wadlington exactly catches the centrality for Dreiser of "the idea that the world is both massively real and thinly unreal": "On the one hand, the much praised solidity of Dreiser's fictional environment underscores a fixed, blank imperviousness to human yearning; on the other hand, this very imperviousness causes the solid world to appear impalpable, transparent before the piercing light of desire."[75] Carrie's rocking and singing expresses the real/unreal paradox; even more, Carrie herself embodies the paradox: her characterization is a sustained equivocation on personal reality. More than Dreiser is willing openly to acknowledge, he shows Carrie herself as an illusory object of desire.

Carrie becomes most real, most realized, in performance. Lester Cohen observes that "As an actress Carrie begins to discover that her 'independence' is to be found in role-playing. Her sense of self can arise only from her ability to be as others see her."[76] This does not contradict Dreiser's view of roles as the epiphenomena of desire: Carrie's stage performances are effective because she can signify desire. She is a medium through which desire reveals itself, although not an altogether neutral medium, since she can represent desire only because she also feels it. But she most authentically feels and represents desire within the frame of a fiction— reading *Père Goriot*, acting on stage.

Wadlington, discussing this problem, discerns "a deep-structured active principle" in Dreiser's characters. Its function is to perform "one task above all: comparing a present external reality with some innate paradigm of ideality." Thus:

> When an occasion appears to offer a correspondence to the internal paradigm, as it does, for example, in Carrie's early stage triumph as Laura, there is a surface, absorbed passivity even as the spark of recognition ignites; but this surface passivity merely allows the full play of the real, buried life that arises from the depths.[77]

Still, it seems that Carrie is *so* latent that she needs the manifest content of a fiction to become fully real. In her role as Laura she responds intensely to the cue of her fictitious name: "At the sound of her stage name Carrie started. She began to feel the bitterness of the situation. The feelings of the outcast descended upon her. She hung at the wing's edge, wrapt in her own mounting thoughts. She hardly heard anything more, save her own rumbling blood" (p. 180). Carrie can go furthest both into and out of herself *as* Laura. Her talent for conveying "natural pathos" stirs a sympathetic response:

> Hurstwood began to feel a deep sympathy for her and for himself. He

could almost feel that she was talking to him. He was, by a combination of feelings and entanglements, almost deluded by that quality of voice and manner which, like a pathetic strain of music, seems ever a personal and intimate thing. Pathos has this quality, that it seems ever addressed to one alone.   (p. 183)

Dreiser's point is that such a representation of pathos can *never* be addressed to one alone, since it is an evanescent embodiment of a universal, ideal form. Carrie's effect on Hurstwood is structurally parallel to the effect the "old tunes" had on her (as discussed in section 3 above); Carrie mediates, through her role, an anonymous, communal desire that is the most authentic thing about her. Wadlington rightly notes that "The 'emotional greatness' specifically ascribed to Carrie Meeber is at base a capacity to desire."[78]

The reader, however, can hardly accept Dreiser's ascription of greatness to Carrie—except as an instance of more special pleading—because of what Dreiser himself reveals as the basically accidental quality of her emotional power. Throughout, Carrie is a sort of Pathos Mary, the carrier of a powerful affect. Her success as an actress is founded on an accident:

> She practiced her part ruefully, feeling that she was effectually shelved. At the dress rehearsal she was disconsolate.
> "That isn't so bad," said the author, the manager noting the curious effect which Carrie's blues had upon the part. "Tell her to frown a little more when Sparks dances."
> *Carrie did not know it* [my italics], but there was the least show of wrinkles between her eyes and her mouth was puckered quaintly.
> "Frown a little more, Miss Madenda," said the stage manager.
> Carrie instantly brightened up, thinking he had meant it as a rebuke.
> "No; frown," he said. "Frown as you did before."
> Carrie looked at him in astonishment.
> "I mean it," he said. "Frown hard when Mr. Sparks dances. I want to see how it looks."
> It was easy enough to do. Carrie scowled. The effect was something so quaint and droll it caught even the manager.
> "That *is* good," he said. "If she'll do that all through, I think it will take."   (p. 420)

Carrie does do it all through and it does take. Here and elsewhere she is portrayed almost as an effect without a cause, with the result being "miraculous so far as Carrie's fortune was concerned" (p. 422).

The function of the intellectual, Ames, in the novel is largely to articulate what Carrie, so to speak, carries. Late in the novel, at a point where Dreiser feels the need to bring Carrie into sharper focus, Ames tells her that her disposition is suited to comedy-drama because she is "sympathetic" in her nature (p. 455). Carrie is sympathetic, but not in the usual modern sense of the word—she displays rather a minimum of compassion and fellow-feeling. She is not *personally* sympathetic. But she does have a real force of sympathy in an obsolete but, for Dreiser's characterization, very appropriate meaning of the word: "A (real or supposed) affinity between certain things, by virtue of which they are similarly or correspondingly affected by the same influence, affect or influence one another (esp. in some occult way), or attract or tend towards each other."[79]

The "influence" that Carrie is affected by, and through which she affects others, is pathos—the touch of nature that makes the whole world kin. But it is a common relation of all to an underlying form rather than a relation of each to each; that pathos "seems ever addressed to one alone" is an illusion intrinsic to its particular nature. Carrie likes the "pathetic strain" of music for exactly the reason she is herself like music: " 'I don't know what it is about music,' she started to say, moved by the inexplicable longings which surged within her; 'but it always makes me feel as if I wanted something—I—' " (p. 456). Ames replies that he *knows* how she *feels* and once more appeals to her to use her talent for pathos in a better way. Her problem is that she doesn't know what she feels, nor does she know what, in and out of the theater, she represents.

Ames tries to explain to Carrie the source of her power: it is, literally, the significance of her face. It signifies pathos and arouses longing: "the expression in your face is one that comes out in different things [i.e., it expresses a form]. You get the same thing in a pathetic song, or any picture which moves you deeply. It's a thing the world likes to see, because it's a natural expression of its longing" (457). This is, Ames tells her, her "natural look," but it is far from it feeling natural to her; she longs "to be equal to this feeling written upon her countenance" (p. 457). There is a gap between what she represents and what she comprehends.

Carrie's success on the stage is the direct result of what she represents. Had the book been written and set later she might well have been a film star, like the more consciously expressive Garbo. Note the parallel with the effect of "The Face of Garbo," as analyzed by Roland Barthes: "Garbo still belongs to that moment in cinema when capturing the human face still plunged audiences into the deepest ecstasy, when one literally lost oneself in a human image as one would in a philtre, when the force represented a kind of absolute state of the flesh, which could be neither reached nor renounced." "Garbo offered to one's gaze a sort of Platonic Idea of the human creature."[80] Ames explains to Carrie that she is a representation of a sort of Platonic Idea of desire:

> "The world is always struggling to express itself," he went on. "Most people are not capable of voicing their feelings. They depend upon others. That is what genius is for. One man expresses their desires for them in music; another one in poetry; another one in a play. Sometimes nature does it in a face—it makes the face representative of all desire. That's what has happened in your case."
>
> He looked at her with so much of the import of the thing in his eyes that she caught it. At least, she got the idea that her look was something which represented the world's longing.   (p. 458)

There is an interesting bit of stylistic casuistry in this passage. Carrie is conflated with musicians, poets, and playwrights as an instance of genius. Yet musicians, poets, and playwrights express in the active tense, whereas Carrie represents in the passive tense—nature, not Carrie, is the agent. Like the artists, Carrie is important because she enables the articulation of feelings; the difference is that, in her case, the enablement is, again, accidental. Carrie only barely catches Ames's explanation of her significance, and that only through his look. What is unconvincing about Dreiser's evaluation of Carrie as an emotional genius is not that she is a success—we can think of many "stars" who owe their fame to a certain look and Ames offers a precise explanation for the phenomenon. But genius (to use Dreiser's word) depends on active expression, not merely on passive representation.

It is Dreiser himself who actively articulates the emotions that Carrie passively represents. Like the author who tells her to frown, Dreiser rescues Carrie's diffuse emotionality by embedding it in a structure that can effectuate it. But Dreiser, in devaluing ethos and glorifying pathos, wants to argue an essential *artistic* value for raw, unstructured feeling. This he can assert but not demonstrate; hence the casuistry. Carrie cannot, in fact, ever be quite equal to the feeling written (passive case) upon her countenance.

The problem is basically that of how to represent, without satirically undercutting, a character important only for what she represents. Carrie is realized in her tropistic responses; she is convincingly exonerated for following "the call of the ideal" (p. 455)—of the ideal form of desire. Even her passive dreaminess can be seen, like Whitman's loafing, as a means of inviting the soul to drift with the current of desire:

> Thus in life there is ever the intellectual and the emotional nature— the mind that reasons, and the mind that feels. Of one come the men of action—generals and statesmen; of the other, the poets and dreamers— artists all.
>
> As harps in the wind, the latter respond to every breath of fancy, voicing in their moods all the ebb and flow of the ideal.
>
> Man has not yet comprehended the dreamer any more than he has the ideal. For him the laws and morals of the world are unduly severe. Ever hearkening to the sound of beauty, straining for the flash of its distant wings, he watches to follow, wearying his feet in travelling. So watched Carrie, so followed, rocking and singing.
>
> And it must be remembered that reason had little part in this. Chicago dawning, she saw the city offering more of loveliness than she had ever known, and instinctively, by the force of mood alone, clung to it. In fine raiment and elegant surroundings, men seemed to be contented. Hence, she drew near these things. Chicago, New York; Drouet, Hurstwood; the world of fashion and the world of stage—these were but incidents. Not them, but that which they represented, she longed for. Time proved the representation false.   (p. 473)

This purple passage seems to me more justified than such passages in

Dreiser are generally conceded to be. It sums up the novel's double perspective, displaying a thoroughly convincing Chicago, New York, Hurstwood, and Drouet who are yet so many shadows on the wall of the Platonic cave. But Dreiser resists his own logic, by which he should recognize Carrie as not only the dreamer who longs after illusory representations of the ideal form of desire, but as herself one of the illusory representations, as one who, at her most real, is dream as well as dreamer.

Howells, with his ethical awareness, could never have been guilty of such a willful misrecognition. However, as I have shown in chapter 3 and as I will show in the next section, Howells' emphasis on ethos led him into his own style of special pleading, while Dreiser's emphasis on pathos led him into recognitions beyond Howells' range.

5. Dreiser and Howells: Two Modes of Realism

Dreiser and Howells shared a critical realism which set them off from the popular romancers of the late nineteenth century. Yet Dreiser was one of the few American realists whom Howells failed in any way to acknowledge, while Dreiser thought only one of Howells' novels genuinely realistic.[81] One can, in fact, detect a polar opposition between Howells' realism of ethos and Dreiser's realism of pathos. Since Howells and Dreiser most obviously diverge in intention when they are most parallel in plot, a discussion of three parallel plot sequences should clarify the differences between their two modes of realism.

a. The sequence in *Sister Carrie* in which Hurstwood steals the money from Fitzgerald and Moy and runs off with Carrie has obvious parallels to Bartley's loss of Halleck's money and his abandonment of Marcia in *A Modern Instance*. In both cases, the specific action is the end result of a process; in both the action is caused by a mixture of subliminal, not consciously chosen, intention and of an accident—the shutting of the safe, the losing of the wallet—which forces the issue. But against Bartley, as against George Eliot's Tito, the judgment is clear: they are to blame for letting the process develop to the point where such an accident could have such an effect. Their wills are diseased through their having allowed impulsiveness to become habitual. As with William James in *Principles*, the psychology of habit is an ethical psychology. This is its significance.

The process which leads to the closing of the safe on Hurstwood is no more complex or interesting in its development than Bartley's loss of the wallet. But, as Robert Penn Warren lucidly shows, Dreiser was careful to muddle any possibility of determinate ethical judgment:

> [Hurstwood] is holding the money in his hand, debating the theft, when the lock of the safe clicks. Had he pushed the door? He does not know. In this brilliant moral and psychological study, what is the nature of Hurstwood's guilt? Is the slamming of the door an accident or an alibi, a trap of fate or a masking of the unconscious decision to steal?[82]

Richard Lehan speculates provocatively on the effect point of view has in Howells' summoning and Dreiser's deflecting of ethical response. The fact that the ending of *A Modern Instance* is told from Marcia's point of view, rather than from Bartley's, clearly establishes the "Christian sense of right and wrong" which Marcia represents. But "by telling the story from Hurstwood's own point of view, and telling it sympathetically, Dreiser turned the genteel novel upside down."[83] But this has it backwards. For Howells, Marcia's impulsive passion is almost as wrong as Bartley's impulsive abandonment. Both are, literally, self-indulgent. The reader's ethical response to Bartley is governed by Howells' ethical structuring of Bartley's consciousness. It is from *inside* this consciousness that we are forced to react against it, and if our reaction is traditional it is not trite.

Moreover, in *Sister Carrie*, a greater use of Mrs. Hurstwood's point of view would probably strengthen rather than reduce our sympathy with Hurstwood's actions. For she is depicted, more from Dreiser's than Hurstwood's point of view, as a coldly calculating self-seeker, a character of the sort whom Howells detested fully as much as Dreiser. Hurstwood perceives only the irritation she causes him, for he is himself too coldly calculating a self-seeker to produce a valid ethical judgment.* If Mrs. Hurstwood is a Dreiserian villain, it is not for her selfishness so much as for the conventional limitations of her desire. Our last view of her shows a complacency based merely on social status and financial security: "Mrs. Hurstwood nestled comfortably in her corner and smiled. It was nice to be the mother-in-law of a rich young man—one whose financial state had borne her personal inspection" (p. 469).

How, from a Dreiserian point of view, could one possibly sympathize with a character whose desires can be so patly satisfied? Mrs. Hurstwood is content with conventional rewards, with the rewards of the conventional. Dreiser characteristically identified convention with habit and habit with ethics— which is why the still, small voice of conscience is, in *Sister Carrie*, a dead letter:

> The victim of habit, when he has neglected the thing which it was his custom to do, feels a little scratching in the brain, a little irritating something which comes of being out of the rut, and imagines it to be the prick of conscience, the still, small voice that is urging him even to righteousness. If the digression's unusual enough, the drag of habit will be heavy enough to cause the unreasoning victim to return and perform the perfunctory thing. "Now, bless me," says such a mind, "I have done my duty," when, as a matter of fact, it has merely done its old, unbreakable trick once again.   (p. 84)

Dreiser's sardonic description of irrational habit doing its unbreakable trick is a total inversion of the still, small voice as perceived by George Eliot, How-

---

*Before Hurstwood loses control over his life, his point of view is rather like that of his wife. They are mirror-image antagonists.

ells, and William James. For them the voice marshalled rational principle and self-restraint against the urgings of irrational impulse.

Thus it is that Hurstwood's forced break with the habit patterns of Chicago, job, home, and family leads him to a self-destruction which does not call for ethical judgment. Its effect on others is wholly positive: Mrs. Hurstwood and her children lose nothing financially while they gain freedom from a presence that had become highly disagreeable to them; Carrie once again falls upward. Everything works out beautifully for everyone but Hurstwood. And Hurstwood is destroyed not by a moral flaw but for the more serious offense, in Dreiser's cosmos, of making an error in the game of life. To put it another way, Hurstwood's decline is morally significant as an illustration of the rules of the game, whereas his previous prosperity was both morally and esthetically uninteresting: it had affirmed nothing but the ability of convention to uphold and endow with a certain social status an essentially hollow man.[84] By stepping out of his role, the performance of "the perfunctory thing," Hurstwood begins a process of decline that gains him the sympathy we all must have with the losing game. Paradoxically, over the course of his descent into the dark of Potter's Field, Hurstwood is forced out of the nullity of his previous habitual existence and takes on the dignity that comes from an unprotected encounter with unmediated reality. His unheroic decline and death mark, in an odd way, his finest hour.

Hurstwood's fall is more engaging than his prosperity because Dreiser's strength is his rendering of the pathos of process. We participate most intensely in Hurstwood's consciousness *after* his fatal error because Dreiser is less interested in the process which led to it than in the fatality of the process consequent to the act. Howells, whose strength is in representing ethical sequence, beautifully describes Bartley up to the moment of his fatal action. Thereafter Howells loses interest in Bartley; he never returns to his point of view and throws off the news of his death as an ironic afterthought.

b. Every step in Howells' perfectly developed representation of the process of the breakdown in the Hubbards' marriage is controlled by ethical judgment. They go wrong because they do wrong. Bartley's self-serving rationalizations are a prime instance; as with Tito Melema, they form part of the case against him. Dreiser, in *Sister Carrie*, indeed depicts this sort of rationalizing— but he makes no ethical point of it. When Hurstwood announces to Carrie that they must move into a cheaper flat she begins to rationalize, but with an effect altogether different than in Howells:

> It really affected her more seriously than anything that had yet happened. She began to look on Hurstwood wholly as a man, and not as a lover or husband. She felt thoroughly bound to him as a wife, and that her lot was cast with his, whatever it might be; but she began to see that he was gloomy and taciturn, not a young, strong, and buoyant man. He looked a little bit old to her about the eyes and mouth now, and there were other things which placed him in his true rank, so far as her estimation was concerned. She began to feel that she had made a

mistake. Incidentally, she also began to recall the fact that he had
practically forced her to flee with him.   (p. 318)

Howells could forgive a character for such cruel perceptions (after sufficient atonement), but Dreiser does not need to. The irony of Carrie's after-the-
fact judgment of Hurstwood is pointed in the wonderful "Incidentally," but
Dreiser does not blame Carrie for blaming Hurstwood. *Son cosas de la vida.*
An even more devastating passage maintains the same ethical neutrality:
"Carrie saw things were wrong with him. He was not so handsome when
gloomy. The lines at the sides of the eyes were deepened. Naturally dark of
skin, gloom made him look slightly sinister. He was quite a disagreeable figure" (pp. 324–325). This passage comes just when the focus of the book is
beginning to shift to Hurstwood. Dreiser can, without satire or blame, have
Carrie feel this way; he can represent it as a perfectly natural way to feel, in
fact, just as he is about sympathetically to explore Hurstwood's consciousness, a consciousness defined by the chill of the losing game.

For Dreiser, the conflict between Carrie and Hurstwood is a game characterized by a gradually shifting balance of power:

> At last three days came in which a storm prevailed, and he did not
> go out at all. The snow began to fall late one afternoon. It was a regular
> flurry of large, soft, white flakes. In the morning it was still coming
> down with a high wind, and the papers announced a blizzard. From out
> the front windows one could see a deep, soft bedding.
> "I guess I'll not try to go out today," [Hurstwood] said to Carrie
> at breakfast. "It's going to be awful bad, so the papers say."
> "The man hasn't brought my coal, either," said Carrie, who ordered
> by the bushel.
> "I'll go over and see about it," said Hurstwood. This was the first
> time he had ever suggested doing an errand, but, somehow, the wish to
> sit about the house prompted it as a sort of compensation for the
> privilege.
> . . . .
> Hurstwood sat and read by his radiator in the corner. He did not try to
> think about his need of work. This storm being so terrific, and tying up
> all things, robbed him of the need. He made himself wholly comfort-
> able and toasted his feet.
> Carrie observed his ease with some misgiving. For all the fury of the
> storm she doubted his comfort. He took his situation too philosophical-
> ly.   (pp. 334–335)

Carrie's observation at the end of the passage is cruel in its cool objectivi-
ty, but it is also quite accurate. It is supported even by the sound effects, the
dispiriting thunk of Hurstwood's settling all too much down: "He made himself wholly comfortable and toasted his feet." The entire passage does not
condemn either Hurstwood or Carrie ethically, but conveys perfectly the process of their tropistic interaction. Neither Carrie's growing contempt nor
Hurstwood's growing apathy are shown as anything but the natural result

of their temperaments and conditions. No one is to blame, least of all the weather, which is central to the process of Hurstwood's defeat without there being the slightest suggestion of pathetic fallacy. As Hurstwood goes to his suicide, Dreiser tells us: "A heavy snow was falling—a fine, picking, whipping snow, borne forward by a swift wind in long, thin lines" (p. 467). What points the sentence is its deliberate refraining from point. The irony is that the beauty of this "fine, picking, whipping snow" is as real as the people unlucky enough to be whipped by it. We cannot protest against snow, we cannot accuse it of an unethical fall.

c. Dreiser's political and social writings are, for the most part, politically and ethically obtuse. Howells, in contrast, developed a relatively sophisticated and responsible insight into the contradictions between American democratic ideals and American capitalistic realities. Yet the financial and political manipulations of Dreiser's Frank Cowperwood come alive, whereas the ethical complications of Silas Lapham's business dealings do not (as opposed to Silas' social complications, which are thoroughly convincing). Howells tries to force ethical significance out of seemingly recalcitrant materials, whereas Dreiser's interest is in the game as it is played.

The streetcar strike scenes in *A Hazard of New Fortunes* and *Sister Carrie* illustrate the difference. Howells is as aware as Dreiser of the economic forces which lead to and determine the outcome of the strike. But this is not enough. Howells must key the scene up to ethical melodrama; the passage describing Conrad Dryfoos' death as he tries to protect the crippled radical Berthold Lindau is impressive but flawed.

> The officer whirled his club, and the old man threw his left arm up to shield his head. Conrad recognized Lindau, and now he saw the empty sleeve dangle in the air, over the stump of his wrist. He heard a shot in that turmoil beside the car, and something seemed to strike him in the breast. He was going to say to the policeman, "Don't strike him! He's an old soldier! You see he has no hand!" but he could not speak, he could not move his tongue. The policeman stood there; he saw his face; it was not bad, not cruel; it was like the face of a statue, fixed, perdurable, a mere image of irresponsible and involuntary authority. Then Conrad fell forward, pierced through the heart by that shot fired from the car.[85]

Lindau's gesture of trying to protect his head from the police with the arm crippled in the Civil War is, as irony and symbolism, quite evident—too much so if we hold Howells to the standards of his own criticism, with its attacks on "effectism."[86] The impressionistic rendering of Conrad's fatal wound is finely done—"something seemed to strike him in the breast"—but it does not fit easily into the same stylistic universe with the stock melodramatic phrase "pierced through the heart." Quite the best thing in the passage is the politically acute representation of the policeman, "a mere image of irresponsible and involuntary authority"—but there is a false note even here. In the context of Conrad's intercession on behalf of Lindau, of his being "pierced," and of his dying for the sins of others, the policeman's resemblance to Pontius Pilate is inescapable. The problem is not that such symbolism is in itself illegitimate but that it is not stylistically or philosophically at home in this novel. It has the air of a last-minute forced intrusion from the realm of melodramatic romance.

Basil March later spells out the suggestions of Christian allegory in the scene:

> But Conrad—yes, he had some business there; it was his business to suffer there for the sins of others. Isabel, we can't throw aside that old doctrine of the Atonement yet. The life of Christ, it wasn't only in healing the sick and going about to do good; it was suffering for the sins of others! That's as great a mystery as the mystery of death. Why should there be such a principle in the world? But it's been felt and more or less dumbly, blindly recognized ever since Calvary. If we love mankind, pity them, we even *wish* to suffer for them.   (p. 393)

This passage is not supported by the rest of the novel, by the ambience of Howells' created world. Religious humanism is here abandoned for a weak rhetorical shadow of religious mystery: the overall effect is like that of the over-obvious and banalized echo of "my Father's business."

But throughout most of this and of other Howells novels the whole push of his style is against irrationality, mystery, passion. When he feels compelled to fall back on the mysterious irrationality of Christ's passion, he can only write empty rhetoric. When Howells tries to dramatize such passion he descends to melodrama; when Howells' characters attempt to discuss first and last things the effect is of a line of chatter thrown up against the breath of the furies.

Dreiser goes the opposite direction in his streetcar strike; he achieves his intense effect through a careful low-keying of the sequence, a calculated avoidance of melodrama, a deliberate reduction of it to the commonplace. (We might almost say that Dreiser's scene works in accordance with Howells' critical theories.) Hurstwood is pulled off the streetcar he has been operating in a scene that has the feel of exact reality:

> "Let go of me," he said, falling on his side.
>
> "Ah, you sucker," he heard some one say. Kicks and blows rained on him. He seemed to be suffocating. Then two men seemed to be dragging him off and he wrestled for freedom.
>
> "Let up," said a voice, "you're all right. Stand up."
>
> He was set loose and recovered himself. Now he recognized two officers. He felt as if he would faint from exhaustion. Something was wet on his chin. He put up his hand and felt, then looked. It was red.
>
> "They cut me," he said, foolishly, fishing for his handkerchief.
>
> "Now, now," said one of the officers. "It's only a scratch."
>
> . . . .
>
> He walked over and looked out. It was an ambulance, backing in.

He saw some energetic charging by the police and arrests being made.

"Come on, now, if you want to take your car," said an officer. . . .

He walked out, feeling rather uncertain of himself. He was very cold and frightened.

"Where's the conductor?" he asked.

"Oh, he's not here now," said the policeman.

Hurstwood went toward the car and stepped nervously on. As he did so there was a pistol shot. Something stung his shoulder.

"Who fired that?" he heard an officer exclaim. "By God, who did that?" Both left him, running toward a certain building. He paused a moment and then got down.

"George!" exclaimed Hurstwood, weakly, "this is too much for me." He walked nervously to the corner and hurried down a side street.

"Whew!" he said, drawing in his breath.

A half block away, a small girl gazed at him.

"You'd better sneak," she called.   (pp. 403-404)

We are left to infer a relation between the missing conductor and the ambulance. The impressionistic technique used in Hurstwood's delayed re-actions to his cut chin and his bullet wound is in perfect consonance with the random, happenstance quality of the entire scene. Howells tries to impose coherence on his scene by framing it with Christian allegory. But Dreiser gives us a series of jump cuts, showing the scene, from the point of view of a par-ticipant, *as* discontinuous and incoherent. What most authenticates Hurst-wood's reaction is his lack of any. Like most onlookers or even participants in such melees, his primary response is benumbment. The principle of such re-sponse has been caught, in a far more extreme instance, by W. H. Auden:

There are events which arouse such simple and obvious emotions that an AP cable or a photograph in *Life* magazine are enough and poetic comment is impossible. If one reads through the mass of versified trash inspired, for instance, by the Lidice Massacre, one cannot avoid the feeling that what was really bothering the versifiers was a feeling of guilt at not feeling horrorstruck enough. Could a good poem have been written on such a subject? Possibly. One that revealed this lack of feel-ing, that told how when he read the news, the poet, like you and I, dear reader, went on thinking about his fame or his lunch, and how glad he was that he was not one of the victims.[87]

March makes after-the-fact sense out of the riot he has witnessed by evok-ing the nostrum of atonement; Hurstwood makes after-the-fact sense out of the riot he was shot in by dosing himself with the narcotic of mass culture: the press is his wafer.[88]

He trudged doggedly on until he reached the flat. There he entered and found the room warm. Carrie was gone. A couple of evening papers were lying on the table where she left them. He lit the gas and sat down. Then he got up and stripped to examine his shoulder. It was a mere scratch. He washed his hands and face, still in a brown study, apparently, and combed his hair. Then he looked for something to eat, and finally, his hunger gone, sat down in his comfortable rocking-chair. It was a wonderful relief.

He put his hand to his chin, forgetting, for the moment, the papers.

"Well," he said, after a time, his nature recovering itself, "that's a pretty tough game over there."

Then he turned and saw the papers. With half a sigh he picked up the "World."

"Strike spreading in Brooklyn" he read. "Rioting Breaks out in All Parts of the City."

He adjusted his paper very comfortably and continued. It was one thing he read with absorbing interest. (p. 405)

The other side of the coin of Dreiser's celebration of desire and of the illusory glamour of the city was his perfect awareness of the urban anomie, of the anesthetizing of affect, phenomena which are both mirrored in and partly caused by the mass media. Hurstwood lacks the *sang froid* of Eliot's newspaper reader in "Portrait of a Lady," but they share the condition of narcosis. Both inhabit Plato's cave. For Eliot's newspaper readers on the London tube, in "Four Quarters," the press *is* the shadow on the wall:

> Only a flicker
> Over the strained time-ridden faces
> Distracted from distraction by distraction
> Filled with fancies and empty of meaning
> Tumid apathy with no concentration.[89]

Hurstwood forgets the paper momentarily when he touches the cut on his chin, a nonverbal sign of a non-journalized riot. But the newspaper version transforms the blur of experience into coherence through draining it of its reality.

6. *An American Tragedy*: Sympathy and Discomfort

Donald Davidson wrote in his review of *An American Tragedy* that it was "a book from which may be gained, as from George Eliot's *Romola*, an overpowering sense of the reality of evil."[90] One might ask whether "evil" is an appropriate term, however, given J. W. Krutch's claim that Dreiser "sloughed off once and for all the implications of the theory that man is primarily a moral animal and he did this much as the behaviourists in psychology sloughed off the soul." Krutch characterizes Clyde Griffiths as "a fate-driven criminal . . . brought unjustly to justice. At no point in all the vast and closely woven story does any motive based upon moral, social, or religious abstractions count."[91]

Yet Davidson's comparison to *Romola* is revealing: Clyde Griffiths *is* a soul-brother of Tito Melema. The difference is not in what they are but in how they are to be evaluated. Moreover, Krutch was only half-right about the amorality of *An American Tragedy*. Motives based on moral, social, and religious abstractions count heavily, though only so far as they yield what William James would call their cash value; they are never taken on faith. Dreiser brings ethical motives into play while simultaneously downplaying his usual special pleading on behalf of pathos. Yet ethos is never used for purposes of judgment; ethos in *An American Tragedy* moves the reader only insofar as it is subsumed under pathos. Another contemporary reviewer might be taken as Dreiser's ideal reader: "You will not admire Clyde Griffiths; you will not even approve of him; but you will be desperate in his desperation and, defenceless as he, you will seek as eagerly to break through the thin wall which keeps him from his happiness."[92]

The reader cannot admire or approve of Clyde because he resembles too closely the prototypical nineteenth-century villain of "self": Dreiser tells us that "Clyde was as vain and proud as he was poor";[93] that evasion and concealment were native to his disposition (p. 92); that he "had a soul that was not destined to grow up" (p. 169); that he had an "immature and really psychically unilluminated mind" (p. 188); and that his was "a naturally selfish and ambitious and seeking disposition" (p. 296). These editorial comments, though devastating, shock us far less than does Clyde in action. For example, we see him preparing to lie about a college education: "On the instant he proposed to claim it, if asked, and then look up afterwards what, if anything, he was supposed to know about it—what, for instance, he might have studied. He had heard of mathematics somewhere. Why not that?" (p. 318). Or, when he calls Roberta after having found the name of a reputed abortionist, his manner is "redolent of a fairly worth-while achievement" (p. 395). The achievement proves as empty as his elation over procuring some supposed abortion pills, when he finds "some central and detached portion of the ego within himself congratulating him upon his luck and undaunted efficiency in such a crisis as this" (p. 378). Ellen Moers has shown Dreiser's use of Freud in *An American Tragedy* and Dreiser probably draws his usage of "ego" from Freud. However, the process of Clyde's self-delusive consciousness is entirely consonant with the traditional Victorian analysis of egoism. The fatuousness of Clyde's self-congratulations reminds us of Frank Osbaldistone's moment and of Willoughby Patterne's career, of weakness— except, of course, that Clyde is especially inept, which is hardly a redeeming feature.

Clyde has enough of a conscience to experience occasional "misgivings": "But now, so thrilled was he at the possibility of a reencounter with Sondra, he decided that he would cancel this last evening engagement with Roberta, although not without some misgivings as to *the difficulty as well as the decency of it*" (p. 330, my italics). Of course, as the italicized passage shows, logistical problems preempt moral ones. But Clyde has just enough moral sensitivity to give him a continuous need for the resources of bad faith. Clyde is highly reminiscent of Tito and Bartley as "he . . . casuistically argued with himself" (p. 385), or as he employs "once more evasion—tergiversation with himself" (p. 468). He is trying to delude himself as much as Roberta as he uses "sly and yet muddy tergiversation" to come up with a "false and morally meretricious . . . plan" (p. 388).

Clyde even has two selves, perhaps on the model of Freud's id and superego; their psychomachia, however, resembles more the Victorian colloquy between "self" and the still, small voice of conscience, between lower and higher self. Clyde tries not to listen to the "evil hint of an evil spirit" (p. 440), he tries to shut out the insinuations of "the genie of his darkest and weakest side," "some darker or primordial and unregenerate nature of his own" (p. 464), and give heed to the voice of his "darker fears or better impulses" (p. 466) (a wonderfully Dreiserian conjunction). True, Clyde's darker self speaks with an irrationality and potential violence more extreme than usual in the Victorian colloquy, but this merely adds a darker tone to the color of Clyde's temptations; it does not change the structure of his engagement with them.

We see both the similar structure and the darker tone in Clyde's semi-aware *fear* of his own consciousness. At one point Clyde leaves his room, "feeling that he was walking away from the insinuating thought or suggestion that had so troubled him up to now" (p. 442). In an extraordinary passage:

> He took his straw hat and went out, almost before any one heard him think, as he would have phrased it to himself, such horrible terrible thoughts.
>
> . . . .
>
> He walked and walked—away from Lycurgus—out on a road to the southeast which passed through a poor and decidedly unfrequented rural section, and so left him alone to think—or, as he felt, not to be heard in his thinking. (p. 461)

But even for this dread-filled malaise of consciousness we can find such near-parallels in Victorian fiction as Dickens' portrayal of the obsessive Carker in *Dombey and Son*.

In some respects Dreiser seems to weight the scales against his inept, self-centered protagonist even more than do the Victorian masters. For, against Clyde's evasions and tergiversations, Dreiser places the painfully authentic pathos, entrapment, and terror of Roberta. There is a terrible irony in Dreiser's paralleling of Sondra Finchley's and Roberta's letters. The one is as empty and noisy as a 1920s' musical comedy and has just that much vision of human pain and limitation: "This morning when I was riding a bird flew right up under Dickey's heels. It scared him so that he bolted, and Sondra got all switched and scwatched. Isn't Clydie sorry for his Sondra?" The other is inarticulate and uncertain, but almost unbearably eloquent, in its unconscious statement of sorrow and fear:

> Dear Clyde,
> I am nearly ready for bed, but I will write you a few lines. I had such a tiresome journey coming up that I was nearly sick. In the first place I

didn't want to come much (alone) as you know. I feel too upset and uncertain about everything, although I try not to feel so now that we have our plan and you are going to come for me as you said.

(pp. 433–434)

(A formalist approach could make much of the high *i*'s in Sondra's letter; it tweets like a canary. Roberta's letter, in contrast, is heavy with down-pulling *e*'s and low *u*'s. The difference in emotional registers is total—it could be diagrammed.)

It would seem that the interaction of Clyde's pervasive bad faith and Roberta's intensely authentic pathos ought to make the reader feel a repulsion toward Clyde proportionate to the pity Roberta evokes. Dreiser's extraordinary *tour de force* is that, instead, he puts the (ideal)[94] reader into an intense and uncomfortable empathy with Clyde. This is a much greater challenge than the inversion of ethos and pathos in Carrie's fall upwards. Rather than inverting sympathies in *An American Tragedy*, Dreiser complicates and intensifies them to create a world tragically fatal in its boundaries. The tragic complication of this world is precisely that its social structure, and perhaps even its metaphysical structure, blocks the sympathetic impulse. It is a mousetrap world, constituted as if to tempt, entrap, and ultimately destroy the desiring self.

One of the great moments in *An American Tragedy* is the scene in which Roberta, visiting her mother, hesitates to act on an impulse to unburden herself about her increasingly dubious and compromising relation with Clyde. Roberta is not yet pregnant, but she has already sensed Clyde's increasing evasiveness and indifference and is deeply troubled about it. Even a first reader of the novel senses how dangerous her admission of the relationship would be to Clyde and, desperate in Clyde's desperation, must helplessly watch the dime fall. What is so original in this scene is that we are agonized to see Clyde given away while we are still entirely in sympathy with Roberta. All this is immensely subversive to traditional ethics: we very much want Roberta to refrain from doing something which is in no way ethically wrong so as to protect a character who is in danger because of his wrong treatment of her. We hope she won't tell, we fear for Clyde when she does—but we have no desire whatever to blame her for it. Why is this? It can only be because we have participated in, even entered into a measure of complicity with, a consciousness so much at cross-purposes with Roberta's. We have identified at least partially with Clyde's consciousness, on grounds so peculiar they deserve emphasis: we participate in Clyde's consciousness while fully aware of its pervasive bad faith because of the force of the desire he directs toward a factitious object. Even more paradoxically, we share feelings with an emotional solipsist.

In *Notes on Life* Dreiser wrote:

Feelings, emotions are to each one of us the most important things in our own lives. On our emotions depend our relations to everything outside of us and, ultimately, our happiness or unhappiness. Fear, envy

... all these and more, and in combinations of unfathomable complexity, are the realities of our life, more real to us than either the interior
fundamental instincts of self-preservation and sex or the exterior objects toward which our emotions are directed. Thus we can see that
each lives in a little world of his own, having in common with others
only the basic urges of the body and an exterior world which satisfies
or frustrates them.   (*Notes*, p. 81)

If everyone were as emotionally self-bounded as this passage suggests[95] there
would be no reason to write or read novels. The activity of *An American
Tragedy*, like that of *Adam Bede*, is to subvert the universal tendency toward
self-enclosure by means of the force of sympathy. The chief moral quality of
Dreiser's narrative voice is its objectively sympathetic understanding of the
misunderstandings of Clyde and Roberta. They can never see each other as
clearly as the narrator sees both.

The narrative voice is both technically and morally necessary to the novel
precisely because it fills in the space between the semi-solipsists who popu-
late the narration.[96] In some of the finest effects in the novel the characters
either totally deny sympathetic awareness or come ever so close to achieving
it. The near achievement of sympathy is, if anything, more painful, since we
want so strongly but never achieve the release of a completed *act* of sympathetic involvement, an act of love. Here is where the "gap of indeterminacy"
is located in Dreiser's fiction. The reader must break through the shell of
solipsism that encompasses the characters and it is the function of the narrative voice to guide him in so doing.

Clyde's solipsism, at its worst, easily puts Tito and Bartley in the shade
(not to mention Marcher and Densher). Dreiser catches it wonderfully and
awfully in the passage in which Clyde finds himself on the train platform with
Roberta "as the result of her persistent and illogical demands" (p. 472).
Roberta, pregnant, helpless, at the end of her resources, illogically wants
Clyde to marry her after his outstandingly inept attempts to arrange an abortion have, inevitably, failed. Clyde here evidences an extreme of the withholding of sympathy; to go any further would lead into the territory of writers
other than Dreiser: to psychopathic and sociopathic violence.

Clyde's more usual feelings toward Roberta are a muddle of ambivalence:
he pulls toward her some moments, pushes away at others, and sometimes the
push-pull is almost evenly balanced. Roberta is ambivalent as well; in the
early stages of the relationship her repressions and desires mutually block
each other: "At the same time within her was that overmastering urge of re-
pressed and feared desire now knocking loudly for recognition" (p. 289). As
one current momentarily predominates her response is tropistic: "For the
moment the moral repulsion was so great that unconsciously she endeavored
to relinquish herself from his embrace" (p. 289). "Clyde sensed how deep
was this sudden revolt" (p. 289) but only because it blocks his own desire,
not because he understands Roberta's fear.

Throughout, Dreiser shows the lovers' conflict with a kinesthetic immediacy. The following passage, centered on Clyde's insistence that Roberta let him visit her room, is a complex of interacting tropistic responses, of pulls and pushes, flights and returns. But all are governed by the game neither character is fully conscious of playing, the game of sexual politics:

> At once, and with an irritated shrug of the shoulders, as she now saw, he turned and started to leave her, saying as he did so, "Oh, that's all right, if that's the way you feel about it." And Roberta, dumbfounded and terrified, stood there.
>
> "Please don't go, Clyde. Please don't leave me," she exclaimed suddenly and pathetically, her defiance and courage undergoing a deep and sad change. "I don't want you to. I love you so, Clyde. I would if I could. You know that."
>
> "Oh, yes, I know, but you needn't tell me that" (it was his experience with Hortense and Rita that was prompting him to this attitude). With a twist he released his body from her arm and started walking briskly down the street in the dark.
>
> And Roberta, stricken by this sudden development which was so painful to both, called "Clyde!" And then ran after him a little way, eager that he should pause and let her plead with him more. But he did not return. Instead he went briskly on. And for the moment it was all she could do to keep from following him and by sheer force, if need be, restrain him. Her Clyde. And she started running in his direction a little, but as suddenly stopped, checked for the moment by the begging, pleading, compromising attitude in which she, for the first time, found herself. For on the one hand all her conventional training was now urging her to stand firm—not to belittle herself in this way—whereas on the other, all her desire for love, understanding, companionship, urged her to run after him before it was too late and he was gone. . . . And yet so binding were the conventions which had been urged upon her up to this time that, though suffering horribly, a balance between the two forces was struck, and she paused, feeling that she could neither go forward nor stand still.   (p. 292)

The most authentic language for Dreiser's characters is, once again, body language. Clyde's first utterance, as he well knows, is false in both its clauses: it is *not* all right and Roberta does *not* feel that way about it. To genuinely talk to Roberta, Clyde would need to recognize that she is a separate person. But, in fact, she is for him only a surface off which he bounces his resentment at his sexual timidity with two women as unlike Roberta as any could be.[97] In the outcome, Roberta goes bankrupt in surrogate payment for Hortense's sexual stinginess. There is something quite awful in the politics and economics of sexual relationship, and Dreiser spares us nothing in his revelation of it. Here is Clyde worrying whether Roberta will be willing to buy dear and sell cheap:

> For, as he now darkly and vaguely thought, if he sought a relationship which her prejudices and her training would not permit her to look up-

on as anything but evil, was he not thereby establishing in some form a claim on her part to some consideration from him in the future which it might not be so easy for him to ignore? For after all he was the aggressor—not she. And because of this, and whatever might follow in connection with it, might not she be in a position to demand more from him than he might be willing to give? . . . Therefore should he proceed to demand—or should he not? And if he did, could he avoid that which would preclude any claim in the future?   (pp. 295–296)

In an immensely painful scene, the pregnant Roberta realizes Clyde is lying to her but realizes, too, that she cannot afford an open confrontation:

And while she might urge, in the last analysis she could not force him to do anything. He might just go away alone, as he had once said in connection with inadvertently losing his job because of her. And how much greater might not his impulse in that direction now be, if this world here in which he was so much interested were taken away from him, and he were to face the necessity of taking her and a child too. It made her more cautious and caused her to modify her first impulse to speak out definitely and forcefully, however great her necessity might be.   (p. 414)

Meanwhile, Clyde has structurally similar reasons for circumspection:

And so disturbed was he by the panorama of the bright world of which Sondra was the center and which was now at stake, that he could scarcely think clearly. Should he lose all this for such a world as he and Roberta could provide for themselves—a small home—a baby, such a routine work-a-day life as taking care of her and a baby on such a salary as he could earn, and from which most likely he would never again be freed! God! A sense of nausea seized him. He could not and would not be so easily tumbled about his ears by her and because of one false step on his part. It made him cautious and for the first time in his life caused tact and cunning to visualize itself as a profound necessity.   (p. 414)

Roberta and Clyde both know they need to be "cautious." Both must suppress strong feelings, both must hold back, as a false step could precipitate them into an abyss. The conflicting and balanced suppressions give the passage a suffocating effect. Dreiser conveys almost physically the terrible mutual constraints of Clyde and Roberta, the pathos of these two conflicting vortices of feeling midway in a process which will lead to their dying, incommunicado.

Even more excruciating are the moments in which Clyde does approach a sympathetic awareness of Roberta. His failure to sustain these moments entraps him more firmly in the fantasy world of his desires. Clyde is momentarily tender to Roberta, feeling "genuinely moved by his own dereliction," only because "He could for some reason almost see himself in Roberta's place" (p. 360). It is as Roberta reflects his own experience that she emotionally reaches him: "There was about Clyde at times a certain strain of tenderness, evoked by experiences, disappointments, and hardships in his own life, which came out to one and another, almost any other, under such circumstances as these" (p. 361). But if Clyde nearly apprehends Roberta by seeing his own reflection in her, he comes quickly up against the limits of a self-enclosed mode of sympathy. Dreiser implicitly demonstrates that a breakthrough to any other mode would have to be a break away from the limits of "self." Clyde's sympathy for Roberta can go nowhere. It is ultimately as technically sentimental as when Carrie is moved by Père Goriot's fictional sorrows while Hurstwood moves to suicide: such self-reflective sympathy only acts as self-confirmation. Clyde could be taken as an object lesson of the partial truth of the Victorian dogma that self-negation is essential to self-enlargement. Why should Clyde pity Roberta more than himself when he pities her as himself?

Moreover, it is Clyde's very "condition of mingled sympathy and opposition" (p. 368), another variation on tropistic response, that precipitates the crisis of the novel. Clyde feels just enough for Roberta to make love to her to console her for his not feeling more. The love-making causes her pregnancy, which links Clyde permanently to her (in a sense she does take Clyde down with her as she drowns), while it pushes him emotionally to the furthest possible distance from her. In the event, Clyde's type of sympathy, though it brings him as close as he comes to the boundaries of his solipsistic isolation, proves destructive: since this sympathy is itself a form of solipsism it reinforces rather than hinders Clyde's tendency to use Roberta as a surface off which he can project his own fears and desires. If Sondra was "the one girl of this upper level who had most materialized and magnified for him the meaning of that upper level itself" (p. 308), Roberta is all too identified with the "basement world" (p. 190) from which Clyde desperately seeks to escape. In *Sister Carrie* and *An American Tragedy* Dreiser portrays the basement world, with its "promise of a restricted and difficult life" (p. 472) so vividly as to induce in the reader a claustrophobia similar to that Carrie and Clyde feel as they attempt to break free.

A major difference between *Sister Carrie* and *An American Tragedy* is that, when Carrie feels Hanson as a negative force, we are to take it as a genuine insight on her part. Hanson *is* a negative force and Carrie grows in awareness by understanding this. Though we feel differently about Hurstwood, Carrie's turn away from him is based on an accurate if cruel assessment; rejection of his increasing parasitism is essential to her growth, even if this growth is toward a realization of the futility of the satisfaction she seeks. But Clyde's rejection of Roberta is not portrayed as a cruel necessity of self-enlargement, but as a sign of Clyde's solipsistic self-entrapment. For Roberta is no Hanson, nor yet a Hurstwood. Her relationship with Clyde comes about as the result of her own pathetic attempt to escape from the basement world. As much as Clyde or Carrie, she is one of Dreiser's seekers. She does become dependent on Clyde and is forced by circumstances to try to make him respect convention—but only as the last resource of her desperation. Moreover,

Hurstwood had manipulated and almost forced Carrie into their relationship, whereas, in *An American Tragedy*, Clyde is the "aggressor."

Thus, although we are led to share Clyde's horror of the basement world, we see Roberta not as embodiment but as victim of it. Our sympathy for Clyde's predicament does not contradict but carries over into our sympathy for Roberta's. So, throughout, our sympathy with Clyde is compounded by our discomfort at the limitations of his sympathy. Clyde is as much a solipsist as Carrie, but his solipsism is problematic while hers is incidental. Solipsism in *Sister Carrie* is merely symptomatic of Dreiser's version of Platonic romanticism, but in *An American Tragedy* it is thematic: it is part of the novel's constructed pattern of meaning and value.

The death scene compounds the ironies of sympathy that Dreiser has developed throughout the novel. Clyde strikes out at Roberta in a tropistic rejection of his fantasy image of her as the embodiment of constriction and restraint (earlier in the scene he has desubstantialized her "to a shadow or thought really, a form of illusion more vaporous than real" [p. 489]). But he is equally rejecting her unwanted *sympathy*: "And then, as she drew near him, seeking to take his hand in hers and the camera from him in order to put it in the boat, he flinging out at her, but not even then with any intention to do other than free himself of her—her touch—her pleading—consoling sympathy—her presence forever—God!" (p. 492). Then Clyde's own sympathy reasserts itself, at least minimally, only to cause her death: "rising and reaching half to assist or recapture her and half to apologize for the unintended blow—yet in so doing completely capsizing the boat—himself and Roberta being as instantly thrown into the water" (pp. 492–493). Clyde then fails, more or less intentionally, to rescue her, so that the scene structurally recapitulates the pregnancy sequence: Clyde rejects, he sympathetically responds to the pain his rejection causes, his response leads to disaster, and he bails out, becoming responsible by attempting to disclaim responsibility.

But, as always in Dreiser, the concept of responsibility is enveloped in ambiguity. By the time Clyde reaches shore he is already uncertain whether or not he has "murdered" Roberta. This is not mere rationalization; he truly does not know, and a careful reading of the scene leaves any honest reader in a state of equal uncertainty. Though Clyde premeditated Roberta's murder, even to details of the way in which her death in fact happens, the death itself results not from his carrying out his plan but from tropistic movements of both his repulsion *and* sympathy. His responsibility is clearest in what he does *not* do—attempt to aid the drowning Roberta. We cannot comfortably and unequivocally term Clyde either guilty or innocent: we have observed too closely a process which resists abstract fixation.[98]

For another irony of Clyde's self-centeredness is that he has so little self to center. His most persistent traits are his evasiveness, his bad faith, his unawareness. He relates to the world like a cathode-ray tube, picking up and focusing into his own image all the social illusions within range. The last major irony of *An American Tragedy* is the attempt of everyone, friends as well as foes, to make sense out of Clyde by fixing "a temperament that was as fluid and unstable as water" (p. 309) into place. Earlier, Clyde himself tries to fight off his temptation by assuring himself that "He was not a murderer and never could be" (p. 451). Later the assertions get weaker—"He was not like that. . . . He was no such person" (p. 461). After the fact he is uncertain about what he is not, but no more certain about what, if anything, he is. Others are sure: "he was an unmitigated villain—a reptilian villain!" (p. 502). Roberta's father and mother have no choice, within their conventions, than to construe the muddled and pathetic relationship of Roberta and Clyde into the simple melodrama of "a city seducer and betrayer . . . who had been able to seduce her by a promise of marriage" (p. 513). These categories come ready-made.[99]

However one construes Clyde's degree of guilt, Dreiser makes it nearly impossible to judge a personality so lacking in character. Thus the entire courtroom scene, as convincing a representation of reality as any in our literature, is all the same a gigantic farce; prosecution and defense are both reconstructing events as they did not take place caused by individuals who did not exist. Dreiser shows that a "real" trial consists of a tissue of fictions. For the purpose of reaching truth, the prosecutor might just as well have arraigned what Powys called the "cloud of invisible eidola, airy images of . . . grosser desire," for to Dreiser these images are central to any guilt of Clyde's. What Dreiser, then, has put on trial is the ethos that underlies and justifies trials.

6. Stein's "Melanctha": An Education in Pathos

1. Stein as Radical Empiricist

There is a passage in "Melanctha," the great middle story of Gertrude Stein's *Three Lives*, that captures a long moment of silent tension between its two central characters: "They sat there then a long time by the fire, very silent and not loving, and never looking to each other for it. Melanctha was moving and twitching herself and very nervous with it. Jeff was heavy and sullen and dark and very serious in it."[1] The "it" that they react to in such different ways has the same antecedent as in Henry James's late fiction, the complex of relations between two complex characters. The passage concentrates not on Melanctha's feelings toward Jeff or Jeff's toward Melanctha but on a *tertium quid*, the mood created by their momentary antagonism. The objectification of mood is an explicit principle in "Melanctha": "It was not the power of Melanctha's words that held him, for, for them, he had his answer, it was the power of the mood that filled Melanctha, and for that he had no answer" (p. 151). In "Melanctha," mood is a phenomenological reality. Stein has recognized, like William James in his later philosophy, "the way in which certain moods and feelings pervade [the] world-field as a whole."[2] Mood is a precipitate of relations but relations are as real as entities. "Melanctha" is a radically empiricist fiction.

Stein's fascination with both William and Henry James is well known.[3] In *The Autobiography of Alice B. Toklas* Stein acknowledges Henry James as "quite definitely . . . her forerunner" but maintains that her interest in him was a late development.[4] In fact in her first novel, the posthumously published *Q.E.D.*, two central characters discuss Milly Theale and Kate Croy and are loosely paralleled to them.[5] Jamesian thematic and stylistic influences carry over into "Melanctha," which is, in some ways, a rewriting of *Q.E.D.*[6] Later, Stein charmingly cited Henry James in response to T. S. Eliot's malicious query about who was her authority for her habit of splitting infinitives.[7] Finally, there is a possibility that Stein may have tried to send a copy of *Three Lives* to Henry James, though no record exists of his having received it.[8]

William James acknowledged his copy in a somewhat ambiguous letter:

I have had a bad conscience about "Three Lives." You know (?) how hard it is for me to read novels. Well, I read 30 or 40 pages, and said "this is a fine new kind of realism—Gertrude Stein is great! I will go at it carefully when just the right mood comes." But apparently the right mood never came. I thought I had put the book in my trunk, to finish over here, but I don't find it on unpacking. I promise you that it shall be read *some* time! You see what a swine I am to have pearls cast before him! As a rule reading fiction is as hard to me as trying to hit a target by hurling feathers at it. I need *resistance*, to cerebrate![9]

It is uncertain from his syntax whether James means to cite *Three Lives* as an exception to or a confirmation of his difficulty in reading fiction. If the latter, he may well be the only reader who ever complained of meeting insufficient resistance in Stein's fiction. A fascinating passage of *The Autobiography of Alice B. Toklas* recounts how Stein received a letter from a man in Boston who claimed to have "appropriated" William James's copy of *Three Lives*, complete with James's marginal notes. Subsequent correspondence proved unsatisfactory, however, so these notes, if they ever existed, appear to be lost to literary history.[10]

William James was "the important person in Gertrude Stein's Radcliffe life."[11] What she "completely learned" from him was "that science is continuously busy with the complete description of something, with ultimately the complete description of anything with ultimately the complete description of everything."[12] She responded to James's rejection of the temptation to premature closure of ideas: "Keep your mind open, he used to say, and when some one objected, but Professor James, this that I say, is true. Yes, said James, it is abjectly true."[13] Later, when James visited Paris, she showed him her post-impressionist paintings: "He looked and gasped. I told you, he said, I always told you that you should keep your mind open."[14] Along with Henry James, Flaubert, and Cézanne, William James was a central influence on *Three Lives*.[15]

Published shortly before William James's posthumous masterpiece, *Essays in Radical Empiricism*, "Melanctha" has in common with it the attempt to penetrate the structure of the empire of flux so as to become acquainted with the nature of things. Such an acquaintance, according to Justice Holmes, emerges, despite the limitations of his prose style, in James's philosopher ally, John Dewey: "Although Dewey's book is incredibly ill-written, it seemed to me after several rereadings to have a feeling of intimacy with the inside of the cosmos that I found unequaled. So me-thought God would have spoken had he been inarticulate but keenly desirous to tell you how it was."[16]

Dewey's inarticulateness was unintentional, but in "Melanctha" what seems inarticulate in the narrative style and in the speech of the characters results from Stein's striving to represent faithfully the inside of a human relationship. The unusualness of the prose style of "Melanctha" comes from Stein's avoidance of those conventions of articulation that misrepresent actuality, rather than from any self-conscious preciousness of style.[17] Donald

Sutherland notes how the articulate but lighter-than-air language and characters of *Q.E.D.* transpose into "the sure grasp of the personal cadences of a character's thought and feeling that makes the analyses in 'Melanctha' a direct expression of character in movement."[18] Jeff Campbell and Melanctha Herbert seem to be inarticulate but keenly desirous to tell you how it was, as opposed to the characters of *Q.E.D.* —"white American college women, whose speech and thought are bound to be at odds with their feeling."[19]

But Stein is not drawing on the primitivistic convention which, by associating honesty with simplicity, reduces and condescends to its characters. In fact, Stein reversed the convention; Jeff and Melanctha are not only more honest than their *Q.E.D.* counterparts but more complex and intelligent. Their slowed-down, clotted-up, doubling-back syntactic patterns enable their groping but profound phenomenological explorations, their personal, desperately self-interested variation on "the re-instatement of the vague to its proper place in our mental life" (*Principles*, I, 254). These characters reveal themselves to us, John Malcolm Brinnin notes, "as the rhythms in which they speak or think are quickened or relaxed or endlessly repeated." The result is an extraordinary "immediacy," "a continual sense of hearing or overhearing the particular quality of consciousness that belongs to each subject." [20] Donald Sutherland argues that in her later writings Stein comes as close to delivering the *ecceitas* and the *haecceitas* of phenomena as anyone since Duns Scotus,[21] but I believe that one feels this phenomenological authenticity equally strongly in "Melanctha" (albeit the focus is limited to the phenomena of personal relationship).

I would suggest that Thornton Wilder's fine description of how we follow Stein's process of consciousness in *Four in America* almost exactly describes how we trace the tortuosities of consciousness in Jeff and Melanctha:

> *Four in America* is not a book which is the end and summary of her thoughts about the subjects she has chosen; it is the record of her thoughts, from the beginning, as she "closes in" on them. It is *being written* before our eyes; she does not, as other writers do, suppress and erase the hesitations, the recapitulations, the connectives, in order to give us the completed fine results of her meditations. She gives us the process.[22]

The difference is, of course, that *Four in America* is a wearisome tracing of the process of Stein's thoughts whereas "Melanctha" is a great *imitation* of the movements of two consciousnesses, consciousnesses redeemed from self-indulgence and triviality by the pressure of their relationship.[23]

In reading "Melanctha" one experiences something with the feel of direct reality. Stein herself argues that readers respond not to a matching of their reality, since no two people's worlds can match, but to "the vitality of a thing which sounds to them like someone else's knowing."[24] I think that in "Melanctha" one finds this vitality of authenticity, but also a representation of typical experience. Stein herself asserted that all real knowledge is common knowledge and that its source is experience:

Now what we know is formed in our head by thousands of small occasions in the daily life. By "what we know" I do not mean, of course,
what we learn from books, because that is of no importance at all. I
mean what we really know, like our assurance about how we know anything, and what we know about the validity of the sentiments, and
things like that. All the thousands of occasions in the daily life go into
our head to form our ideas about these things.

This knowledge can become charged with intensity when it is authentically
recognized in writing, but not by means of any external "inspiration":

That is the moment of Recognition. Like God on the Seventh Day we
look at it and say it is good. That is the moment that some people call
inspiration, but I do not like the word inspiration, because it suggests
that someone else is blowing that knowledge into you. It is not being
blown into you; it is very much your own and was acquired by you in
thousands of tiny occasions in your daily life.[25]

In "Melanctha" we can feel the desperation and heroism of Jeff's and
Melanctha's only momentarily successful efforts to recognize the life they are
living. This life is special only because of their special need to recognize it:

"Melanctha" . . . remains a landmark performance by a white American
author dealing with the Negro as a person of complexity and bewilder-
ing passions, not as a pawn in a propaganda treatise for social reform.
Gertrude's treatment of the love affair between Jeff Campbell and
Melanctha Herbert was written in terms of the democracy of human
feelings.[26]

"Melanctha" is simple through complication, a formula Stein derived from
William James:

I like a thing simple, but it must be simple through complication.
Everything must come into your scheme; otherwise you cannot achieve
real simplicity. A great deal of this I owe to a great teacher, William
James. He said "Never reject anything. Nothing has been proved. If you
reject anything, that is the beginning of the end as an intellectual." He
was my big influence when I was at college. He was a man who always
said, "Complicate your life as much as you please, it has got to simpli-
fy."[27]

Edmund Wilson saw something like this formula as what Sherwood Anderson and Ernest Hemingway learned from Stein. Notable in the writings of all
three was "a distinctively American development in prose": "a naiveté of
language, often passing into the colloquialism of the character dealt with,
which serves actually to convey profound emotions and complex states of
mind."[28] Wilson later distinguished Stein's *Three Lives* from its model story,
"Un Coeur Simple," for its greater intimacy with the inside:

What is most remarkable in these stories—especially if we compare them with such a typically naturalistic production as Flaubert's "Un Coeur Simple," in which we feel that the old family servant has been seen from a great distance and documented with effort—is the closeness with which the author has been able to identify herself with her characters. In a style which appears to owe nothing to that of any other novelist, she seems to have caught the very rhythms and accents of the minds of her heroines.[29]

Or one might say that "Melanctha" has the phenomenological intensity of *Madame Bovary* without that book's brilliant but self-protective hedge of irony. There is little American fiction in which characters are so intensely realized as in "Melanctha."

2. Understanding Wandering

> "Understanding is the best thing in the world
> Between a boy and a girl." —Ray Charles

"Melanctha" is radically empiricist in plot and language as well as in characterization. *Q.E.D.* works out its plot with the neatness of a syllogism, but the plot of "Melanctha" is in tune with the nonrationally structured world described in William James's *A Pluralistic Universe*:

> I myself find no good warrant for even suspecting the existence of any reality of a higher denomination than that distributed and strung-along and flowing sort of reality which we finite beings swim in. That is the sort of reality given us, and that is the sort with which logic is so incommensurable.[30]

Stein carefully works out her plot to disconnect the major characters: both Jeff and Melanctha know Jane Harden, Jeff is strongly affected by Jane Harden's evaluation of Melanctha, and Melanctha reacts bitterly to Jeff's Jane-influenced criticism—but the three never appear in a scene together. A "well-made" plot would have rounded off the pattern by having Melanctha react directly upon Jane. Melanctha has major relationships with Rose Johnson and Jem Richards, neither of whom directly intersect with Jeff Campbell. These characters are, it is true, thematically related. Jem Richards is too fast for Melanctha, in obvious contrast to Jeff, who is too slow; the riddle of Melanctha's relation to Rose Johnson is explained by the outcome of her relation to Jeff.[31] But this is, precisely, a distributed and strung-along pattern of relations. In a "well-made" plot the thematic parallels would be reinforced by a complex of cross-relations among the characters. *Q.E.D.* has such cross-relations; "Melanctha" deliberately avoids them.

But the phenomenological originality of "Melanctha" shows most in its language. John Wild's commentary on William James emphasizes how he redefined the terms for knowledge:

> In any report of observations on lived existence, we are constantly

presented with terms like *being, feeling*, and *understanding* whose meaning has to be taken for granted. The observer is apt to suppose that these terms stand for objects whose meanings are as yet vague, and which may be clarified by further observations. But this is not true.

These terms do not stand for objects. They stand for living experiences that are known, always vaguely, by direct acquaintance.[32]

James himself, it should be recalled, defined consciousness not as an entity but as a function, the function of "knowing."[33] The key terms in "Melanctha" are "knowledge," "power," "wisdom," "real knowing," "understanding," "learning," "feeling," and "wandering." All these terms, including the first four—which are generally thought of as substantive states of being—Stein uses in the experiential, functional, processual sense defined by James and Wild. And "wandering," seemingly the least intellectual of words, is, in "Melanctha," always the most so: "wanderings after wisdom" (p. 97).

Though "wandering" and the other key terms take on strong sexual associations, they are not mere sexual euphemisms. Sutherland points out that what makes Stein's method of verbal association "accurate and not euphemistic is that the subject is literally feeling, all feeling, inasmuch as all the passions are one. . . . The readiness, slowness, concentration or absent-mindedness, domination or dependence in sexual feeling are about the same as in all the other activities of a character."[34]

Stein, like Whitman, redefines by dissociation. Stein, in fact, recognized Whitman as a pioneer dissociater: "He wanted really to express the thing and not call it by its name." When you name anything you "include emotions as well as things"[35] so that the phenomenon is pervaded by stock associations. Thus, the writer must go on "with this exceeding struggle of knowing really knowing what a thing was really knowing it knowing anything I was seeing anything I was feeling so that its name could be something, by its name coming to be a thing in itself as it was but would not be anything just and only as a name" (*Lect.*, p. 242). Nouns, the grammatical form of nomination, indicate a hasty, careless perception, a perception inaccurate because it lacks intensity:

> As I say a noun is the name of a thing, and therefore *slowly* if you if you feel what is inside that thing you do not call it by the name by which it is known. Everybody knows that by the way they do when they are in love and *a writer should always have that intensity of emotion about whatever is the object about which he writes.* And therefore I say it again more and more one does not use nouns.
>
> (*Lect.*, p. 210; my italics)[36]

From Stein's point of view, then, some of the more "realistic" substantive terms for describing sexual life might be intellectual euphemisms. In overcoming such limiting conventions "a separating way" of writing "may help a great deal, indeed it may, it may, it may help very much" (*Lect.*, p. 22).

It is the reliance on conventional thought, feeling, and moral response—on conventional nomination—which makes the nineteenth-century English novel such an easy (non-resistant, as it were) read: "When I was a child I was always completely fascinated by the sentence, he who runs may read. In England running and reading is one because any one can read, and since any one can read does it make any difference how or why they run" (*Lect.*, pp. 16–17). In Stein's view, English writing works within conventions, accepted by reader and writer alike, of what the "daily island life" is all about (*Lect.*, pp. 14–15). In contrast is the American mode, as typified by Henry James as well as Whitman:

> And so this makes it that Henry James just went on doing what American literature had always done, the form was always the form of the contemporary English one, but the disembodied way of disconnecting something from anything and anything from something was the American one. The way it had of often all never having any daily living was an American one. (*Lect.*, p. 53)

So Stein: "And then I went on to what was the American thing the disconnection and I kept breaking the paragraph down, and everything down to commence again with not connecting with the daily anything and yet to really choose something" (*Lect.*, p. 54).

In "Melanctha" what Stein really chooses is a new, more accurately perceived, set of terms for sexual relations.[37] In her "wanderings" Melanctha seeks "the ways that lead to wisdom" (p. 96), a wisdom that involves "knowledge and power" (p. 97). She seeks because "Melanctha all her life was very keen in her sense for real experience" (p. 97). Sexual experience teaches the reality of power, the power of others and of oneself. Jane Harden illuminates for Melanctha the interrelation of desire and power: "She would be with other people and with men and with Melanctha, and she would make Melanctha understand what everybody wanted, and what one did with power when one had it" (p. 106). The quest has an Odyssean tinge: Melanctha began "to discover men and learn their natures and their various ways of working" (p. 95).[38] This is not "sex education" (talk of nominalizing!) but sex *as* education, an opening into the ways of the world, things as they are. Sex is the ancilla to knowledge.

This is why, in a book where sex is so central a motivation, where style is so pervaded with sexual implications, even *double entendre*, there is so little explicit physical sexual action.[39] It is impossible to say at what particular moment Melanctha changes from inexperienced student to accredited teacher of the ways that lead to wisdom, because this moment occurs somewhere between the lines of the narrative. Unequivocal sexual actions go little beyond hand-holding and kissing (pp. 131, 133). Stein's real interest is in sex as relational nexus. Sex enables the exploration of self—self, that is, in the radical empiricist sense defined by Wild, conceived "not as an isolated substance, but as a field, always stretched out toward others."[40]

"Melanctha" fictionally develops a "field conception of the human self"[41] like that implicit in William James's philosophy. Even Stein's special treatment of this self in sexual terms has a parallel in James's *Principles*:

> The most peculiar social self which one is apt to have is in the mind of the person one is in love with. The good or bad fortunes of this self cause the most intense elation and dejection—unreasonable enough as measured by every other standard than that of the organic feeling of the individual. To his own consciousness he *is* not, so long as this particular social self fails to get recognition, and when it is recognized, his contentment passes all bounds.   (*Principles*, I, 294)

So the loving self is the most intensified version of the relational self, the field conception of self. It is also the self at its most vulnerable, as open to rejection as acceptance. Thus cowardice can be very much an issue in sexual experience. Melanctha, in her inexperienced state, has the usual fear of sexual encounter: "It was a strange experience of ignorance and power and desire. Melanctha did not know what it was that she so badly wanted. She was afraid, and yet she did not understand that here she really was a coward" (p. 96). Her desire and fear counterpoise each other as she adopts the attitude of a spectator: "Melanctha liked to wander, and to stand by the railroad yard, and watch the men and the engines and the switches and everything that was busy there, working" (pp. 97–98). Sexual curiosity, in Stein's language, is contextualized with travel (shipping docks as well as railroad yards are a favorite "wandering" place), adventure, "successful power" (p. 96) (here seen in work), and dynamism ("Hullo sis, do you want to sit on my engine" [p. 98]).

Melanctha refuses such invitations, remaining for the moment, like other watchers, in a passive spectatorial condition that Stein associates with emotional cowardice and laziness:

> For the lazy man whose blood flows very slowly, it is a steady soothing world of motion which supplies him with the sense of a strong moving power. He need not work and yet he has it very deeply; he has it even better than the man who works in it or owns it. Then for natures that like to feel emotion without the trouble of having any suffering, it is very nice to get the swelling in the throat, and the fullness, and the heart beats, and all the flutter of excitement that comes as one watches the people come and go, and hears the engine pound and give a long drawn whistle.   (p. 98)

This passage is not a metaphor for vicarious sexuality but an extended simile; it broadens the conception of sexual experience by exploring its parallels to the world of work, a world given its own full value. The implicit simile conveys a typical stage of experience: the adolescent's suspension and vicarious fascination before the adult world of work and of sexual experience. In both cases the adolescent feels the power and adventure of it perhaps better than the person who works or owns, but fears the potential complications and suffering.

Spectatorship is a form of cowardice too natural, too inevitable to be culpable; it is, after all, an exploratory passivity, a way-station on the wandering after wisdom. Besides, "Railroad yards *are* a ceaseless fascination" (p. 98; my italics). Stein here outflanks the tendency of language to decontextualize, to split off and arbitrarily reduce and demean the dimensions of experience. Her words wander after wisdom by wandering away from their previous associations. This strategy of dissociation must underlie some of Stein's claim in *The Autobiography of Alice B. Toklas* that "Melanctha" "was the first definite step away from the nineteenth century and into the twentieth century in literature."[42]

3. Real Experience: "The Squeeze of This World's Life"

Both the process and the result of understanding is the registering of new emotional frequencies: Melanctha "learned a little in these days to know joy, and she was taught too how very keenly she could suffer" (p. 106). In the ethics of intensity joy and suffering are synonyms, parallel variants on the underlying value of intensity *per se*. Suffering has a slight edge; Melanctha's name recalls less mellowness than the melancholia appropriate to one who "was always full with mystery and subtle movements and denials and vague distrusts and complicated disillusions" (p. 89). Jeff Campbell, as Melanctha's student, extends the demonstration that there can be no learning unaccompanied by pain. In Stein's prolonged, luminous representation, Jeff cannot learn passion except by submitting himself to the tropistic tensions of attraction and repulsion, desire and obstruction. If the self is a field that opens out to others, what traverses this field are kinetic charges, more often deflected than complete in their circuit.

The basis for the model is nicely established by William James, in his *Some Problems in Philosophy:*

> The word "activity" has no content save those experiences of process, obstruction, striving, strain, or release, ultimate *qualia* as they are of the life given us to be known. No matter what "efficacies" there may really be in this extraordinary universe it is impossible to conceive of any one of them being either lived through or authentically known otherwise than in this dramatic shape of something sustaining a felt purpose against felt obstacles, and overcoming or being overcome.[43]

Jeff Campbell's main purpose becomes his relationship with Melanctha, but the relationship is defined by the obstructions their opposed values and rhythms present (see section 4 below). Or, to put it another way, Melanctha is the obstruction that activates Jeff through his inability to overcome her.

In Stein's first presentation of Jeff, he is happily unencumbered:

> Dr. Jefferson Campbell was a serious, earnest, good young joyous doctor. He liked to take care of everybody and loved his own colored people. He always found life very easy did Jeff Campbell, and every-

body liked to have him with them. He was so good and sympathetic, and he was so earnest and so joyous. He sang when he was happy, and he laughed, and his was the free abandoned laughter that gives the warm broad glow to negro sunshine.

Jeff Campbell had never yet in his life had real trouble.

(pp. 110–111)

Clearly this is what is wrong with him! Personally and socially vibrant and joyous, Jeff exhibits, nevertheless, a lack of depth and full reality. His goodness, sympathy, earnestness, and joyousness—real enough and valuable enough in themselves—are, at the same time, a control on his relationships, a protection against the danger, risk, and pain of passionate relationship. Jeff is genuinely ethical, but his ethical control over relationships is a shield against real experience. Needing real trouble in his life, he finds Melanctha.

One of Melanctha's purposes in the novel is to put both Jeff and the reader through a process of education in pathos. Jeff's interest in Melanctha is piqued, aroused, partially consummated, partially retreated from, rearoused yet more intensely, teased, finally pervaded by despair, partially salvaged by resignation, and transformed at last into strength.[44] Jeff emerges a different man. If we cannot point to any single, decisive moment of change, it is because his transformed identity is presented less in terms of a substantive result than of the curve of the process. Moreover, as with William James's gradually mutating self, the transformation does not negate the original self: "The identity which the *I* discovers, as it surveys this long procession, can only be a relative identity, that of a slow sifting in which there is always some common ingredient retained" (*Principles*, I, 372). Still, for the later Jeff the world has a different feel and weight than for his earlier self.

At one stage of Jeff's understanding a mood of despair pervades his world-field. This despair has a palpable weight and depth; it envelops Jeff's world in heavy dreariness:

> He felt very sick and his heart was very heavy, and Melanctha certainly did seem very ugly to him. Jeff was at last beginning to know what it was to have deep feelings. He took care a little longer of Jane Harden, and then he went to his other patients, and then he went home to his room, and he sat down and at last he had stopped thinking. He was very sick and his heart was very heavy in him. He was very tired and all the world was very heavy to him, and he knew very well now at last, he was really feeling. He knew it now from the way it hurt him. He knew very well that now at last he was beginning to have understanding.

(p. 144)

The weight on Jeff is not purely subjective and private; it has enough of an objective presence that he must try to hide it from Melanctha. This, however, is impossible since, at this moment, the weight is intrinsic to Jeff's identity. It expresses itself, if not in words, quite clearly in physical attitude and in eloquent silence:

> There was a weight in Jeff Campbell from now on, always with him,
> that he could never lift out from him to feel easy. He always was trying
> not to have it in him and he was always trying not to let Melanctha feel
> it, with him, but it was always there inside him. Now Jeff Campbell al-
> ways was serious, and dark, and heavy, and sullen, and he would often
> sit a long time with Melanctha without moving.   (p. 171)

The field of self that Jeff opens to Melanctha cannot but be thickened by this
weight, itself a reflex of their relation. The weight's obstruction becomes one
of the ultimate *qualia* of Jeff's present relational activity. Thus, Jeff's silence
is not a closure of the dialogue between himself and Melanctha but part of its
process.

As the relationship goes bad it becomes a kind of emotional addiction to
Jeff. He vacillates, trapped by his longing for Melanctha, tortured by his
awareness of the breakdown between them: "Jeff Campbell knew very well
too now inside him, he did not really want Melanctha, now if he could no
longer trust her, though he loved her hard and really knew now what it was to
suffer" (p. 189). When Jeff finally writes to Melanctha, intending to break off
the relationship, he acts out the phenomenology, as described by William
James, of an intensely painful decision:

> In the fifth and final type of decision, the feeling that the evidence is
> all in, and that reason has balanced the books, may be either present or
> absent. But in either case we feel, in deciding, as if we ourselves by our
> own willful act inclined the beam; in the former case by adding our
> living effort to the weight of the logical reason which taken alone,
> seems powerless to make the act discharge; in the latter, by a kind of
> creative contribution of something instead of a reason which does a
> reason's work. The slow dead heave of the will that is felt in these in-
> stances makes of them a class altogether different subjectively. . . . Sub-
> jectively and phenomenally, the *feeling of effort* . . . accompanies these.
> Whether it be the dreary resignation for the sake of austere and naked
> duty of all sorts of rich mundane delights, or whether it be the heavy
> resolve that of two mutually exclusive trains of future fact, both sweet
> and good . . . one shall forever-more become impossible, while the other
> shall become a reality, it is a desolate and acrid sort of act, an excursion
> into a lonesome moral wilderness. If examined closely its chief differ-
> ence . . . appears to be that in other cases the mind at the moment of
> deciding on the triumphant alternative dropped the other one wholly
> or nearly out of sight, whereas here both alternatives are steadily held
> in view, and in the very act of murdering the vanquished possibility the
> chooser realizes how much in that instant he is making himself lose. It
> is deliberately driving a thorn into one's flesh; and the sense of *inward
> effort* with which the act is accompanied is an element which sets
> [this] type of decision in strong contrast with the previous varieties,
> and makes of it an altogether peculiar form of mental phenomenon.
>   (*Principles*, II, 534)

After Jeff's slow dead heave of the will—of which Stein's language de-
livers the full weight—he feels a kind of freedom and relief; but it is a dull,
heavy kind of relief, associated with an acrid, dreary, depleted mood. He is in
a desolate, lonely emotional wilderness, the seeming peace of which is sodden
and factitious, proceeding from an anesthesis rather than a resolution of his
turmoil:

> Jeff was all locked up and quiet now inside him. It was all settling
> down heavy in him, and these days when it was sinking so deep in him,
> it was only the rest and quiet of not fighting that he could really feel
> inside him. Jeff Campbell could not think now, or feel anything else in
> him. [See section 4 below for the conflict in Jeff between thinking and
> feeling. Now both are momentarily negated.] He had no beauty nor
> any kind of goodness to see around him. It was a dull pleasant kind of
> quiet he now had inside him. Jeff almost began to love this dull quiet in
> him, for it was more nearly being free for him than anything he had
> known in him since Melanctha Herbert first moved him. He did not find
> it a real rest yet for him, he had not really conquered what had been
> working so long in him, he had not learned to see beauty and real good-
> ness yet in what had happened to him, but it was rest even if he was
> sodden now all through him.   (p. 193)

Jeff's strong dead heave of the will, then, proves all too dead until, in a
finely pathetic fallacy, his mood breaks up with the winter. He responds to
spring in the fashion traditional from Chaucer to William Carlos Williams:

> It was very early now in the southern springtime. The trees were just
> beginning to get the little zigzag crinkles in them which the young buds
> always give them. The earth was wet and rich and smelling for them.
> The birds were making sharp fresh noises all around them. The wind
> was very gentle yet urgent to them. And the birds and the long earth-
> worms, and the negroes, and all kinds of children, were coming out
> every minute farther into the new spring, watery, southern sunshine.
>   (p. 195)

"Than longen folk to goon on pilgrimages": "Jeff Campbell too began to feel
a little his old joy inside him. The sodden quiet began to break up in him. He
leaned far out the window to mix it all up with him. Was it Melanctha Herbert he had just seen passing by him?" (p. 195). And the process begins again,
of desire, doubt, and desperate rationalization, all grounded in Jeff's intense
ambivalence:

> What a fool he was to throw her from him. Did he know she did not
> really love him. Suppose Melanctha was now suffering through him.
> Suppose she would be really glad to see him. And did anything else he
> did, really mean anything now to him? What a fool he was to cast her
> from him. And yet did Melanctha Herbert want him, was she honest to

him, had Melanctha ever loved him, and did Melanctha now suffer by
him? Oh! Oh! Oh! and the bitter water once more rose up in him.

(p. 195)

Jeff's suffering revives him; it puts him through a rapid alternation of all
the previous zigzag stages of his passion:

> All that long day, with the warm moist young spring stirring in him,
> Jeff Campbell worked, and thought, and beat his breast, and wandered,
> and spoke aloud, and was silent, and was certain, and then in doubt and
> then keen to surely feel, and then all sodden in him; and he walked, and
> sometimes he ran fast to lose himself in him rushing.   (p. 195)

Jeff cannot finally resolve his passion until he is able to conjoin it to his
ethos, for ultimately, in however tortuous a fashion, Stein does refer her
phenomenology of pathos back to ethos—as I shall argue in the next section.
But Jeff has learned in his education in pathos the *sine qua non* defined in
James's *Some Problems of Philosophy*: "The belief in the genuineness of each
particular moment in which we feel the squeeze of this world's life . . . is an
Eden from which rationalists seek in vain to expel us."[45]

4. Melanctha and Jeff: Pathos vs. Ethos

William James denied the possibility of a valid "ethical philosophy dogmati-
cally made up in advance."[46] Ethics must meet experience in all its variegated
forms. As Herbert Schneider notes, James's emphasis on the experiential basis
of ethical philosophy helped John Dewey "to formulate a 'psychological
ethics' based, not on precepts, but on actual, active desires."[47] Much of the
running philosophical debate between Jeff and Melanctha centers on ethics:
Jeff's belief in a preformulated conventional ethics is opposed to Melanctha's
belief in an ethics of intensity that dares the risk of desire. Melanctha scorns
Jeff's respectable definition of love:

> ". . . Miss Melanctha, I certainly do believe strong in loving, and in be-
> ing good to everybody, and trying to understand what they all need to
> help them." "Oh I know all about that way of doing Dr. Campbell, but
> that certainly ain't the kind of love I mean when I am talking. I mean
> real, strong, hot love Dr. Campbell, that makes you do anything for
> somebody that loves you."   (p. 122)

To Melanctha, Jeff's sort of love is merely a cowardly evasion, not a true
good:

> "You certainly are just too scared Dr. Campbell to really feel things
> way down in you. All you are always wanting Dr. Campbell is just to
> have a good time, and yet always to certainly keep yourself out of
> trouble. It don't seem to me Dr. Campbell that I admire that way to do
> things very much. It certainly ain't any more to me Dr. Campbell, but

that you certainly are awful scared about really feeling things way
down in you, and that's certainly the only way Dr. Campbell I can see
that you can mean, by what it is that you are always saying to me."

(p. 123)

And, in one of the loveliest sentences in "Melanctha," the debate becomes
epistemological: " 'Tell me just straight out how much do you care about
me, Miss Melanctha.' 'Care about you Jeff Campbell,' said Melanctha slowly.
'I certainly do care for you Jeff Campbell less than you are always thinking
and much more than you are ever knowing' " (p. 132). Jeff's response to this
is appropriate; he becomes "silent with the power of Melanctha's meaning"
(p. 132).

The passage is parallel to Milly's reproof of Lord Mark, who was "familiar
with everything but conscious, really of nothing." But there is more of a
parallel with "The Beast in the Jungle." Melanctha is Jeff's preceptor in the
ethics of intensity, as May wished to be with Marcher. Both Jeff and Marcher
are deficient in passion; both want an impossibly preformulated and articulated statement of the tacit and unsayable. But there is a major difference.
Jeff, operating in high good faith, discovers real experience by submitting
himself to the squeeze of this world's life; he becomes a true student in the
school of passion.

The most extraordinary thing in this extraordinary story is Stein's creation
of two characters who, without their seeming in any way falsely idealized,
she represents as struggling nobly toward right understanding. As much as
Milly Theale and Lambert Strether, Melanctha and Jeff are aristocrats of the
spirit, exemplary in virtue as in error. The most intense element of "Melanctha" is their never fully realized attempt to "work out together what they
meant by what they were always saying to each other" (p. 142). Their difficulty is that they are working in such ultimate terms, straining to compre-
hend fully and become morally responsible for their tropistic impulses—as
opposed to characters such as Howells' whose consciousnesses rarely reach
beyond rationalization and self-deception. In trying to make sense of their
own relationship Jeff and Melanctha attempt to name the non-substantive, to
track the transitive in flight, to denote feelings of "and," "if," "but," and
"by."[48] And, too, the feeling of "sort of feeling": "In all these ways he just,
by his nature, did, what he sort of felt Melanctha wanted" (pp. 142-143).
Their spoken language doubly reflects this preformulative consciousness, for
not only does it reflect directly, in its torsion of syntax, the tropistic pulsations passing between them, but these pulsations are what they are talking
about. Their discourse is an effort to understand the waxing and waning of
their feelings of relation.

As happens frequently in real life, though less often in fiction, the fatal
flaw in this relationship is that it is emotionally out of synch. Stein had been
fascinated to discover that a theater audience's emotion is always behind or
ahead of the play. This causes a peculiar sort of nervousness:

nervousness is the certain proof that the emotion of the one seeing and the emotion of the thing seen do not progress together.

Nervousness consists in needing to go faster or to go slower so as to get together. It is that that makes anybody feel nervous.   (*Lect.*, p. 95)

This is an esthetic theory but it is surely directly applicable to the dilemma of two people who are trying mutually to construct an ideal relationship. They may demand mutuality of each other, but the inevitable flaw is "the excitement and nervousness and the being behind or ahead in one's feeling" (*Lect.*, p. 99).

What is so culpable about being behind or ahead in a relationship is that it reveals an insufficient awareness of the other's feelings. Stein, as a good Jamesian, held "that habits of attention are reflexes of the complete character of the individual" (*Lect.*, p. 138). It was precisely this idea in James that Howells and Babbitt felt reinforced classical ethics. But Stein uses the idea to articulate pathos:

> I began to get enormously interested in hearing how everybody said the same thing over and over again with infinite variations but over and over again until finally if you listened with great intensity you could hear it rise and fall and tell all that there was inside them, not so much by the actual words they said or the thoughts they had but the movement of their thoughts and words endlessly the same and endlessly different.   (*Lect.*, p. 138)

As in Whitman we listen to the lull and hum of a valvèd voice for the purpose of disclosing "the complete rhythm of a personality" (*Lect.*, p. 147). What is crucial then is "the way the emotion progresses" (*Lect.*, p. 105). Readers of Stein's later fiction are bothered not only by its obscurity, but by the fact that it consists essentially of a single voice progressing, and meeting resistance only from its own self-enclosed doublings-back and second guesses. In "Melanctha," on the other hand, two quite different emotional rhythms clash: "He was silent, and this struggle lay there, strong, between them. It was a struggle, sure to be going on always between them. It was a struggle that was as sure always to be going on between them, as their minds and hearts always were to have different ways of working" (p. 153). And the clash generates a dialectic:

> "I certainly do very badly want to be right, Melanctha, the only way I know is right Melanctha really, and I don't know any way, Melanctha, to find out really whether my old way, the way I always used to be thinking, or the new, the way you make so like a real religion to me sometimes, Melanctha, which way is certainly the right way for me to be always thinking."   (p. 159)

At conflict are not only two systems of ideas but two different modes of emotional progression. What some critics have called repetition in her writing, Stein defines as part of this emotional progression—an always-varying insistence, not a repetition: "Then we have insistence insistence that in its emphasis can never be repeating, because insistence is always alive and if it is alive it is never saying anything in the same way because emphasis can never be the same" (*Lect.*, p. 171). What makes the disagreement so excruciating is that it implicates the characters' life rhythms, their will to live: "No matter how often what happened had happened any time any one told anything there was no repetition. This is what William James calls the Will to Live. If not nobody would live" (*Lect.*, p. 169).

In "Melanctha," however, one rhythm can *affect* another: the Jeff we see near the end of the story is a Jeff reconstituted by his relationship with Melanctha and partially converted to her ethical philosophy. The power of Melanctha's definition of how much she cares for him silences, at least momentarily, his compulsion toward the logical and ethical formulation of all admissible experience: "Dr. Campbell sat there very quiet; with only a little thinking and sometimes a beginning feeling" (p. 133). Jeff is learning to know rather than think, to respond in terms of what he sort of feels. This is part of the process of, as he later writes to Melanctha, "how hard I been trying to think and feel right for you" (p. 147). Melanctha's lesson of intensity has taken hold—"I got a new feeling now, you been teaching to me . . . just like a new religion to me, and I see, perhaps, what really loving is like" (p. 158)—but the trouble is that it has not entirely displaced his more conventional ethical set. Jeff articulated these values early in the story:

> "No I ain't got any use for all the time being in excitements and wanting to have all kinds of experience all the time. I got plenty of experience just living regular and quiet. . . . I don't believe much in this running around business and I don't like to see the colored people do it. I am a colored man and I ain't sorry, and I want to see the colored people like to live regular and work hard and understand things, and that's enough to keep any decent man excited." (p. 117)

Melanctha responds to Jeff's ambivalence with the partial rejection which becomes the cause of his education in suffering (see section 3 above).

It might seem as if Jeff's original ethical set were merely a straw man to be demolished by the force of Melanctha's pathos. Certainly, in Stein's later critical writing the Melanctha values of excitement and intensity are continually reaffirmed, whereas the Jeff values of remembering right and living regular are continually denigrated:

> We in this period have not lived in remembering, we have lived in moving being necessarily so intense that existing is indeed something, is indeed that thing that we are doing. And so what does it really matter what anybody does. The newspapers are full of what anybody does and anybody knows what anybody does but the thing that is important is the intensity of anybody's existence. (*Lect.*, p. 182)[49]

In *Narration* Stein argues, as she did in *Lectures in America*, that the genius of English fiction is its soothing fictional remembering right of everyone living regular their daily island life: "as it is a daily life lived every minute of the day it is a soothing thing to say and mostly what the English have had to say has been that it has been a soothing thing to say that they live every minute of the day even when the day has been a difficult day." In contrast, the genius of American fiction is its response to the American sense of excitement: "The American not living every minute of every day in a daily way does not make what he has to say be soothing he wants what he has to say to be exciting, and to move as everything moves, not to move as emotion is moving but to move as anything that really moves is moving."[50] The stability of language English fiction derived from the stability of life is cut loose from in American fiction:

> If you watch as I have watched all through the history of American literature you will see how the pressure of the non daily life living of the American nation has forced the words to have a different feeling of moving. . . . They got the words to express moving and in England the words even when they were most active were words that expressed arrested motion or a very slow succession. In the American writing the words began to have inside themselves those same words that in the English were completely quiet or very slowly moving began to have within themselves the consciousness of completely moving, they began to detach themselves from the solidity of anything.

Words, as it were, become excited and forget to remember, with the result that "words left alone more and more feel that they are moving and all of it is detached and is detaching anything and in this detaching and in this moving it [American writing] is being in its way creating its existing."[51]

In her assertion of intense immediacy and her dismissal of continuity in relationship, Melanctha might be taken as a portrait of the artist—certainly of the artist of *What are Masterpieces*:

> The thing that one gradually comes to find out is one has no identity that is when one is in the act of doing anything. Identity is recognition, you know who you are because you and others remember anything about yourself but essentially you are not that when you are doing anything. I am I because my little dog knows me but, creatively speaking the little dog knowing that you are you and your recognizing that he knows, that is what destroys creation.[52]

In fact, Jeff Campbell, not Melanctha, is the character Stein based on herself.[53] And the clash of ideas, as of emotional rhythms, is dialectical. Jeff does learn the lesson of pathos, he accepts its necessity and its virtue, but he does not abandon, so much as reshape, his original ethos. His ethos is ultimately strengthened by having to come to terms with "actual, active desires" and to incorporate the ethics of intensity. Jeff is even able, without self-righteousness, to see the flaw in Melanctha's assumption of heroic passion.

The problem with intensity for intensity's sake is that it encourages its own special form of bad faith:

> "You certainly Melanctha, you ain't got down deep loyal feeling, true
> inside you, and when you ain't just that moment quick with feeling,
> then you certainly ain't ever got anything more there to keep you, it
> is, that you ain't ever got any way to remember right what you been
> doing, or anybody else that has been feeling with you. You certainly
> Melanctha, never can remember right, when it comes to what you have
> done and what you think happens to you."   (p. 180)

When Melanctha drifted away from Jane Harden it was because she "never
could remember right when it came to what she had done and what had happened" (p. 107). So Melanctha's strength in intensifying a relation is counter-
balanced by her weakness in sustaining one, a weakness that cannot be written off as creative discontinuity. Moreover, by her demands on the present
moment Melanctha forces Jeff into bad faith. This bad faith is the reverse of
John Marcher's selfish egoism, since it is Melanctha rather than himself Jeff
tries to protect, but it goes much against the grain of his innate honesty:

> Jeff did not like it very well these days, in his true feeling. He knew
> now very well Melanctha was not strong enough inside her to stand any
> more of his slow way of doing. And yet now he was not honest in his
> feeling. Now he always had to show more to Melanctha than he was
> ever feeling. Now she made him go so fast, and he knew it was not real
> with his feeling, and yet he could not make her suffer so any more be-
> cause he always was so slow with his feeling.   (p. 163)

"Now," "now," "now," "now": there is an excess of immediacy, intensity
has become forced and feverish. Melanctha goes as much too fast as Jeff,
previously, had gone too slow. Part of the meaning of the moment must be
its historical provenance as well as its intensity.

For that matter, not remembering right is an offense against the ethics of
intensity. Honesty of feeling is central to this ethos, and Melanctha's forgetting falsifies past feelings. Also, though Melanctha's emotional immediacy
is a true value, she presumes too much on it. She begins to play the role of
martyr and of Lady Bountiful, forcing Jeff into the role of suppliant. This
goes counter to another principle implicit in the ethics of intensity; it circles
back, indeed, to the temptation built into the Victorian ethos: self-abnegation as a form of egoism. Jeff sees the wrongness of this: "And it certainly
must never be any kind of feeling, of one only taking, and one only just
giving, Melanctha, to me" (p. 192). Jeff remembers right, that "we did begin
fair, each not for the other but for ourselves, what we were wanting" (p.
178). Mutuality is fair play in the game of desire.

This is not to say that Stein represents Jeff as "better" than Melanctha;
he is strong in one way, she in another. Truth in "Melanctha" is on Jeff's
side, Melanctha's side, and somewhere in between, in the gap of indeterminacy. The ethics of intensity resist convenient codification. But it is clear that
Melanctha, because she cannot remember right, is wounded by the relationship whereas Jeff, because he reconstitutes himself in terms of it, is strength-

ened. Jeff finds real wisdom by accepting the pain of his now-unreciprocated love:

> Slowly Jeff found it a comfort in him to have it hurt so, and to be good to Melanctha always. Now there was no way Melanctha ever had had to bear things from him, worse than he now had it in him. Now Jeff was strong inside him. Now with all the pain there was peace in him. Now he knew he was understanding, now he knew he had a hot love in him, and he was good always to Melanctha Herbert who was the one who had made him have it. Now he knew he could be good, and not cry out for help to her to teach him how to bear it. Every day Jeff felt himself more a strong man, the way he once had thought was his real self, the way he knew it. Now Jeff Campbell had real wisdom in him, and it did not make him bitter when it hurt him, for Jeff knew now all through him that he was really strong to bear it.   (pp. 204-205)

The seven "nows" of this passage have a contextual meaning far different from the four insistent "nows" noted in a previous passage—for here the moment is part of the structure of the self. "Now," here, incorporates the past, combines intensity with duration and refers it back to social as well as personal ethos:

> Jeff had behaved right and he had learned to have a real love in him. That was very good to have inside him.
> Jeff Campbell never could forget the sweetness in Melanctha Herbert, and he was always very friendly to her, but they never any more came close to one another. More and more Jeff Campbell and Melanctha fell away from all knowing of each other, but Jeff never could forget Melanctha. Jeff never could forget the real sweetness she had in her, but Jeff never more had the sense of a real religion[54] for her. Jeff always had strong in him the meaning of all the new kind of beauty Melanctha Herbert had once shown him, and always more and more it helped him with his working for himself and for all the colored people.
> (pp. 206-207)

So we come full circle to an ethos which now includes and is authenticated by a real understanding of pathos.

Stein's later work is even more innovative, and sometimes as interesting as the early masterpiece, "Melanctha." But it lacks the special, beautifully sustained dialectical tension of that story. James R. Mellow observes that though "Jefferson Campbell's comfortable moral assumptions are similar to the author's . . . Gertrude Stein also underscores the hypocrisy of her own position."[55] The relationship is more complicated than that, in fact, because though Jeff's and Gertrude Stein's moral assumptions do correlate, so, as we have seen, do Melanctha's moral assumptions and Stein's *esthetic* assumptions. "Melanctha" beautifully develops the conflict between Jeff and Melanctha[56] at the same time as it beautifully articulates the conflict within Gertrude Stein.

In Stein's later writings, however, the split is not within the work, but between it and the writer:

> Gertrude Stein was determined, in her time, to stay with the twentieth century, come what might, but only in her art. For personal comfort she sat amongst Renaissance furniture, a devotion to the Republican Party, and fundamentally the moral views of a lady of 1902. We all need some sort of ballast for navigating the present, some distance from which to see it straight, some still point of continuity from which to measure or count off the chaotic events of the moment, but at least Gertrude Stein used her residual nineteenth century habits as a personal comfort, while as an artist she could risk taking on the twentieth century directly.[57]

This, from Donald Sutherland, is wonderfully said and seems true so far as it goes—but surely divorces of this sort have some court costs. Stein never ceased to value intensity, and "Melanctha," in its tensions between life and life, life and art, and ethos and pathos, is arguably the most intense of her writings, or indeed of any American writing of this century.

Conclusion

The danger of constructing a character—whether in life or fiction—too exclusively around ethos is that one tends to accept historically contingent limits as natural and essential, to ground value and identity in a *status quo* the solidity of which is merely apparent.[1] The danger of constructing a character too exclusively around pathos is that one tends to narrow into solipsism or dissipate into a "fluid emotionalism."[2] The writings examined in this study all operate within a gap of indeterminacy created by the polar tensions of ethos and pathos.

Whitman balances his radical pathos with a sympathy that incorporates traditional ethical relationships, but he shows those very relationships as the precipitates of a passional impulse. Whitman's world, then, is one in which ethos is enabled by pathos. Whitman's basing of human relationship on the recognition and sharing of hidden desire was a moral as well as esthetic breakthrough of the greatest importance. But the single *sustained* relationship throughout Whitman's "Song" *must* be that of the continually negotiated relationship of writer to reader. For the negation of traditional ethos destroys the possibility of any shared social field within which his fictional characterizations could establish continuous relationships. Outside of the relation of Whitman's persona to the reader, Whitman's world is too fluid to permit the resistances essential to sustained relationship, the sense of the claims, of the necessary encroachments of the other. The phantasmal sympathetic self can enclose the other, but it meets resistance only from within—from its competing impulses. A world of such nearly pure pathos might seem impossible in a novel but there it is, minus the sympathy, in William Burroughs' *Naked Lunch*.[3]

For none of the novelists in this study is such a purity of pathos—such a breakdown of the ethical outline of the self into its fluid impulses—possible or, ultimately, right. Howells, I have argued, overbalances in the other direction, negating desire to affirm the historically contingent ethical values which his own fiction puts into doubt. The best of Howells' fiction carries on a homiletic Victorian mode. He is frequently brilliant in his insight into the devious mental strategies of selfishness. But there is less energy in Howells' fiction than in the great Victorians because of his diminished confidence, his inability to find, even with the gap of indeterminacy, a convincing ethical base.

In Henry James the tension between ethos and pathos becomes excruciating—as witness the many anguished critical responses. In James's fiction the possibility of genuine relationship is usually defined in opposition to the venality of socially (generally monetarily) motivated relationships. Yet the attempt—the never quite realized attempt—is to establish a society of two (or at the most a few) based on a commitment to the risk of relationship. Desire, in James, is powerfully affirmed, but only as it is forced to define itself in relation to the irreducibility of others and to what I have called the biological imperatives. In demanding such relationship James implies an ethics of passion, an ethics of intensity.

Dreiser, in contrast, follows out the line of pathos until it discloses itself as a dead end, and only then recoils into something like a traditional ethos. What emerges is an implied rule of relationship: that the socially constituted self pursuing socially constituted realities[4] results in illusion compounded. This is the theme of *An American Tragedy*. Yet, as illusory as are the objects of desire, as false as is the consciousness pursuing them, desire itself is neither denied nor reduced in Dreiser's fiction. Desire is the very engine of life, though in Dreiser's ironic vision it is very much like a *Ding an sich*; it underlies all phenomena but is invisible behind their collective envelope. Desire, in general, is truth; desire, in particulars, is a necessary fiction. But Dreiser's vision does not deny the possibility of a desire free from illusion; this possibility exists somewhere in the gap of indeterminacy suggested in Jennie Gerhardt's relinquishments[5] and in Clyde Griffiths' not-quite-accomplished sympathy for Roberta.

Finally, Stein's "Melanctha" fictionally contrives for us a school for passion but also the final necessity to incorporate its lessons into an ethical structure. Jeff's days will not "have been but as isolated beads loosely strung on the thread of his desire."[6] But, of course, his discipline is founded on the poignancy of loss.

These qualified, indeterminate resolutions of the tension between ethos and pathos seem to me options about as live as any offered in the years after. Fitzgerald enriched the Dreiserian theme of Platonic desire, modulated in *The Great Gatsby* as glamour, but Fitzgerald's elegant mythology, lyrical style, and finely tuned ironies deflect the sense of life in his novels even as they decorate it.[7] And Hemingway's brilliant ironies, luminous in individual stories, seem in the stories *en masse* and in the novels uncomfortably like a character armor, a version of the stoical defensiveness William James deplored. Only Faulkner, with his perverse sympathy for non-negotiable spiritual demands, seems in retrospect to have engaged the theme with a power equal to that of the writers studied here.[8]

In contemporary American fiction, the tension between ethical and passional claims seems almost to have dissolved because of the negation of the pole of ethos. The tension in current fiction is more, as Tony Tanner describes it, between a freedom close to terrifying formlessness and forms merely arbitrary and imprisoning.[9] Contemporary fiction and criticism tends to treat character itself as a malignant fiction, as in Leo Bersani's assertion that character is only a fragment of a person and "has the factitious coherence of all obsessions."[10] Whatever the truth may be (I feel Bersani presents only a partial truth), the outcome of this view of identity is those figures of current fiction who struggle to justify the most minimal claim to existence, and never quite manage to do so.

In some ways this recent fiction brilliantly addresses a world hollowed out by mass culture and technology,[11] and shows an impressive stylistic and intellectual energy in the effort. But these fictions—the fictions of Barth, Barthelme, and Pynchon—feel, to me, light and thin in contrast to those of James, Dreiser, and Stein. And of another direction of contemporary fiction, the valorization of unrestrained impulse, Bersani himself remarks that "consciousness liberated from the restrictive continuities of character may also be consciousness abandoned to the brutal if illusory omnipotence of masturbatory fantasies."[12] Given a choice of fictions, one might legitimately prefer that typified by the irresolvable tension of ethos and pathos. I believe that this fiction, as I have described it, mirrors and potentiates us differently—but not less accurately and, perhaps, a good deal more fully—than many dazzling recent performances.[13]

Notes

Preface

1. For the concept of "the gap of indeterminacy" see Wolfgang Iser, *The Implied Reader* (Baltimore: Johns Hopkins University Press, 1974). Iser notes: "The right mode of conduct can be extracted from the novel through the interplay of attitudes and discoveries; it is not presented explicitly. And so the meaning of the novel is no longer an independent, objective reality; it is something that has to be formulated by the reader" (p. 44). Another way of putting this is that the novel has more to do with the *esprit de finesse* than the *esprit de géométrie*.

2. Cf. Alan Friedman's analysis of literary openness in *The Turn of the Novel* (London: Oxford University Press, 1970).

3. See, for instance, George Levine, "Realism Reconsidered" (in John Halperin, ed., *The Theory of the Novel* [New York: Oxford University Press, 1974], pp. 242, 248–249 et seqq.), for a moderate but trenchant argument against confusing literary realism with reality. See also Roland Barthes, *S/Z* (trans. Richard Miller [New York: Hill and Wang, 1974], pp. ix–xii and pp. 3–217), for an all-out assault on conventions of the "real."

4. A parallel would be E. H. Gombrich's idea of schema and correction in *Art and Illusion* (Princeton: Princeton University Press, 1960).

5. See Martin Price, "The Logic of Intensity: More on Character" (*Critical Inquiry*, 2 [Winter 1975], 369–379), for a critically sophisticated defense of emphasizing fictional characterization. Price argues that "the logic of intensity" (the phrase is from one of Henry James's prefaces) depends on some concept of character. He notes: "clearly, one may feel that character is not the medium in which destiny is realized; the logic of intensity is to be found in the language, and style becomes fatality. But no fatality is very interesting that produces automatic victims; *there must be a sense of sufficient resistance or at least of sufficient complexity*" (p. 379; my italics).

6. See Price, p. 377: "What strikes me about much recent criticism is its rather puritanical fear of character, as if a reader who shows interest in a character of any complexity must be irresistibly drawn into regarding the character for its own sake or as a real person."

7. A perceptive analysis of how writers cue readers to certain moral interpretations can be found in Sheldon Sacks, *Fiction and the Shape of Belief* (Berkeley: University of California Press, 1964).

Introduction

1. S. H. Butcher, trans., *Aristotle's Theory of Poetry and Fine Art* (New York: Dover, 1951), pp. 122–123.

2. Ibid., p. 340.

3. Aristotle, *The Rhetoric of Aristotle*, trans. Lane Cooper (New York: Appleton-Century-Crofts, 1960), p. 77.

4. Ibid., p. 230.

5. See Madeleine Doran, *Endeavors of Art* (Madison: University of Wisconsin Press, 1954), pp. 232–238.

6. Aristotle, *Aristotle's Theory of Poetry and Fine Art*, p. 29.

7. Ibid., p. 53.

8. Irving Babbitt, *Rousseau and Romanticism* (New York: Meridian Books, 1955), p. 50.

9. Edwin H. Cady, *The Road to Realism* (Syracuse: Syracuse University Press, 1956), p. 149.

10. Charles L. Crow, "Howells and William James: 'A Case of Metaphantasmia' Solved," *American Quarterly*, 27 (May 1975), 169–177; William J. Free, "Howells' 'Editha' and Pragmatic Belief," *Studies in Short Fiction*, 3 (Spring 1966), 285–292. Also see William McMurray, *The Literary Realism of William Dean Howells* (Carbondale: University of Southern Illinois Press, 1967). McMurray's thesis is that "Howells' literary realism closely resembles James's pragmatism" (p. ix).

11. Henry James, *The Letters of Henry James*, ed. Percy Lubbock (London: Macmillan, 1920), II, 83. Richard Hocks's *Henry James and Pragmatistic Thought* (Chapel Hill: University of North Carolina Press, 1974) presents a full and satisfying reading of Henry's affinities to William's pragmatic philosophy.

12. William James, *The Letters of William James*, ed. Henry James (Boston: Little, Brown, 1926), I, 299. (The editor of this volume was William James's son.)

13. Henry James, *Henry James Letters*, I, 1843–1875, ed. Leon Edel (Cambridge, Mass.: Belknap Press, 1974), p. 273; from a letter to Charles Eliot Norton.

14. William Dean Howells, *W. D. Howells as Critic*, ed. Edwin H. Cady (London: Routledge and Kegan Paul, 1973), pp. 200–201.

15. Frederick J. Hoffman, in "William James and the Modern Literary Consciousness" (*Criticism*, 4 [Winter 1962], 1–13), sees William James as an exemplar of the modern literary consciousness—especially in that "the general attitude toward the self has changed from regarding it as substance to analyzing it as process" (p. 1). I disagree with some of Hoffman's conclusions but concur with his view of James as a philosopher of process. Throughout this study my own interest is more in James the radical empiricist than in James the pragmatist. The two masterpieces by James on which I draw the most are *Principles of Psychology* and *Essays in Radical Empiricism*.

As James W. Edie notes, the phenomenologists have drawn heavily on *Principles of Psychology*, which anticipated many of their central ideas ("William James and Phenomenology," *The Review of Metaphysics*, 23 [March 1970], p. 489). John Wild traces these ideas as they are developed in *Principles* and as they receive more formal philosophical definition in *Essays in Radical Empiricism* (*The Radical Empiricism of William James* [Garden

City, N.Y.: Doubleday Anchor, 1970]). A subtly argued account of James as proto-phenomenologist is Bruce Wilshire's *William James and Phenomenology* (Bloomington: Indiana University Press, 1968), which cites James's influence on Husserl (p. 120) and notes James's immense ability to grasp the world *"just* as it appears—no small accomplishment. Phenomenology has been called an exercise in seeing" (p. 6).

Throughout this study I draw on James's extraordinary phenomenological descriptions, since just this sort of description distinguishes the literature I am examining. For a warning about updating James to meet our own needs and for an excellent account of him at Harvard, the reader should consult Bruce Kuklick's *The Rise of American Philosophy* (New Haven: Yale University Press, 1977).

16. John Dewey, "The Development of American Pragmatism" in H. Standish Thayer, ed., *Pragmatism: The Classic Writings* (New York: Mentor Books, 1970), p. 36. Originally published in 1931.

17. William James, *Essays in Radical Empiricism* and *A Pluralistic Universe* (New York: Dutton, 1971), p. 25.

18. Ibid., pp. 46–47.

19. Ibid., p. 4.

20. Ibid., p. 120. Two fascinating articles on James's concept of consciousness are: John Dewey, "The Vanishing Subject in the Psychology of James," *The Journal of Philosophy, Psychology and Scientific Method*, 37 (1940), 589–599; and Milic Capek, "The Reappearance of the Self in the Last Philosophy of William James," *Philosophical Review*, 62 (1953), 526–544.

21. Ralph Barton Perry, *The Thought and Character of William James: Briefer Version* (New York: Harper and Row, 1964), p. 274.

22. Quoted in Perry, p. 306.

23. Quoted in Perry, p. 307.

24. Quoted in Thayer, *Pragmatism*, p. 261.

25. Perry, p. 195.

26. William James, *Principles of Psychology*, 2 vols. (1890; rpt. New York: Dover, 1950), I, 246. Hereafter citations from either volume of *Principles* will be in the text.

27. The following comment, by Alexander Cowie, is rather delightfully overstated and not unsympathetic: "If James could be conceived of as interested in a game of baseball, he would prefer a 'pitcher's battle' to a free-hitting game. His books indeed are like the technical conversation of experts *between* the innings of a game—but the average fan wants action. Conceive of James (if possible) at a prizefight. It would suffice for him to judge from the sparring, the footwork, the weight, the condition of the men, what the outcome should be, and he would leave before the end in full knowledge of the implications involved—with the excited multitude clamoring for the 'kill' " (Alexander Cowie, *The Rise of the American Novel* [New York: American Book Co., 1951] , p. 734).

28. Gordon O. Taylor, *The Passages of Thought* (New York: Oxford University Press, 1969), pp. 5–6.

29. John Dewey, *Reconstruction in Philosophy* (1920; rpt. Boston: Beacon Press, 1957), p. 177.

30. Babbitt, Paul Elmer More, and Stuart Sherman thought of themselves as new humanists. William James, besides being a pragmatist and radical

empiricist, was, like F. C. S. Schiller, a humanist. These two versions of humanism had little but a complex word in common. It would seem that almost any human can be *some* variety of humanist.

31. M. H. Abrams, *The Mirror and the Lamp* (New York: Norton, 1958), p. 134.

32. Ibid., pp. 136, 134.

33. William James, *Letters*, I, 185.

34. Dewey, *Reconstruction*, p. 61.

35. Quoted in Perry, p. 216.

36. Quoted in Perry, p. 216.

37. Perry, p. 217.

38. Compare also *Principles*, II, 308: "The greatest proof that a man is *sui compos* is his ability to suspend belief in the presence of an emotionally exciting idea."

39. William James, *Pragmatism* (1907; rpt. New York: Meridian Books, 1955), p. 113.

40. William James, *Essays on Faith and Morals* (Cleveland: World, 1962), p. 209.

1. The Ethical Imperative: "Self, Self, Self" in Victorian Fiction

1. Daniel Walker Howe, "Victorianism in America" in Howe, ed., *American Victorianism* (Philadelphia: University of Pennsylvania Press, 1976), p. 4.

2. Ibid., p. 6.

3. For contemporary valuations and later revaluations of American writing, see Jay B. Hubbell, *Who Are the Classic American Writers?* (Durham: Duke University Press, 1972).

4. Especially noteworthy was Howells' 1882 essay, which defends James by comparing him favorably to Dickens and Thackeray. The essay caused "vengeful reverberations both in England and America" (Edwin H. Cady, *The Road to Realism* [Syracuse: Syracuse University Press, 1956], p. 220) and James referred in a letter to Howells' "ill starred amiabilities to me" (Henry James, *Henry James Letters*, II, ed. Leon Edel [Cambridge, Mass.: Belknap Press, 1975], p. 406). The Victorian masters were in 1882 as sacrosanct as Mark Twain had discovered the New England Victorians were from his disastrous speech in 1877 on Whittier (see Henry Nash Smith, *Mark Twain: The Development of a Writer* [New York: Oxford University Press, 1967], pp. 94–107). For a full account of the reaction to Howells' essay see Howells, *W. D. Howells as Critic*, ed. Edwin H. Cady (London: Routledge and Kegan Paul, 1973), pp. 57–64.

5. On Howells' relation to Victorian fiction, see chapter 3, especially note 47.

6. Charles Dickens, *Martin Chuzzlewit* (New York: Heritage Press, n.d.), p. 41. Steven Marcus analyzes selfishness as the central theme in *Martin Chuzzlewit* in *Dickens from Pickwick to Dombey* (New York: Basic Books, 1968), p. 225.

7. A. N. Kaul, "Introduction," *Hawthorne*, ed. Kaul (Englewood Cliffs, N.J.: Prentice-Hall, 1966), pp. 8–9.

8. Nathaniel Hawthorne, *The Blithedale Romance* (New York: Norton, 1958), p. 224.

9. Henry James, *The American Essays of Henry James*, ed. Leon Edel (New York: Vintage, 1956), p. 19. The popular American woman writers—E. D. E. N. Southworth, Maria Cummins, Susan Warner, Anna Warner, Augusta Jane Evans Wilson—were equally opposed to "self." Nina Baym emphasizes the repudiation of self-indulgent emotionalism in the nineteenth-century American genre of women's fiction: "Merely to feel strongly is to be at the mercy of oneself and others; it is to be self-absorbed and passive. Although committed to an ethic of social love, the authors differentiated it from self-love and linked love to wisdom, responsibility, rationality, and self-command. From their point of view, the merely feelingful person was selfish and superficial, hence incapable of love" (Nina Baym, *Woman's Fiction* [Ithaca: Cornell University Press, 1978], p. 25). Later in the century, however, "this fiction began to embody a self-expressive ethic, a feminine claim to pleasure and a rebellion against the Victorian ethic of obligation" (Baym, p. 198). Popular fiction appears to follow the same curve as high fiction.

10. *The Compact Edition of the Oxford English Dictionary* (Oxford: Oxford University Press, 1971), p. 2715.

11. In Miriam Allott, ed., *Novelists on the Novel* (New York: Columbia University Press, 1959), p. 87. From the introduction to Scott's *The Fortunes of Nigel*.

12. Quoted in Allott (p. 66), from Scott's review of *Emma*. Reflecting on *Pride and Prejudice*, Scott mused wonderfully, "The Big Bow-wow strain I can do myself like any now going, but the exquisite touch which renders ordinary commonplace things and characters interesting from the truth of the description and sentiment is denied to me" (*The Journal of Sir Walter Scott 1825–26* [Edinburgh, 1939], I, 135).

13. John Halperin, *The Language of Meditation* (Ilfracombe: Roundfield, 1973), p. 27.

14. Karl Kroeber, *Styles in Fictional Structure* (Princeton: Princeton University Press, 1971), p. 22.

15. John Halperin, *Egoism and Self-Discovery in the Victorian Novel* (New York: B. Franklin, 1974), p. ii.

16. U. C. Knoepflmacher, *Religious Humanism and the Victorian Novel* (Princeton: Princeton University Press, 1965), p. 93.

17. J. Hillis Miller, *The Form of Victorian Fiction* (Notre Dame: Notre Dame University Press, 1968), pp. 31, 33, 32, 96, 123.

18. Matthew Arnold, *Literature and Dogma* (New York: Macmillan, 1883), p. 345.

19. Ibid., p. 336.

20. Ibid., p. 329.

21. Ibid., p. 337.

22. U. C. Knoepflmacher traces the emergence of religious humanism and its effect on the Victorian ethos (*Religious Humanism*, passim).

23. Barbara Hardy, "The Change of Heart in Dickens' Novels" in Martin Price, ed., *Dickens: A Collection of Critical Essays* (Englewood Cliffs, N.J.: Prentice-Hall, 1967), p. 39.

24. In George M. Ford, *Dickens and His Readers* (Princeton: Princeton University Press, 1955), p. 82.

25. Ruth M. Vande Kieft, "Patterns of Communication in *Great Expecta-*

tions," in Richard Lettis and William E. Morris, eds., *Assessing* Great Expectations (San Francisco: Chandler, 1960), pp. 178–179.

26. Feuerbach's philosophy developed out of Hegel's and strongly influenced Marx.

27. Ludwig Feuerbach, *The Essence of Christianity*, trans. George Eliot (New York: Harper and Row, 1957), p. 14. Original publication of Eliot's translation: 1854; original publication in German: 1841.

28. Ibid., p. 118.

29. Ibid., p. 21.

30. Ibid., p. 271.

31. Walter E. Houghton, *The Victorian Frame of Mind* (New Haven: Yale University Press, 1957), pp. 238–239.

32. Quoted in John Holloway, *The Victorian Sage* (New York: Norton, 1965), p. 126.

33. Holloway, p. 126.

34. Ford, p. 67.

35. Halperin, *Egoism*, p. 109.

36. Ibid., p. 105.

37. Houghton, p. 293.

38. Marcus, *Dickens*, pp. 81–82.

39. Ibid., pp. 157–158.

40. Leo Bersani, *A Future for Astyanax* (Boston: Little, Brown, 1976), p. 70.

41. Ibid., p. 77.

42. V. S. Pritchett, "The Implacable, Belligerent People of '*Wuthering Heights*' " in Alistair Everitt, ed., Wuthering Heights: *An Anthology of Criticism* (London: Cass, 1967), p. 154.

43. Edwin H. Cady (*The Light of Common Day* [Bloomington: Indiana University Press, 1971], p. 213) sees this as the modernist faith.

44. Lionel Trilling, *The Opposing Self* (New York: Viking, 1959), p. 213.

45. Ibid., p. 216.

46. Ibid.

47. Halperin, *Egoism*, p. 47.

48. Cited in Richard Stang, *The Theory of the Novel in England 1850–1870* (New York: Columbia University Press, 1959), p. 77.

49. See Wolfgang Iser, "Introduction," *The Implied Reader* (Baltimore: Johns Hopkins University Press, 1974), passim.

50. See Halperin, *Egoism*, and Halperin, *The Language of Meditation*, both passim.

51. Sir Walter Scott, *Rob Roy*, ed. Edgar Johnson (Boston: Houghton Mifflin, 1956), pp. 158–159. Johnson calls this passage "a brilliant display of what modern psychologists call *rationalization*" (p. 159).

52. Kroeber, p. 77.

53. W. J. Harvey, *Character and the Novel* (Ithaca: Cornell University Press, 1965), p. 119.

54. Cited in Ford, p. 184.

55. Hardy, "Change of Heart," p. 41.

56. Holloway, pp. 122–123. For perceptive analyses of Eliot's processual style see also: Kroeber, pp. 184 and 194–195; Martin Price, "The Other Self:

Thoughts about Character in the Novel" in Elizabeth and Tom Burns, eds., *Sociology, Literature, and Drama* (Harmondsworth: Penguin Books, 1973), p. 276; and Halperin, *The Language of Meditation*, pp. 57, 71.

57. Holloway, pp. 135, 149, 135.

58. Knoepflmacher, p. 65. Knoepflmacher sees a triumph of Arnold and Hebraism in Eliot's later novels.

59. George Eliot, *Romola* (1863; rpt. Boston: Houghton Mifflin, 1907), I, 155.

60. Ibid., II, 17.

61. Ibid., I, 148-149.

62. Ibid., I, 326.

63. Ibid., I, 329-330.

64. Ibid., I, 161.

65. Ibid., I, 203.

66. Henry James, *The Future of the Novel*, ed. Leon Edel (New York: Vintage, 1956), p. 80. From James's 1873 review of *Middlemarch*.

67. Henry James, *Partial Portraits*, ed. Leon Edel (Ann Arbor: University of Michigan Press, 1970), p. 51.

68. Cited in Kenneth Graham, *English Criticism of the Novel: 1865-1900* (Oxford: Oxford University Press, 1965), p. 110.

69. See William Dean Howells' critical attacks on the excesses of the neo-romantic historical novels of the nineties, especially "The New Historical Romances" in Howells, *W. D. Howells as Critic*, pp. 299-313.

70. Kroeber, p. 153.

71. Knoepflmacher, p. 128.

72. James, *Future*, pp. 115-117. "The Lesson of Balzac" was originally published in 1905.

73. Iser, *Implied Reader*, pp. 113-114.

74. Cited in Iser, *Implied Reader*, p. 113.

75. W. B. Yeats, *The Letters of W. B. Yeats*, ed. Allan Wade (New York: Macmillan, 1955), p. 31.

76. Friedrich Nietzsche, *The Portable Nietzsche*, ed. Walter Kaufmann (New York: Viking, 1954), p. 208. From *Thus Spoke Zarathustra*. See also Eugene Goodheart's brilliant study of *"le culte du moi"* in nineteenth- and twentieth-century literature (*The Cult of the Ego* [Chicago: University of Chicago Press, 1968]).

77. *Portable Nietzsche*, pp. 515-516. From *Twilight of the Idols*. See Jeannette King, *Tragedy in the Victorian Novel* (Cambridge: Cambridge University Press, 1978), chapter 4 ("George Eliot: Pathos and Tragedy"), pp. 70-96 for an analysis of pathos in Eliot's writings. *Romola* gets less attention in King's book than *The Spanish Gypsy* for precisely the reason I have highlighted it—the predominance in it of ethos over pathos. King's examination of pathetic tragedy in Eliot counterbalances my emphasis on Eliot's ethos. But King notes that "for George Eliot, duty can and must conquer passion" and that Eliot's "approach is remedial rather than tragic" (pp. 91-92).

2. Whitman's Body: Kinesthetic Imagery and Sexual Pathos in "Song of Myself"

1. Walt Whitman, *Complete Poetry and Selected Prose*, ed. James E.

Miller, Jr. (Boston: Houghton Mifflin, 1959), p. 29. Hereafter all citations of *Leaves of Grass* will be in the text. Though I am persuaded by Roy Harvey Pearce's arguments for the 1860 edition of *Leaves* and would recommend his facsimile edition (Ithaca: Cornell University Press, 1961) to anyone who wants the richest experience of "Song of Myself," I found that, in practice, none of the passages I quote was significantly altered in Whitman's revisions. Therefore I use Miller's edition, for both its accessibility to readers and its useful inclusion of Whitman's prose. One exception: in the 1860 edition the persona is identified as "Walt Whitman, an American, one of the roughs, a kosmos." The later version—"Walt Whitman, a kosmos, of Manhattan the son"—is notably blander.

2. Richard Chase, *Walt Whitman Reconsidered* (New York: Sloane, 1955), pp. 77, 36.

3. Walt Whitman (anonymously), "Walt Whitman and His Poems" in Francis Murphy, ed., *Walt Whitman* (Harmondsworth: Penguin, 1969), p. 35 (Penguin Critical Anthology). Hereafter cited as Penguin Anth.

4. Cited in Gay Wilson Allen, *The Solitary Singer* (New York: Grove Press, 1955), p. 517.

5. Charles Eliot Norton thought *Leaves* "combines the characteristics of a Concord philosopher with a New York fireman" (Penguin Anth., p. 21). John Kinnaird notes Whitman's "marriage of mythopoeic or symbolic motives with the trafficking language of the ordinary world" (*"Leaves of Grass* and the American Paradox" in Roy Harvey Pearce, ed., *Whitman: A Collection of Critical Essays* [Englewood Cliffs, N.J.: Prentice-Hall, 1962], p. 30).

6. Whitman, *An American Primer* in Penguin Anth., p. 69.

7. Whitman, "Preface, 1876" in *Complete Poetry*, p. 440. My italics.

8. See Allen (*Solitary Singer*, pp. 113–114) for Whitman's love of opera: "Whitman himself came to believe that 'But for the opera I could never have written *Leaves of Grass*.' And he also testified: 'My younger life was so saturated with the emotions, raptures, up-lifts, of so much musical experiences that it would be surprising indeed if all my future work had not been colored by them.' "

9. Cf. Whitman, *American Primer*, Penguin Anth., p. 67: "How vast, surrounding, falling, sleepy, noiseless, is the word Night! It hugs with unfelt yet living arms."

10. Whitman, "Preface, 1876" in *Complete Poetry*, p. 438.

11. Roy Harvey Pearce, *The Continuity of American Poetry* (Princeton: Princeton University Press, 1961), p. 170. Also note the comment: "American poets, however much they have wanted to say yes, have never been able to conceive of doing so until they have said no" (p. 4).

12. See William James, *Principles of Psychology* (1890; rpt. New York: Dover, 1950), II, 345.

13. Ehrenzweig posits a hidden order perceivable through suspension of the intentional, willful consciousness: "The scanning of the total structure often occurs during a temporary absence of mind. One could say that during this gap in the stream of consciousness the ordinary distinctions between good and bad are 'manically' suspended. Oceanic dedifferentiation usually occurs only in deeply unconscious levels and so escapes attention; if made conscious, or rather, if the results of unconscious undifferentiated scanning, rise into consciousness, we may experience feelings of manic ecstacy" (*The*

Hidden Order of Art [Berkeley: University of California Press, 1967], p.
295). Cf. Whitman's "I loafe and invite my soul" and consequent feelings of
manic ecstacy.

14. The displacement does not necessarily imply Ehrenzweig's concept of
a hidden order of art in the unconscious: "It is not necessary to assert a
'hidden order,' although that approach is especially applicable to the two
artists [Whitman and Pollock], in order to defend their seeming formlessness.
Form in life and art is an order, a norm, to the conservative mentality an absolute, which has achieved wide acceptance over a period of time. It freezes
life and art into a mold which becomes life-denying in its denial of flux and
change, but which provides a consoling illusion of permanence or stasis. When
the norm is challenged by social unrest or by artistic exploration, immediately there are warnings, in the hushed tones of Cassandra, of chaos, anarchy,
formlessness. Change or a void triggers emotions and arouses anxieties which
have been cradled in a reassuring illusion. Yet the so-called 'absence of form'
in Whitman and Pollock can be explained and defended as a modernized
realism" (Edwin Haviland Miller, "The Radical Vision of Whitman and
Pollock" in Miller, ed., *The Artistic Legacy of Walt Whitman* [New York:
New York University Press, 1970], p. 59). By way of William James, I am
explaining "Song of Myself" as "modernized realism."

15. Cf. Jacques Derrida on "the *metaphysics of the proper* [*le propre—
self-possession, propriety, property, cleanliness] " (*Of Grammatology*, trans.
Gayatri Spivak [Baltimore: Johns Hopkins University Press, 1976], p. 26).
Since Whitman is in some ways a proto-deconstructionist in his poetic practice it seems appropriate to draw on a deconstructionist critical vocabulary to
discuss him. However, as my arguments here should make clear, I am more
convinced by William James's analysis of subject and substance and am less
certain than the deconstructionists of the impossibility of perception (although I agree that perception is never "raw").

16 William James, *Essays in Radical Empiricism* and *A Pluralistic Universe*
(New York: Dutton, 1971), p. 259. Hereafter cited as *E.R.E.*

17. That is, "The beauty of a thing or its value is no force that can be
plotted in a polygon of compositions, neither does its 'use' or 'significance'
affect in the minutest degree its vicissitudes or destiny at the hands of physical nature" (*E.R.E.*, p. 78).

18. Ibid. My italics.

19. Ibid., p. 79.

20. Ralph Barton Perry, *The Thought and Character of William James:
Briefer Version* (New York: Harper and Row, 1964), pp. 372–373. Cf. Kinnaird's comment, "Whitman had an abnormal susceptibility to touch: nearly
everyone who knew him well remarked that the skin on his rather large and
languorous body seemed unusually soft and pink; in him, as he himself liked
to say was 'the flush of the universe' " (Kinnaird, "*Leaves of Grass* and the
American Paradox," p. 25). Of course, James's kinesthetic emphasis is on
activity, while Whitman's is on passive response.

21. Pearce, *Continuity*, p. 230.

22. John Greenleaf Whittier, *The Complete Poetical Works of John
Greenleaf Whittier* (Boston: Houghton Mifflin, 1904), p. 494. Hereafter cited
in text. "Snow-Bound" was originally published in 1866.

23. "He puts things together as they never have been before; they are re-

lated only by the force of the poetic ego operative on them. There is little or no dramatic effect in the poems, even those with huge casts of characters; for the items which are named in them do not interact, are not conceived as modifying and qualifying one another, so as to make for dramatic tension. They are referred back to their creator, who does with them as his sensibility wills. If we see a relationship, it is because Whitman has made it, not because it was already there for him to discover and report" (Pearce, *Continuity*, p. 166). We might question, however, whether relationships "already there" exist only *because* previously "made" by someone.

24. John Jay Chapman, "Walt Whitman" in Penguin Anth., p. 157.

25. Cf. Kinnaird: "We find that we are really never in a consciously American world, but always within the purely magical universe of Whitman's 'self' and its strange visitations" (*"Leaves of Grass* and the American Paradox," p. 29).

26. Whitman (anonymously), "An English and American Poet" in Penguin Anth., pp. 41–42. My italics.

27. Quoted in Pearce, *Continuity*, p. 82.

28. Hayden White, "The Culture of Criticism" in Ihab Hassan, ed., *Liberations: New Essays on the Humanities in Revolution* (Middletown, Conn.: Wesleyan University Press, 1971), p. 68. Sam B. Girgus ("Culture and Post-Culture in Walt Whitman," *The Centennial Review*, 18 [Fall 1974], 394–400) applies White's idea of avant-garde paratactic structure to Whitman's catalogues. It should be noted, however, that Whitman, like other avant-garde paratactic writers, does privilege *kinesthesia* over sight, sound, and smell, as well as over reflection, judgment, etc.

29. Roger Asselineau describes a passage in "Song of Myself" as "an extreme case where the oneiric character of the evocation and the gratuitousness of the associations almost announce surrealism" ("Style—From Mysticism to Art" in Penguin Anth., p. 396). In fact, there are many such passages and the impulse behind them, as defined by Richard Chase, resembles the surrealist adventure: "He would utterly escape and defy the world's attempt to establish in his shifting psychic economy a superego—to impose upon him this or that conventional 'identity' " (Chase, *Whitman*, p. 51). David J. Wells notes an affinity with, though not an influence from, Rimbaud in "Whitman and Rimbaud" (*Walt Whitman Review* 19, 1 [March 1973], 25–30). Harold W. Blodgett and Sculley Bradley see "The Sleepers" as "perhaps the only surrealist American poem of the nineteenth century" (*Leaves of Grass: Comprehensive Readers Edition* [New York: New York University Press, 1965], p. 424). (I see it as one of two proto-surrealist Whitman poems.)

Whitman, of course, shows none of the surrealistic extremes of *humour noir* and apocalyptic violence. As Eugene Goodheart comments, "Baudelaire, Rimbaud, Nietzsche, Rilke experience the actual world as a violent assault upon their consciousness, and their own violence is a measure of it. Whitman, on the other hand, seems to inhabit a space so expansive and accommodating that his most violent verbal gestures become almost vaporous" (Goodheart, *The Cult of the Ego* [Chicago: University of Chicago Press, 1968], p. 150). I consider Poe the first American surrealist. His mode of descent into the subconscious differs extremely from Whitman's; it is more in key with the apocalyptic tendencies of the European writers Goodheart mentions. Betsy

Erkkila's *Walt Whitman among the French* (Princeton: Princeton University Press, 1980) appeared too late for me to consult in this discussion.

30. Whitman, "Preface to 1855 Edition of 'Leaves of Grass' " in *Complete Poetry*, p. 425.

31. R. P. Blackmur, *Language as Gesture* (London: Allen and Unwin, 1961). Allen notes that Whitman "came to believe that some sort of supreme wisdom could be conveyed not through words but through the musical tones of the words in the mouths of inspired speakers or singers. . . . The fact that he could not understand the language in which the operas were sung, but yet enjoyed them to the point of ecstasy, accounts in part for his literary ambition to convey more than the meanings of the words themselves; somehow by manner, tone, feeling, and implication to write so that he could say: 'The words of my book nothing, the drift of it everything' " (Allen, *Solitary Singer*, p. 115). The Whitman quote is from "Shut Not Your Doors, Proud Libraries." (Note that Whitman did know the plots and action of the operas he enjoyed from studying the librettos [Allen, p. 113].)

32. Whitman, "Preface . . . 1855" in *Complete Poetry*, p. 497.

33. Ibid., p. 415.

34. Whitman, "Democratic Vistas" in *Complete Poetry*, p. 497.

35. Ibid.

36. *E.R.E.*, pp. 21–22.

37. Derrida, *Of Grammatology*, p. 249. Note also Derrida's quotation from Rousseau's *Essay on the Origins of Language*: "Natural sounds are inarticulate" (p. 242). Finally: "What dislocates presence introduces difference and delay, spacing between desire and pleasure. Articulated language, knowledge and work, the anxious research of learning, are nothing but the spacing between two pleasures" (p. 280). Though Whitman (fortunately) has gotta use words, it is arguable that he goes further than Rousseau in reducing the space between desire and pleasure. (Needless to say, Derrida's own view is quite different from what he finds in Rousseau—Derrida doubts the existence of presence of any sort.) Roger Asselineau comments that Whitman's "position might be defined by that formula of André Gide which parodies Descartes's *cogito*: 'I feel therefore I am.' " Asselineau also notes Bernardin de Saint Pierre's early inversion of Descartes: "Je sens, donc j'existe" (1792) (Asselineau, *The Evolution of Walt Whitman: The Creation of a Book* [Cambridge, Mass.: Belknap Press, 1962], pp. 26, 281).

38. D. H. Lawrence, "Poetry of the Present," Penguin Anth., pp. 192–193 (originally published in 1920). Lawrence's italics. Lawrence was later to object strenuously to Whitman's "merging."

39. Cited in Horace Traubel's *Conversations with Walt Whitman* in Penguin Anth., p. 126. My italics.

40. Whitman, "Democratic Vistas" in *Complete Poetry*, p. 500.

41. William Carlos Williams, "An Essay on *Leaves of Grass*" in Pearce, ed., *Whitman*, p. 149.

42. Charles Olson, *Human Universe and Other Essays* (New York: Grove Press, 1967), p. 53. Cf. also: "It is true what the master says he picked up from Confusion [i.e., what Pound picked up from Confucius] : all the thots men are capable of can be entered on the back of a postage stamp. So, is it not the PLAY of a mind we are after, is not that that shows whether a mind is there at all" (Olson, p. 55). Denis Donoghue comments, "the cadence is the

limit of the speaker's breath" ("Walt Whitman" in Penguin Anth., p. 443—excerpted from *Connoisseurs of Chaos*). Muriel Rukeyser asserts that Whitman drew his rhythm from "the relation of our breathing to our heartbeat, and those measured against an ideal of water at the shore" (Rukeyser, "Backgrounds and Sources" in Edwin Haviland Miller, ed., *A Century of Whitman Criticism* [Bloomington: Indiana University Press, 1969], p. 190).

Harold Bloom traces the word breath to its etymological roots as a background for his discussion of English and American romanticism. He asks, "What is a psyche, and what must a text be if it can be represented by a psyche?" and explains: " 'Psyche' is ultimately from the Indo-European root *bhes*, meaning 'to breathe,' and possibly was imitative in its origins. 'Text' goes back to the root *teks*, meaning 'to weave' and also 'to fabricate.' My question thus can be rephrased: 'What is a breath, and what must a weaving or a fabrication be so as to come into being again as a breath?' " (Bloom, *Poetry and Repression* [New Haven: Yale University Press, 1976], p. 1). I have attempted to answer this question for Whitman's text.

43. James, *Principles*, I, 288; Kinnaird, "*Leaves of Grass* and the American Paradox," p. 33.

44. Pearce, *Continuity*, p. 172.

45. Cf. Lionel Trilling on the "insurgent poets from Wordsworth through Baudelaire to Joyce" who "have appealed beyond the institutional barrier to the sense of identity, knowing it to be spunky, alive, resistant—the basic fact and the hardest, hard enough to be the touchstone of every idea. Whitman was such a poet." This sense of identity, though hard, is contradictory enough to need negotiation through "paradox, strangeness and even 'absurdity' " (Trilling, "Sermon on a Text from Whitman" in Penguin Anth., p. 299).

46. Edwin Haviland Miller, "The Radical Vision," pp. 63–64.

47. In terms of Freud's paper, "On Narcissism" (in Freud, *General Psychological Theory*, ed. Philip Rieff [New York: Collier, MacMillan, 1963]). See pp. 57, 69.

48. Cf. James: "The body is the storm center, the origin of coordinates, the constant place of stress in [the] experience-train. Everything circles around it, and is felt from its point of view. The word 'I' then, is primarily a noun of position, just like 'this' and 'here' " (*E.R.E.*, p. 91). It should be evident that I find James's general ideas far more useful for understanding Whitman than James's specific reading of Whitman as an exemplar of "The Religion of Healthy-Mindedness." For this reading see James, *Varieties of Religious Experience* (1902; rpt. New York: Modern Library, 1929), pp. 83–86. James failed to see that his theories were mirrored in his brother's fiction, so it is no wonder that, despite his admiration of Whitman, he failed to recognize Whitman's anticipations of radical empiricist ideas about identity.

49. See Dewey, "The Development of American Pragmatism" in H. Standish Thayer, ed., *Pragmatism: The Classic Writings* (New York: Mentor Books, 1970), p. 37. This is not to say that the relations Whitman extends were exactly what Dewey had in mind.

50. Emily Dickinson, letter to T. W. Higginson, 25 April 1862 (*The Letters of Emily Dickinson*, ed. Thomas H. Johnson [Cambridge, Mass.: Belknap Press, 1958], II, 404). Walter H. Eitner argues that Dickinson would almost certainly have read "Bardic Symbols" (later retitled "As I Ebb'd with the Ocean of Life"), which was published in the April 1860 *Atlantic Month-*

ly. Eitner comments: "There were two 'disgraceful' poets on the scene and the one in Amherst may well have been aware of the other." Dickinson's correspondent Higginson was, after all, a notably conventional, anti-Whitman critic (Eitner, "Emily Dickinson's Awareness of Whitman: A Reappraisal," *Walt Whitman Review*, 22: 3 [September 1976], 111–115).

51. I use "he" as a convenient designation and do not mean to imply Whitman's reader is always male. In Whitman's case, as my argument shows, it would be appropriate for either male or female readers to use "he," "she," "he/she," or "they." The use of "he" to designate the general reader is a convention in process of changing.

52. Leslie Fiedler, "Walt Whitman: Portrait of the Artist as a MiddleAged Hero" in Penguin Anth., p. 354 (excerpted from *No! in Thunder*).

53. Chase, *Whitman*, p. 50. But note that the generalized poet-hero of *Leaves* is also expressing a traditional, abstract American federal identity, as brilliantly argued in Sacvan Bercovitch, *The Puritan Origins of the American Self* (New Haven: Yale University Press, 1975), pp. 181–184. See also Girgus, "Culture and Post-Culture in Walt Whitman." Bercovitch and Girgus revive the federal Whitman but, while I believe their construction a correct one, I do not believe that it cancels out Chase's or my own.

54. Chase, *Whitman*, p. 46. Cf. Derrida's analysis of sexual auto-affection in *Of Grammatology*, pp. 153–155.

55. Pearce, *Continuity*, p. 166.

56. Chase, however, brilliantly describes the Ovidian (metamorphical) and Dionysiac (festive) qualities of "Song of Myself" (see Chase, *Whitman*, pp. 59–60, 72). My reading of Whitman draws inspiration from Chase, Pearce, and Kinnaird, as well as from Edwin Haviland Miller's *Walt Whitman's Poetry* (New York: New York University Press, 1968); nonetheless I differ, to a degree, with all of them.

57. Martin Green, "Twain and Whitman" in Penguin Anth., pp. 424–425. My italics, except for "*to*" and "*as*." In the face of Green's certainty that people just *are* and should not, in writing or reading books, be somebody else, one might almost be inclined to go the whole way with Derrida:

> No doubt that by orienting and organizing the coherence of the system, the center of a structure permits the freeplay of its elements inside the total form. . . .
> Nevertheless, the center also closes off the freeplay it opens up and makes possible. *Qua* center, it is the point at which the substitution of contents, elements, or terms is no longer possible. At the center, the permutation or the transformation of elements . . . is forbidden.

The quote is from Derrida, "Structure, Sign and Play in the Discourses of the Human Sciences" in Richard Macksey and Eugenio Donato, eds., *The Structuralist Controversy* [Baltimore: Johns Hopkins University Press, 1972], p. 248). For center substitute "personality." Ultimately the gap of indeterminacy *between* Green's certainty of personal identity and Derrida's radical doubt of it may be preferable (see note 15, this chapter).

58. George Santayana, "Walt Whitman: A Dialogue" in Penguin Anth., p. 135. My italics.

59. Whitman (anonymously), "Walt Whitman and his Poems" in Penguin Anth., p. 30.

60. Whitman, "Whoever You Are Now Holding Me in Hand" in *Complete Poetry*, pp. 85–86.

61. Whitman, "A Backward Glance o'er Travel'd Roads" in *Complete Poetry*, p. 451. Important critical observations on Whitman's interplay with his readers and on his play with the universalizing possibilities of first- and second-person address can be found in: Philip Y. Coleman, "Walt Whitman's Ambiguities of 'I'," *Papers on Language and Literature*, 5, supplement (Summer 1969), 40–59; James M. Cox, "Autobiography and America," *Virginia Quarterly Review*, 47: 2 (Spring 1971), 267–269; Howard J. Waskow, *Whitman: Explorations in Form* (Chicago: University of Chicago Press, 1966), pp. 157–158; and E. F. Carlisle, "Walt Whitman: The Drama of Identity," *Criticism*, 10: 4 (Fall 1968), 259–276. Finally, Eugene Goodheart argues strongly that Whitman transcended egoism through his "unitary *I*": "Whitman feels no aversion to egoism, because he is nonchalantly at ease in the company of others: he is thus able to achieve an identification of egoism and community" (Goodheart, *The Cult of the Ego*, p. 158). I think Goodheart takes the will for the deed and misses the tension between "I" and "you" in Whitman. But Goodheart powerfully develops the theme of community in the poet's work.

62. Whitman, "Democratic Vistas" in *Complete Poetry*, p. 500.

63. Whitman, "Specimen Days" in Walt Whitman, *Leaves of Grass and Selected Prose*, ed. John Kouwenhoven (New York: Modern Library, 1950), p. 758.

64. Ezra Pound, *The Cantos of Ezra Pound* (New York: New Directions, 1948), p. 6.

65. Henry Adams, *The Education of Henry Adams* (1918; rpt. Boston: Houghton Mifflin, 1961), p. 385.

66. Not to mention Anderson's *Winesburg, Ohio*; Tennessee Williams' *A Streetcar Named Desire* and *The Glass Menagerie*; and the Corydon and Phyllis section of book 4 of William Carlos Williams' *Paterson*.

3. *A Modern Instance*: Pathos Subordinated to Ethos

1. Howells' conspicuous lack of interest in Dreiser probably derived from the same critical philosophy that led to his doubts about Whitman. The ironic method in Crane's *Maggie* obviously implies moral judgment throughout, whereas Dreiser's method as obviously evades and dissolves such judgment (see chapter 5, section 5, for a contrast of the methods of Howells and Dreiser). Ellen Moers (*Two Dreisers* [New York: Viking, 1969], pp. 172, 175–176, 327 n6) examines Howells' and Dreiser's mutual misconceptions about each other. Interestingly, Dreiser praised Howells' *Their Wedding Journey* as genuine realism—confusing it, as Olov Fryckstedt believes, with *A Modern Instance* (Fryckstedt, *In Quest of America: A Study of Howells' Early Development as a Novelist* [Upsala: Ivor Haeggerströms Boktryckeri, 1958], p. 268).

2. William Dean Howells, review of *Drum-Taps* in Francis Murphy, ed., *Walt Whitman* (Harmondsworth: Penguin, 1969), pp. 85–87. Originally published in *The Round Table*, November 1865.

3. Ibid., p. 85. This review is Howells' harshest treatment of Whitman. He liked Whitman as a person and even finally mellowed toward his poetry, though he only qualified, rather than reversed, his misgivings. But note how

different was the tone of Howells' citation of the "ingenious French critic" when he remembered Whitman in *Literary Friends and Acquaintances*, published thirty-seven years after the *Drum-Taps* review: "His [Whitman's] verse seems to me not poetry, but the materials of poetry, like one's emotions; yet I would not misprize it, and I am glad to own that I have had moments of great pleasure in it. Some French critic quoted in the *Saturday Press* (I cannot think of his name) said the best thing of him when he said that he made you a partner of the enterprise, for that is precisely what he does, and that is what alienates and what endears in him, as you like or dislike the partnership" (Howells, *Literary Friends and Acquaintances* [New York: Harper and Row, 1902], pp. 75–76).

Valden Madsden argues that Howells condemned the form rather than the moral content of Whitman's poetry (Madsden, "W. D. Howells's Formal Poetics and His Appraisals of Whitman and Emily Dickinson," *Walt Whitman Review*, 23: 3 [September 1977], 103–109). But Howells could never have approved such a sharp distinction between form and moral vision. Clearly, he regards formless emotion in art as *morally* questionable. Edwin H. Cady notes Howells's ambivalence about Whitman in pieces ranging from 1860 to 1907. In an 1860 review Howells found passages of "profound and subtle significance" along with passages "gross and revolting" (Cady, ed., Howells, *W. D. Howells as Critic* [London: Routledge and Kegan Paul, 1973], pp. 12, 14). None of Howells' comments on Whitman were as unkind as Whitman's remark to Traubel in 1889 that "Howells had 'so little virility' that he was 'unable to follow up radically the lead of his rather remarkable intellect' " (quoted in Edwin Haviland Miller, "Introduction" in Miller, ed., *A Century of Whitman Criticism* [Bloomington: Indiana University Press, 1969], p. xxxiii).

4. Howells, review of *Drum-Taps*, p. 85.

5. Ibid., p. 87.

6. Ibid., p. 88.

7. Ibid. My italics.

8. Whitman, "Preface to 1855 Edition of 'Leaves of Grass'" in Whitman, *Complete Poetry and Selected Prose*, ed. James E. Miller, Jr. (Boston: Houghton Mifflin, 1959), p. 417.

9. Quoted in William Alexander, "Howells, Eliot, and the Humanized Reader" in Morton Bloomfield, ed., *The Interpretation of Narrative*, Harvard English Studies I (Cambridge: Harvard University Press, 1970), pp. 152–153. This article is an excellent analysis of Howells' similarity to and difference from George Eliot.

10. *W. D. Howells as Critic*, p. 468.

11. See Alexander, p. 151.

12. *W. D. Howells as Critic*, p. 464.

13. Ibid., p. 440. Howells believed Thackeray was a sham but saw *Barry Lyndon* as his best novel and its title character as "the most perfect creation of Thackeray's mind" (ibid., pp. 101–102). Barry Lyndon is a first-person Tito Melema, lacking the moral ambiguities implicit in Becky Sharp.

14. Howells, "The Novels of Robert Herrick," *North American Review*, 189 (1909), p. 816. Fryckstedt notes the significance of this passage for Howells' own fiction (*In Quest*, p. 244).

15. Howells, *My Literary Passions* (New York: Harper, 1910), p. 138.

Fryckstedt (pp. 241–243) develops the relation between *Romola* and *A Modern Instance*. I repeat many of the quotes he uses, as they are an essential part of my own argument.

16. *My Literary Passions*, pp. 162–164.

17. Quoted from an unpublished letter in Fryckstedt, p. 242.

18. Quoted in Fryckstedt, p. 242. Smith obviously means Tito, not Romola. Alexander ("Howells, Eliot," pp. 153–154) also quotes this letter. Cf. the anonymous reviewer of *A Modern Instance* who saw Bartley as "a sort of vulgar Tito, without any of the tragic elements involved in George Eliot's great and terrible conception" (quoted in Kenneth E. Eble, ed., *Howells: A Century of Criticism* [Dallas: Southern Methodist University Press, 1962], p. 30—originally published in *Blackwood's Magazine*, 133 [January 1883]).

19. Cady, *The Road to Realism* (Syracuse: Syracuse University Press, 1956), p. 19.

20. Ibid., p. 109.

21. See above (Introduction, section 2), for Howells' ethical reading of *Principles*. Howells' letter to Howard Pyle, a Swedenborgian, constructs an interesting connection: "Are you reading James's *Psychology*? I am, with the interest of knowing his Swedenborgian origin. The book is a most important one. James is one of the few scientific men who do not seem to snub one's poor humble hopes of a hereafter" (Howells, *Life in Letters of William Dean Howells*, ed. Mildred Howells [New York: Doubleday Doran, 1929], II, 14). (Henry James, Sr., was a heterodox Swedenborgian.)

22. William Dean Howells, *A Modern Instance*, edited and with an introduction by William M. Gibson (New York: Houghton Mifflin, 1957), p. 5. Hereafter, citations to the novel and to Gibson's introduction will be incorporated within the text.

23. See *A Modern Instance*, p. 15. See also Charles Dickens' *American Notes*:

> The following dialogue I have held a hundred times: "Is it not a very disgraceful circumstance that such a man as So-and-So should be acquiring a large property by the most infamous and odious means, and, notwithstanding all the crimes of which he has been guilty, should be tolerated and abetted by your citizens? He is a public nuisance, is he not?" –"Yes, sir."–"A convicted liar?"–"Yes, sir."–"He has been kicked and cuffed and caned?"–"Yes, sir."–"And he is utterly dishonorable, debased, and profligate?"–"Yes, sir."–"In the name of wonder, then, what is his merit?"–"Well, sir, he is a smart man."
> (*American Notes* [Greenwich, Conn.: Fawcett, 1961], p. 279)

24. See George Santayana, "The Genteel Tradition in American Philosophy" in *Winds of Doctrine* (London: Dent, 1926), pp. 186–187.

25. This is a recurrent motif in Howells' criticism. See Howells' *Criticism and Fiction* (Cambridge, Mass.: Walker–de Berry, 1962), passim, and "The New Historical Romances," *W. D. Howells as Critic*, pp. 291–313 (originally published in *North American Review*, December 1900). See also Cady's remarks, *W. D. Howells as Critic*, p. 149: "Howells equated romanticism with self-regard."

26. Note that Howells' use of Kinesthesia is always to make an ethical point; the tropistic movements of his characters generally expose "self."

27. Nathalie Sarraute, *The Age of Suspicion*, trans. Maria Jolas (New York: Braziller, 1963), pp. 91–92.

28. I am drawing from a lecture, "Form and Content of the Novel," Sarraute gave at the University of Texas on March 22, 1967. "Tropism," as used here and in the chapters on Dreiser and Stein, describes not a purely physical reflex but a minimal and basic psychological response. It should be admitted that Sarraute would surely find Howells' style rather clumsy, since in *The Age of Suspicion* she complains that Proust's style of sub-conversation was insufficiently minute and immediate.

29. Sarraute, *Age of Suspicion*, p. 95.

30. Marcel Proust, *The Remembrance of Things Past*, quoted in Frederic Jameson, *The Prison-House of Language* (Princeton: Princeton University Press, 1972), p. 54.

31. See William C. Fischer, Jr. ("William Dean Howells: Reverie and the Nonsymbolic Aesthetic," *Nineteenth-Century Fiction*, 25 [June 1970], 1–30) for a convincing analysis of Howells' use of reverie primarily to show ethical vagrancy. In his *Drum-Taps* review Howells declares: "There is a yearning, almost to agony at times, in the human heart, to throw off the burden of inarticulate feeling, and if the poet will not help it in this effort, if, on the contrary, he shall seek to weigh it and sink it down under heavier burdens, he has not any reason to be" (p. 88). It seems clear that the disburdening would occur by means of ethical articulation.

32. Quoted in Gibson, ed., *A Modern Instance*, p. xviii.

33. See Howells' review of *Principles*: "It would be hard for us, at least, to find a more important piece of writing in its way than the chapter on Habit; it is something for the young to read with fear and hope, the old with self-pity or self-gratulation, and every one with recognition of the fact that in most things that tell for good or ill, and much or little in life, we are creatures of our own making. It would be well for the reader to review this chapter in the light of that on the Will, where the notion of free-will is more fully dealt with. In fact the will of the weak man is *not* free; but the will of the strong man, the man who has *got the habit* of preferring sense to nonsense and 'virtue' to 'vice', is a freed will, which one might very well spend all one's energies in achieving. It is this preference which at last becomes the man, and remains permanent throughout those astounding changes which everyone finds in himself from time to time" (*W. D. Howells as Critic*, p. 199). Clearly, Bartley and Marcia have not got the right habits. Note Irving Babbitt's approval of James's chapter on habit, Introduction, section 2.

34. St. Augustine, quoted in William James, *The Varieties of Religious Experience* (1902; rpt. New York: Modern Library, 1929), p. 169. My authority for this outrageous analogy also derives from James: "In judging of the religious types of regeneration which we are about to study, it is important to recognize that they are only one species of a genus that contain other types as well. For example, the new birth may be away from religion into incredulity; or it may be from moral scrupulosity into freedom and license. . . . In all these instances we have precisely the same psychological form of event,—a firmness, a stability, and equilibrium succeeding a period of storm

and stress and inconsistency. In these non-religious cases the new man may also be born either gradually or suddenly" (*Varieties*, pp. 172-173).

35. *Varieties*, p. 177.

36. Howells said of Shakespeare's characters that they work "all the better for being warnings rather than example" (*W. D. Howells as Critic*, p. 431). Fryckstedt argues that "As the novel proceeds we suspect that Bartley is sliding downward because the author deliberately pushes him" (*In Quest*, p. 245).

37. "You didn't intend Bartley for me, but he *is* me, just the same, & I enjoy him to the utmost uttermost, & without a pang" (in Henry Nash Smith and William M. Gibson, eds., *Mark Twain-Howells Letters* [Cambridge, Mass.: Belknap Press, 1970] , I, 412). Howells: "Yesterday I read a great part of *A Modern Instance*, and perceived that I had drawn Bartley Hubbard, the false scoundrel, from myself" (Howells, *Life in Letters*, p. 301). The analogy with Eliot's implicatory characterization of Tito Melema is obvious. In fact, I too feel implicated by Bartley.

38. T. S. Eliot, *Selected Essays* (New York: Harcourt Brace, 1950), p. 424.

39. Cf. Breton: "Beauty will be CONVULSIVE or will not be at all" (André Breton, *Nadja*, trans. Richard Howard [New York: Grove Press, 1960] , p. 160; original publication 1928). This would be the other extreme.

40. See Fischer, "William Dean Howells: Reverie and the Nonsymbolic Aesthetic," passim.

41. Kermit Vanderbilt, "Marcia Gaylord's Electra Complex: A Footnote to Sex in Howells," *American Literature*, 34 (1962), p. 365.

42. See H. D. F. Kitto, *Greek Tragedy* (Garden City, N.Y.: Doubleday Anchor, 1954), pp. 208-209. Kitto remarks: "Sun and Earth, the most elemental things in the universe, have been outraged by these [Medea's] terrible crimes; what will they do? how will they avenge their sullied purity? What Earth will do we shall not be told, but we are told what the Sun does: he sends a chariot to rescue the murderess" (p. 208).

43. In his essay on Herrick's fiction, Howells comments that "details of emotions and behavior long blinked in Anglo-Saxon fiction are not spared; but it is to be noted in the book's behalf that the facts are recognized with a pathological decency" (Howells, "The Novels of Robert Herrick," pp. 813-814). It is consistent with Howells' fiction, letters, and criticism to interpret this to mean that the facts of passion are decent when treated as pathological.

44. Alexander ("Howells, Eliot," pp. 167-168) contrasts Howells' deliberately dispassionate relation to his characters to George Eliot's intense involvement: "This involvement, whatever its dangers and awkwardnesses, is likely, because of its force and concern, to attract and challenge us more than Howells's particular detachment."

45. See Cady (*The Road to Realism*, p. 208) for speculations on the relationship between Howells' illness and the weakness of the conclusion of *A Modern Instance*.

46. See Gibson's "Introduction" (p. xiv) on Howells' representation of the failure of religious faith and of the consequent vacuity of the community ethos. Henry Nash Smith incisively analyzes the shifts in Howells' style between a "vocabulary of empirical cause and effect" and a diction that "sur-

renders to melodrama by invoking a primitive set of theological assumptions"
as instances of his inability fully to escape the inadequacies of the genteel
culture of his time (Smith, *Democracy and the Novel* [New York: Oxford
University Press, 1978], pp. 75–103). The chapter is appropriately titled
"William Dean Howells: The Theology of Realism."

47. Alexander ("Howells, Eliot," p. 168) contrasts the ways Howells and
Eliot represent primal emotion: "The central difference is one of range.
Howells mostly concerns himself with social relations, with conversations,
confusions, rationalizations, acts of conscience, and so on, all treated with a
fine accuracy, subtlety, and relevance, all close to the surface of our experience, most within the range of rationality, and all presented in the terminol-
ogy by which we most usually think and live. Eliot, on the other hand, is
much more concerned with primal emotions, with basic impulses of love,
fear, hate, despair, revenge, with satisfactions in religion, in deep childhood
roots, in work and with the passing of time and with tides and seasons. Leslie
Stephen accurately marked as a distinctive characteristic of her genius her
'constant, though not obtrusive, suggestion of the depths below the surface
of trivial life.' " In the terms I have been using, Eliot mixes ethos and pathos
whereas Howells is too purely committed to ethos.

Cf. also Joseph H. Gardner ("Howells: The 'Realist' as Dickensian,"
Modern Fiction Studies, 16 [Autumn 1970], 323–343), who demonstrates
that Howells was closer to Dickens than he liked to recognize, both in his
favorite theme of selfish egotism and in a tendency to fall back on divine
providence when in a tight spot. Indeed, Gardner maintains, Howells' novels
like *The Son of Royal Langbrith* recall the early, Christmasy Dickens more
than the later, socially sinister one. Henry James might have had something
like this in mind in his blunt 1884 letter to Howells: "They [Daudet, Gon-
court, Zola] do the only kind of work, to-day, that I respect; and in spite of
their ferocious pessimism and their handling of unclean things, they are at
least serious and honest. The floods of tepid soap and water which under the
name of novels are being vomited forth in England, seem to me, by contrast,
to do little honor to our race. I say this to you because I regard you as the
great American naturalist. I don't think you go far enough, and you are
haunted with romantic phantoms and a tendency to factitious glosses, but
you are in the right path" (Henry James, *The Letters of Henry James*, ed.
Percy Lubbock [London, Macmillan, 1920], I, 104–105). For an example
of a romantic phantom and a factitious gloss in Howells' fiction, see my comment on *A Hazard of New Fortunes* in chapter 5, section 5, part c.

48. Without at all wanting to engage the complicated question of whether
American fiction is primarily romance, I find Gertrude Stein's comment appropriate:

> And so this makes it that Henry James just went on doing what
> American literature had always done, the form was always the form of
> the contemporary English one, but the disembodied way of disconnect-
> ing something from anything and anything from something was the
> American one. The way it had of often all never having any daily living
> was an American one.
>
> Some say that it is repression but no it is not repression it is lack of
> connection, of there being no connection with living and daily living be-

cause there is none, that makes American writing what it always has
been and what it will continue to become.
(Gertrude Stein, *Lectures in America* [Boston: Beacon Press, 1967],
pp. 53–54)

If this view is exaggerated it is no more so than the classic passages about
American social thinness and individualist disconnectedness in Tocqueville,
Cooper, Henry James, and D. H. Lawrence. Howells "connects" more, and
more convincingly, than most American novelists but finally, too many of the
connections seem asserted, forced, rather than simply recorded.

4. Henry James: An Ethics of Intensity

1. See chapter 1, section 6, for a commentary on the Balzac essay.
2. Henry James, *The Art of the Novel* (New York: Scribner's, 1937),
p. 12. Hereafter cited in text.
3. James, "The Beast in the Jungle" in James, *The Better Sort* (New York:
Scribner's, 1903), p. 197. Hereafter cited in text.
4. A refrain in the contemporary criticism of James was that he carried
analysis to the extreme of denying his characters the reader's sympathy. An
1881 review of *The Portrait of a Lady* claims: "It might almost be called a
cruel book in its dissection of character and exposure of the nerves and
sinews of human actions" (cited in Roger Gard, ed., *Henry James: The Critical Heritage* [London: Routledge and Kegan Paul, 1968], p. 105). This is a
moderate response; James's analytic technique was frequently condemned
out of hand.
5. Iser, "Introduction," *The Implied Reader* (Baltimore: Johns Hopkins
University Press, 1974), passim; Richard Poirier, *A World Elsewhere* (New
York: Oxford University Press, 1973). It is a world constituted by a use of
language that allows the imagination to envision a freer self, relating more
naturally to others. "The great works of American literature are alive with
the effort to stabilize certain feelings and attitudes that have, as it were, no
place in the world, no place at all except where a writer's style can give them
one" (Poirier, p. ix).
6. In teaching "The Beast in the Jungle" I find that some students are on
to Marcher from the start, some need the overt passage at the end before they
catch on, and some pick it up in between. The most "literary" readers are
sometimes the most credulous, as they have been trained to look more closely
at symbols than characters. Many students find the story quite threatening.
7. Leo Bersani, "The Narrator as Center in 'The Wings of the Dove,'"
Modern Fiction Studies, 6 (1960), p. 144.
8. George E. Dimock, Jr., "The Name of Odysseus" in Charles H. Taylor,
Jr., ed., *Essays on* The Odyssey (Bloomington: Indiana University Press,
1969), pp. 65, 72.
9. See especially: Arlin Turner, "Introduction" to Nathaniel Hawthorne,
The Blithedale Romance (New York: Norton, 1958), pp. 5–23; and Nina
Baym, "*The Blithedale Romance*: A Radical Reading," *Journal of English and
Germanic Philology* 67 (October 1968), 545–569. Joseph J. Firebaugh ("The
Idealism of Merton Densher," *Texas Studies in English*, 27 [1958], p. 147)
compares Densher, Prufrock, and Mauberley as solipsists. The article is an

excellent analysis of the theme of self-protective idealism in *The Wings of the Dove*.

10. See Grover Smith (*T. S. Eliot's Poetry and Plays* [Chicago: University of Chicago Press, 1956] , pp. 25–26) for a discussion of the Jamesian quality in Eliot's early poetry.

11.   He had passed, inconscient, full gaze,
The wide-banded irides
And botticellian sprays implied
In their diastisis;

Which anaesthesis, noted a year late,
And weighed, revealed his great affect,
(Orchid), mandate
Of Eros, a retrospect.

Ezra Pound, "Hugh Selwyn Mauberley," *Selected Poems* (New York: New Directions, 1957), p. 73. See the explication of the sexual theme in these lines by John J. Espey, *Ezra Pound's Mauberley: A Study in Composition* (Berkeley: University of California, 1955), pp. 51–52. Espey compares Mauberley, in the passage above, to Lambert Strether in his relation to Maria Gostrey, but a comparison to John Marcher would be more appropriate. See Espey (pp. 49–61) for a reading of Mauberley "as Pound's condensation of the James novel."

12. "I could not help but reflect that if I hadn't been so noble—if it was nobility—everything would have been different. . . . So, I observed, my nobility (or whatever it was) had had in my world almost as dire a consequence as Cass Mastern's sin had had in his. Which may tell you something about the two worlds" (Robert Penn Warren, *All the King's Men* [New York: Bantam, 1963] , p. 297). Cass Mastern's world was the 1850s and 1860s; his sin was adultery. Jack Burden's "nobility" is actually solipsistic idealism. Robert B. Heilman notes that Jack Burden ends "in a hesitation which is in origin an echo of an old honor, thinned out now into a wavering sentiment, and which is in effect a negation" (Heilman, "*All the King's Men* as Tragedy" in Maurice Beebe and Leslie A. Field, eds., All the King's Men: *A Critical Handbook* [Belmont, Calif.: Wadsworth, 1966] , p. 87—originally published as "Melpomene as Wallflower: or the Reading of Tragedy," *Sewanee Review*, 55 [Winter 1947] , 154-166).

13. Among the best readings of James from this viewpoint is Sallie Sears, *The Negative Imagination* (Ithaca: Cornell University Press, 1968). Sears sees renunciation triumphing but brilliantly analyzes the late novels "as an unresolved debate about the problem and meaning of life, a debate between a voice of yearning and a voice of restriction" (p. xii).

14. In Gard, ed., *Henry James: The Critical Heritage*, p. 335; originally published in *Bookman* (1902) as "The Queerness of Henry James."

15. James, "George Sand: The New Life," *North American Review*, 174 (April 1902), p. 552.

16. In Gard, p. 415; originally published 1905.

17. James, "George Sand," p. 553.

18. James, "The Lesson of Balzac," *The Future of the Novel*, ed. Leon Edel (New York: Vintage, 1956), p. 111.

19. Ibid., p. 110.

20.   Say something to us we can learn
By heart and when alone repeat.
Say something! And it says, 'I burn.'
But say with what degree of heat.
Talk Fahrenheit, talk Centigrade.

From Robert Frost, "Take Something Like a Star," *Selected Poems of Robert Frost* (New York: Holt, 1965), pp. 269–270.

21. At the beginning of the crucial interview May Bartram "was the picture of a serene, exquisite, but impenetrable sphinx." Later she spoke "with the perfect straightness of a sibyl" ("The Beast in the Jungle," pp. 220, 230).

22. Michael Shriber, "Cognitive Apparatus in *Daisy Miller, The Ambassadors* and Two Works by Howells: A Comparative Study of the Epistemology of Henry James," *Language and Style*, 11 (1969), p. 225.

23. The best account of William James's radical empiricism is John Wild's *The Radical Empiricism of William James* (Garden City, N.Y.: Doubleday Anchor, 1970).

24. "I was lost in the wonder of the extent to which all my life I have (like Monsieur Jourdain) unconsciously pragmatised" (cited in F. O. Matthiessen, *The James Family* [New York: Knopf, 1947], p. 343; letter from Henry to William, 1907).

25. Richard A. Hocks, *Henry James and Pragmatistic Thought* (Chapel Hill: University of North Carolina Press, 1974). Hocks illuminatingly discusses "the Jourdain relationship" and William's letter attacking Henry's "third manner" (see pp. 15–37). Hocks' book carefully and convincingly relates the mode of thinking of the two brothers. Hocks notes that, despite its attack, we have in William's letter on the third manner "simply one of the most beautifully exact descriptions of the late 'Jamesian' method anywhere to be found" (Hocks, p. 22).

26. R. W. Short, "The Sentence Structure of Henry James," *American Literature*, 17 (May 1946), p. 79.

27. Short, p. 80. On James's style, see also: Seymour Chatman, *The Later Style of Henry James* (Oxford: Oxford University Press, 1972); Ian Watt, "The First Paragraph of *The Ambassadors*: An Explication," *Essays in Criticism*, 10 (July 1960), 250–274; Dorothea Krook, *The Ordeal of Consciousness in Henry James* (Cambridge: Cambridge University Press, 1962); Jane P. Tompkins, " 'The Beast in the Jungle': An Analysis of James's Late Style," *Modern Fiction Studies*, 16 (1970), 184–191. Krook stresses the self-consciousness of the style, and sees an affinity with the idealist philosophy of the nineteenth century. All the other analyses stress the relational, transitive quality of the style.

28. William James, *The Letters of William James*, ed. Henry James (Boston: Little, Brown, 1926), II, 278.

29. Bruce Kuklick asserts that, although William James was "passionately interested in the welfare of individuals" and in "creating the widest possible area of freedom in which people could operate," he "did not even develop a reasonable account of moral argument, and his social and political philosophy was negligible" (*The Rise of American Philosophy* [New Haven: Yale University Press, 1977], p. 309). Kuklick notes that James reflected the Harvard philosophy department's lack of interest in social thought: "One may search

without success in the work of Royce and James for references to the social
theorists who were, in many cases, their contemporaries. Marx, Tönnies,
Durkheim, Veblen, Pareto, and Weber meant little in the Harvard philosophy
department" (pp. 313–314). George R. Garrison and Edward H. Madden
("William James—Warts and All," *American Quarterly*, 29 [Summer 1977],
207–221) show the provincialities and class biases in James's thought. It is
arguable, of course, that Henry James was even more naïve than his brother
about politics and society, so that this mutual deficiency confirms their relation *a fortiori*. Until there has been a more thorough investigation of Henry
James's social and political ideas, however, any generalization about them is
suspect. (Millicent Bell notes this lack of data in "Henry James, the Man Who
Lived," *Massachusetts Review*, 14 [Spring 1973], p. 393.)

What is certain is that Henry James goes beyond the weakness Bruce Wilshire finds in William James's account of the self: "He [William] does not tell
us nearly enough about its [the body as self's] relationships in its role as the
social self" (*William James and Phenomenology* [Bloomington: Indiana University Press, 1968], p. 138). This role is what Henry focuses on. Just such an
insight was needed to complete the emphasis on relationship of William
James's philosophy. William James defended his radical empiricism against
the accusation of solipsism by pointing to the continual relationship function
of consciousness: "Against [the] rationalistic tendency to treat experience as
chopped up into discontinuous static objects, radical empiricism protests. It
insists on taking conjunctions at their 'face-value,' just as they come. Consider, for example, such conjunctions as 'and,' 'with,' 'near,' 'plus,' 'towards.'
While we live in such conjunctions our state is one of *transition* in the most
literal sense. We are expectant of a 'more' to come, and before the most *has*
come, the transition, nevertheless, is directed *towards* it. I fail otherwise to
see how, if one kind of more comes, there should be satisfaction and feeling
of fulfillment; but disappointment if the more comes in another shape. One
more will continue, another more will arrest or deflect the direction, in which
our experience is moving now. We can not, it is true, *name* our different
living 'ands' or 'withs' except by naming the different terms towards which
they are moving us, but we *live* their specifications and differences before
these terms explicitly arrive" ("Is Radical Empiricism Solipsistic?" *Journal of
Philosophy, Psychology and Scientific Method*, 2 [1905], pp. 235–238). My
argument is that in Henry James's fiction our relation of "and," "with,"
"plus," and "towards" is with another person, and the failure of a character
to perceive and respond with intensity to this already existent relation of self
and other constitutes a variety of solipsism and bad faith.

30. Henry James, *What Maisie Knew* (Garden City, N.Y.: Doubleday
Anchor, 1954), p. 150. The passage is notorious.

31. George H. Mead, *Mind, Self, and Society* (1934; rpt. Chicago: University of Chicago Press, 1972), p. 182. The book is a compilation of student
notes on Mead's lectures, mixed with selections from his manuscript. Though
not an "influence" on Henry James (or vice versa), Mead elaborated his basic
concepts from 1900 to 1915, roughly at the same time that James was writing his late novels.

32. Mead, p. 48.

33. James, *The Wings of the Dove* (New York: Scribner's, 1902), I, 29.
Hereafter cited in text.

34. James is obviously playing on: "We have left undone those things whiche we oughte to have done, and we have done those thinges which we ought not have done, and there is no health in us" (*The First and Second Prayer Books of Edward VI* [London: Dent, 1957], p. 348). The Victorian seducer does things he ought not to have done; Marcher has left undone those things which he ought to have done; and Croy has evidently committed both sins although we only find out the specifics about the latter. At any rate, sin is traditionally a negation, as in the above powerfully negative passage from *The Book of Common Prayer*.

35. William James, "The Will to Believe," *Essays on Faith and Morals* (Cleveland: World, 1962), p. 56.

36. Charles Sanders Peirce, "How to Make Our Ideas Clear" in H. Standish Thayer, ed., *Pragmatism: The Classic Writings* (New York: Mentor Books, 1970), p. 85 (originally published in *Popular Science Monthly*, 1878). James picks this up in James, *Pragmatism* (1907; rpt. New York: Meridian Books, 1955), p. 43.

37. William James, *Pragmatism*, p. 133.

38. Mead, p. 201.

39. Ibid., p. 200.

40. William James, *Essays in Radical Empiricism* and *A Pluralistic Universe* (New York: Dutton, 1971), p. 248.

41. The Russian formalists argue that art "defamiliarizes" reality in order to force us to perceive it fully as opposed to our usual automatic responses (see Lee T. Lemon and Marion J. Reis, eds., *Russian Formalist Criticism* [Lincoln: University of Nebraska Press, 1965]). William James loved to defamiliarize traditional philosophical arguments and common-sense presuppositions. Cf. Coleridge: "Mr. Wordsworth, on the other hand, was to propose to himself as his object to give the charm of novelty to things of everyday, and to excite a feeling analogous to the supernatural by awakening the mind's attention from the lethargy of custom and directing it to the loveliness and the wonders of the world before us; an inexhaustible treasure, but for which, in consequence of the film of familiarity and selfish solicitude, we have eyes yet see not, ears that hear not, and hearts that neither feel nor understand" (Samuel Taylor Coleridge, *Biographia Literaria* [London: Dent, 1956], p. 169).

Milly Theale, like William James, is a romantic in the sense Coleridge defines. It is an attitude central to Emerson, as William James noted: "This faith that in a life at first hand there is something sacred is perhaps the most characteristic note of Emerson's writings. . . . The world is still new and untried. In seeing freshly, and not in hearing of what others saw, shall a man find what truth is" (quoted in F. O. Matthiessen, *The James Family*, p. 455).

42. James, "The Will to Believe," *Essays on Faith and Morals*, p. 56.

43. Michael Polanyi notes that the evolutionary emergence of man "is accompanied at every step by an additional liability to miscarry." "Inanimate nature is self-contained, achieving nothing, relying on nothing and, hence, unerring. This fact defines the most essential innovation achieved by the emergence of life from the inanimate. A living function has a result which it may achieve or fail to achieve. Processes that are expected to achieve something have a value that is inexplicable in terms of processes having no

such value. The logical impossibility of such explanation may be affiliated to the dictum that nothing that *ought* to be, can be determined by knowing what *is*" (Polanyi, *The Tacit Dimension* [Garden City, N.Y.: Doubleday Anchor, 1967], pp. 50, 44).

44. William James, "Is Life Worth Living? " *Essays on Faith and Morals*, p. 28.

45. Frank Moore Colby's comment is classic: "A year ago, when Henry James wrote an essay on women that brought to our cheek the hot, rebellious blush, we said nothing about it, thinking that, perhaps, after all, the man's style was his sufficient fig-leaf, and that few would see how shocking he really was. And, indeed, it has been a long time since the public knew what Henry James was up to behind that verbal hedge of his, though half-suspecting that he meant no good, because a style like that seemed just the place for guilty secrets" (in Gard, p. 335; originally published as "The Queerness of Henry James," *Bookman*, 1902). The essay on women is James's "George Sand: The New Life" (see notes 14 and 15).

46. ". . . James knows, as his creations so often do not, that this manipulation is the essence, the ultimate germ of the evil the whole of his work condemns, and it is nowhere more brutal than when fronted by the kindest regard and backed by a benevolent will" (William H. Gass, "The High Brutality of Good Intentions," *Fiction and the Figures of Life* [New York: Vintage, 1972], p. 184). The fineness of Gass's insight into Henry James is matched only by the completeness of his misunderstanding of William James and of pragmatic philosophy.

47. Kierkegaard remarks: "all immediacy, in spite of its illusory peace and tranquillity, is dread, and hence, quite consistently, it is dread of nothing. . . . / Despair, just because it is wholly dialectical, is in fact the sickness of which it holds that it is the greatest misfortune not to have had it. . . . / Those . . . who say that they are in despair are generally such as have a nature so much more profound that they must become conscious of themselves as spirit, or such as by the hard vicissitudes of life and its dreadful decisions have been helped to become conscious of themselves as spirit" (Sören Kierkegaard, *Fear and Trembling and the Sickness unto Death* [Garden City, N.Y.: Doubleday Anchor, 1955], pp. 158–159). This is apposite to Milly, except that Milly is too well-mannered to advertise her despair or proclaim her spirituality.

48. Leon Edel, *Henry James: The Middle Years* (Philadelphia: Lippincott, 1962), pp. 386–387; Edel, *Henry James: The Master* (Philadelphia: Lippincott, 1972), pp. 137–139. Milly is assimilated to a specific icon: the portrait of Lucrezia Panciatichi (see Miriam Allott, "The Bronzino Portrait in Henry James' *The Wings of the Dove*," *Modern Language Notes*, 68 [January 1953], pp. 23–25).

49. Sallie Sears has an especially fine analysis of the tensions in James's late novels (Sears, *The Negative Vision*).

50. Mead, p. 164.

51. Henry James, *Henry James Letters*, ed. Leon Edel (Cambridge, Mass.: Belknap Press, 1974), I, 208. See also Edel, *Henry James: The Untried Years* (Philadelphia: Lippincott, 1953), p. 322.

52. Mead, p. 384.

53. Ibid., p. 385.

54. Ibid., p. 386.

55. This is true of James's *best* critics. Ruth Bernard Yeazell sees the conclusions of *The Ambassadors* and *The Wings of the Dove* as renunciatory and negative, but she is more upset by the nature of Maggie's victory in *The Golden Bowl*. As she notes, "the direct link between imaginative sympathy and self-sacrifice—that link so crucial to the moral vision of George Eliot and of the earlier James himself—is in *The Golden Bowl* strangely broken" (Yeazell, *Language and Knowledge in the Late Novels of Henry James* [Chicago: University of Chicago Press, 1976], pp. 110, 114). Sallie Sears finds James's imagination "negative" rather than "tragic" because his protagonists are passive and renunciatory. Yet Maggie's active triumph is demonically manipulative and sadistic (Sears, pp. 129, 130–133, 193–202). Joseph Firebaugh, in his otherwise excellent article, comes up with an extraordinary solution to Merton Densher's dilemma: "He hasn't the courage of his sin. Had he taken the strong line, he would have had the advantage of possessing both Kate and Milly; and they would each have had the advantage of possessing him" (Firebaugh, p. 148). We have certainly come a long way from the contemporary critic who, misreading the original ending of *The Portrait of a Lady* as implying that Isabel eventually yielded to Goodwood, attacked her "ignoble surrender to selfish passion" (in Gard, p. 96; the review was by R. H. Hutton, *Spectator*, 1881).

For James as a solipsist see: Leo Bersani, "The Narrator as Center in *The Wings of the Dove*," and "The Jamesian Lie," *Partisan Review*, 36 (Winter 1969), 53–79; and Quentin Anderson, *The Imperial Self* (New York: Vintage, 1971), pp. 166–200. For other perspectives see: John Goode, "The Pervasive Mystery of Style: *The Wings of the Dove*" and Gabriel Pearson, "The Novel to End All Novels: *The Golden Bowl*," both in John Goode, ed., *The Air of Reality* (London: Methuen, 1972). Jane P. Tompkins responds thus to the stereotype of James's bloodlessness: "This stereotype has its identifiable causes in James's fiction, but as any attentive reader of James knows, there is greater depth and intensity in one of his novels than many people experience in their whole lives" (Tompkins, " 'The Beast in the Jungle': An Analysis of James's Late Style," *Modern Fiction Studies*, 16 [1970], p. 185). After completing this chapter, I caught up with two readings of *The Wings of the Dove* that seemed to me especially accurate: Kenneth Graham, *Henry James: The Drama of Fulfillment* (Oxford: Oxford University Press, 1975); and John Carlos Rowe, *Henry Adams and Henry James: The Emergence of a Modern Consciousness* (Ithaca: Cornell University Press, 1976).

5. Dreiser: Pathos as Ethos

1. Stuart P. Sherman, "The Naturalism of Mr. Dreiser" in George J. Becker, ed., *Documents of Modern Literary Realism* (Princeton: Princeton University Press, 1963), p. 455.

2. Ibid.

3. Ibid., p. 456.

4. Irving Babbitt, *Rousseau and Romanticism* (New York: Meridian Books, 1955), p. 92. Hereafter cited in text.

5. Babbitt, "The Critic and American Life" in *On Being Creative* (Boston: Houghton Mifflin, 1932), p. 202 (originally published in *Forum*, February 1928).

6. Sherman, p. 462.

7. Ibid., p. 459.

8. Ibid., p. 464.

9. Theodore Dreiser, *Letters of Theodore Dreiser*, ed. Robert H. Elias (Philadelphia: University of Pennsylvania Press, 1959), I, 204.

10. Howard Mumford Jones in Jack Salzman, ed., *Theodore Dreiser: The Critical Heritage* (New York: David Lewis, 1972), p. 701. Jones's article originally appeared in the *Atlantic Monthly*, 1946. Hereafter, when citing from Salzman's valuable collection, I shall put the original source and year of publication at the end of the note.

11. Dreiser, *Letters*, I, 254.

12. Theodore Dreiser, *Notes on Life*, ed. Marguerite Tjader and John J. McAleer (University: University of Alabama Press, 1974), p. 256. Hereafter cited in the text as *Notes*.

13. Salzman, p. 29: *New York Times Saturday Review*, 1907. See section 4 for how Dreiser does, in fact, complicate the facts as they are with notions of things as they should be esthetically.

14. Salzman, p. 50: *San Francisco Argonaut*, 1907.

15. Salzman, p. 90: *Dial*, 1912.

16. Salzman, p. 68: Floyd Dell, *Chicago Evening Post Literary Review*, 1911.

17. Sherman, pp. 457–458.

18. For evidence that, contrary to mythology, *Sister Carrie* received relatively favorable reviews, see Jack Salzman, "Introduction" to Theodore Dreiser, *Sister Carrie*, ed. Salzman (Indianapolis: Bobbs-Merrill, 1970), pp. xx–xxiii. See also Salzman, "The Publication of *Sister Carrie*: Fact and Fiction," *The Library Chronicle of the University of Pennsylvania*, 33 (Spring 1967), 119–133. Salzman shows that the famous suppression of *Sister Carrie* existed mostly in Dreiser's imagination.

19. Salzman, pp. 52, 26: *North American Review*, 1907; Frederick Taber Cooper, *Bookman*, 1907.

20. Salzman, p. 28: Harrison Rhodes, *Bookman*, 1907.

21. Theodore Dreiser, *Sister Carrie*, ed. Jack Salzman, p. 10. See Cathy N. and Arnold E. Davidson ("Carrie's Sisters: The Popular Prototypes for Dreiser's Heroine," *Modern Fiction Studies*, 23 [Autumn 1977], p. 403) on Dreiser's inversion of the self-sacrificing heroine of sentimental romance.

22. Salzman, p. 184: *Chicago Journal*, 1914.

23. Salzman, pp. 233–234: Randolph Bourne, "Dreiser as Hero," *New Republic*, 1915.

24. Salzman, p. 44: *New Orleans Picayune*, 1907.

25. Gordon O. Taylor, *The Passages of Thought* (New York: Oxford University Press, 1969), p. 147.

26. Donald Pizer, *The Novels of Theodore Dreiser* (Minneapolis: University of Minnesota Press, 1976), pp. 74–75.

27. Taylor, pp. 149–150.

28. Ellen Moers, *Two Dreisers* (New York: Viking, 1969), p. 168.

29. See Pizer (p. 158) and Moers (pp. 248–255) on Dreiser's use of Loeb.

30. Dreiser, *Letters*, I, 62.

31. Salzman, p. 148: *Nation*, 1913.

32. Dreiser, *The "Genius"* (1915; rpt. Cleveland: World, 1946), p. 367.

33. Salzman, p. 248: Floyd Dell, *New Review*, 1915.

34. Julian Markels, in "Dreiser and the Plotting of Inarticulate Experience" (*Massachusetts Review*, 2 [Spring 1961], 431–448), brilliantly analyzes
Dreiser's success in rendering inarticulate experience and his difficulty with
articulate experience.

35. Salzman, p. 103: H. L. Mencken, *New York Times Book Review*,
1912.

36. Salzman, pp. 16–17: *Newark Sunday News*, 1901.

37. Dreiser, *Sister Carrie*, p. 15. Hereafter cited in text.

38. See Moers, p. 150.

39. Ibid., pp. 148–149.

40. Salzman, p. 7: William Marion Reedy, *St. Louis Mirror*, 1901. See
Davidson and Davidson ("Carrie's Sisters," p. 400) on Dreiser's subversion of
the convention of virginity.

41. William Dean Howells, *A Hazard of New Fortunes* (New York: Signet,
1965), p. 27.

42. See Markels, "Inarticulate Experience," passim.

43. Salzman, p. 236: Bourne, "Dreiser as Hero."

44. William James, *The Letters of William James*, ed. Henry James (Boston: Little, Brown, 1926), II, 234 (letter to Dickinson Miller, 1905). Hereafter in citing letters the date of the letter will be given at the end of the
note.

45. Quoted in Richard Ellman and Charles Feidelson, Jr., *The Modern
Tradition* (New York: Oxford University Press, 1965), pp. 268–269. Excerpted from Dreiser, *Newspaper Days or a Book about Myself*, 1922.

46. Salzman, p. 236: Bourne, "Dreiser as Hero."

47. Salzman, p. 276: Mencken, *Smart Set*, 1916.

48. Dreiser, *The "Genius,"* p. 728.

49. Salzman, p. 226: J. C. Powys, *Little Review*, 1915.

50. Roger Asselineau, "Theodore Dreiser's Transcendentalism" in G. A.
Bonnard, ed., *English Studies Today*, 2nd series (Bern: Francke Verlag,
1961), p. 241. Dreiser's transcendentalism derives primarily from Emerson
and Thoreau, but he also acknowledged Whitman as a literary liberator in
his letters (see Dreiser, *Letters*, I, 253, 327–328).

51. Pizer, pp. 181–182.

52. Moers, pp. 110–111.

53. See David Brion Davis' essay, "Dreiser and Naturalism Revisited" (in
Alfred Kazin and Theodore Shapiro, eds., *The Stature of Theodore Dreiser*
[Bloomington: Indiana University Press, 1955], pp. 225–236) for an illumi-
nating analysis of Dreiser as pietist.

54. Quoted in Ralph Barton Perry, *The Thought and Character of William
James* (Boston: Little, Brown, 1935), I, 486.

55. William James, *Letters*, I, 256 (1886).

56. Dreiser, *Letters*, I, 308.

57. Dreiser, *Letters*, I, 287 (1920). See Pizer (pp. 10–15 et seqq.) on
Dreiser's fascination with life as a game and with contrast as a law of life.

58. Dreiser, *Letters*, II, 719 (1935).

59. Salzman, pp. 7–8: Reedy, 1901.

60. Dreiser, *Letters*, III, 889 (1940).

61. F. O. Matthiessen, *The James Family* (New York: Knopf, 1947), p. 313.

62. Lars Ahnebrink, "Dreiser's 'Sister Carrie' and Balzac," *Symposium*, 7 (November 1953), 306–322.

63. Salzman, p. 130: *Chicago Record-Herald*, 1913. See also Salzman (p. 89: *Nation*, 1912) for Sister Carrie as Rastignac. Dreiser mentions Balzac's powerful impression on him in *Letters*, I, 211–212. See also: Pizer, pp. 19, 44; and Richard Lehan, *Theodore Dreiser: His World and His Novels* (Carbondale: Southern Illinois University Press, 1969), p. 86. Lehan notes that, in the holograph of chapter 46 of *Sister Carrie*, Ames discusses Lucien de Rubempré.

64. Dreiser, *Letters*, I, 214.

65. See Guy Szuberla ("Dreiser at the World's Fair: The City without Limits," *Modern Fiction Studies*, 23 [Autumn 1977], 369–379) on Dreiser's "urban sublime."

66. Quoted in Moers, p. 227. From *A Hoosier Holiday*.

67. Robert Penn Warren, *Homage to Theodore Dreiser* (New York: Random House, 1971), p. 86.

68. Albert Thibaudet, excerpted in Gustave Flaubert, *Madame Bovary*, Norton Critical Edition, ed. Paul deMan (New York: Norton, 1965), pp. 378–379.

69. Quoted in W. A. Swanberg, *Dreiser* (New York: Bantam, 1967), pp. 88–89. For Dreiser's use of popular song and popular culture see Moers, pp. 99–102 et seqq.; Warren, pp. 150–151.

70. Charles Augustin Sainte-Beuve, excerpted in *Madame Bovary*, Norton Critical Edition, p. 331. From an 1857 review.

71. T. S. Eliot, "Portrait of a Lady," *The Complete Poems and Plays* (New York: Harcourt, 1952), p. 10.

72. Salzman, pp. 488–490: T. S. Powys, *Dial*, 1926.

73. For the relation of pathos to inarticulateness see Northrop Frye, *Anatomy of Criticism* (Princeton: Princeton University Press, 1957), pp. 38–39.

74. George Levine, "Realism Reconsidered" in John Halperin, ed., *The Theory of the Novel* (New York: Oxford University Press, 1974), p. 242.

75. Warwick Wadlington, "Pathos and Dreiser," *The Southern Review*, n.s. (Spring 1971), p. 426. Along with the books by Moers, Warren, and Pizer I found this an excellent reading of Dreiser. The essay also develops an innovative and persuasive definition of pathos.

76. Lester Cohen, "Locating One's Self: The Problematics of Dreiser's Social World," *Modern Fiction Studies*, 23 (Autumn 1977), p. 367.

77. Wadlington, "Pathos," p. 423.

78. Ibid., p. 427.

79. *The Compact Edition of the Oxford English Dictionary* (Oxford: Oxford University Press, 1971), p. 3207.

80. Roland Barthes, "The Face of Garbo," *Mythologies* (New York: Hill and Wang, 1972), p. 56.

81. Moers, pp. 172, 175–176, 327 n6.

82. Warren, p. 22.

83. Lehan, *Theodore Dreiser*, p. 242.

84. See Pizer (pp. 75-76) on Hurstwood as social role-player.

85. Howells, *A Hazard of New Fortunes*, p. 368.

86. See William Dean Howells, *Criticism and Fiction* (Cambridge, Mass.: Walker-de Berry, 1962), p. 69.

87. W. H. Auden, excerpted in Ellman and Feidelson, *The Modern Tradition*, pp. 210-211.

88.   Faun's flesh is not for us,
         Nor the saint's vision.
         We have the press for wafer;
         Franchise for circumcision

Ezra Pound, "Hugh Selwyn Mauberley," *Selected Poems* (New York: New Directions, 1957), p. 63.

89. T. S. Eliot, "Burnt Norton," *The Complete Poems and Plays*, p. 120. The distractions could be advertising posters instead of, or as well as, newspapers, but this does not alter the essential meaning. On Dreiser's representation of urban anomie see also: Jay Martin, *Harvests of Change* (Englewood Cliffs, N.J.: 1967), pp. 254-255; and Larzer Ziff, *The American 1890's* (New York: Viking, 1968), pp. 339-341. Hart Crane's version was:

      I think of cinemas, panoramic sleights
      With multitudes bent toward some flashing scene
      Never disclosed, but hastened to again,
      Foretold to other eyes on the same screen. . . .

Hart Crane, *The Complete Poems of Hart Crane* (Garden City, N.Y.: Doubleday Anchor, 1958), p. 3.

90. Salzman, p. 466: Donald Davidson, *Nashville Tennessean*, 1926.

91. Salzman, p. 470: Joseph Wood Krutch, *Nation*, 1926.

92. Salzman, p. 474: *Detroit Free Press*, 1926.

93. Dreiser, *An American Tragedy* (New York: Bantam, 1964), p. 18. Hereafter cited in text.

94. In teaching *An American Tragedy* I have found that many students are repelled by Clyde Griffiths—but it is his ineptitude rather than his immorality that upsets them. They appear not to want to associate themselves, imaginatively, with a loser, lest the bad luck rub off. Students react in the same way to Tommy Wilhelm (in Saul Bellow's *Seize the Day*)—a character who hurts only himself, but is threateningly vulnerable.

95. Swanberg's biography reveals Dreiser's sometimes extraordinary insensitivity to the feelings of others. Instances are too numerous to cite, but see especially p. 320.

96. William J. Handy analyzes the artistic function of Dreiser's narrative voice in *Sister Carrie* (see Handy, "A Reexamination of Dreiser's *Sister Carrie*," *Texas Studies in Literature and Language*, 1 [Autumn 1959] , 380-389).

97. Warren (p. 136) notes Clyde's rage when Roberta, the *one* woman he had successfully dominated, begins to become demanding. Pizer (pp. 250-258) finely analyzes the irony and pathos of Clyde's human sympathy toward Roberta combined with his worship of Sondra as iconic figure.

98. See Warren (pp. 125, 128, 131); Moers (pp. 228-230, 248-255); and Pizer (pp. 75-81, 233-235) for major insights into the relation between identity and responsibility in Dreiser.

99. See Pizer (p. 267) for an analysis of Dreiser's ironic use of these cultural stereotypes.

6. Stein's "Melanctha": An Education in Pathos

1. Gertrude Stein, *Three Lives* (New York: Vintage, 1936), p. 170. Hereafter cited in the text.

2. John Wild, *The Radical Empiricism of William James* (Garden City, N.Y.: Doubleday Anchor, 1970), p. 299.

3. The influence of Henry James on the development of Stein's prose style is persuasively argued in the chapter on Stein in Richard Bridgman's *The Colloquial Style in America* (New York: Oxford University Press, 1966), pp. 165–194. See notes 5 and 6 below for a specific thematic influence on "Melanctha." The influence of William James is a standard topic of Stein criticism. See, for instance: Michael J. Hoffman, "Gertrude Stein and William James," *The Personalist*, 47 (Spring 1960), 226–233; Donald Sutherland, *Gertrude Stein* (New Haven: Yale University Press, 1951), pp. 1–18 et seqq.; Sutherland, "Gertrude Stein and the Twentieth Century" in Robert Bartlett Haas, ed., *A Primer for the Gradual Understanding of Gertrude Stein* (Los Angeles: Black Sparrow Press, 1971), p. 142; James R. Mellow, *Charmed Circle* (New York: Avon, 1974), pp. 46–50, 181–183; Wendy Steiner, "The Steinian Portrait," *Yale University Library Gazette*, 50 (1975), 30–45. Sutherland and Steiner especially emphasize the phenomenological side of James's influence.

4. Gertrude Stein, *The Autobiography of Alice B. Toklas* in *Selected Writings of Gertrude Stein*, ed. Carl van Vechten (New York: Modern Library, 1962), p. 73. Hereafter cited as *Auto.*

5. See Gertrude Stein, *Fernhurst, Q.E.D., and Other Early Writings* (New York: Liveright, 1971), p. 121. Adele compares Helen to Kate Croy: "I know there is no use in asking for an explanation. Like Kate Croy she would tell me 'I shall sacrifice nothing and nobody' and that's just her situation, she wants and will try for everything, hang it all, I am so fond of her that I am willing to help as far as within me lies." Stein's earlier description of Helen evokes a somewhat watered-down (because American) version of Kate Croy: "She was the American version of the English handsome girl. In her ideal completeness she would have been unaggressively determined, a trifle brutal and entirely impersonal; a woman of passions but not of emotions, capable of long sustained action, in-capable of regrets. In this American edition it amounted at its best to no more than brave bluff" (pp. 54–55).

6. See Richard Bridgman ("Melanctha," *American Literature*, 33 [November 1961], 350–359) for the parallels between *Q.E.D.* and "Melanctha." The description of Helen in note 5 above fits Melanctha, not excepting the bluff. So Melanctha is, in a sense, a transmutation of Kate Croy.

7. Mellow, *Charmed Circle*, p. 345.

8. Ibid., p. 181. Stein tried to visit James at Rye but James was not disposed to see visitors at the time (Mellow, p. 258). Toklas too was interested in James, and corresponded with him (in her pre-Stein years) about the possibility of writing a dramatization of *The Awkward Age* (*Auto.*, p. 1).

9. Donald Gallup, ed., *The Flowers of Friendships: Letters Written to Gertrude Stein* (New York: Knopf, 1933), pp. 50–51.

10. *Auto.*, pp. 75–76.

11. Ibid., p. 73.

12. Stein, *Lectures in America* (Boston: Beacon Press, 1967), p. 156. I am well aware of the danger of using Stein's later critical theory, *Lectures in America* and *Narration*, as a frame for her early fiction. In no case, however, have I derived an interpretation of Stein from her later work and projected it backwards. Rather, I have looked for confirmations of readings I had already arrived at, but expressed, of course, with the inimitable Steinian piquancy and wit.

13. *Auto.*, p. 74.

14. Ibid., p. 75.

15. Stein describes Flaubert, Cézanne, and Henry James as influencing her toward the idea "that in composition one thing was as important as another thing" in "A Transatlantic Interview. 1946" in Haas, *Primer*, pp. 15–16. Leon Katz argues that Stein reacted against James's philosophy after 1908, and defined herself as an idealist. This change he sees revealed by the entries in her notebook (of which he is preparing an edition): "Gertrude, during the writing of *The Making of Americans*, was in full flight from James and from pragmatism. Her personal admiration for James and her continuing interest in him is evident in several notebook entries . . . but her revolt from his teaching is one of the important bases of the whole book." She writes, for instance, "When Leo [Stein] said that all classification was teleological I knew I was not a pragmatist. I do not believe that, I believe in reality as Cézanne or Caliban believe in it. I believe in repetition. Sterne gave me the feeling of it" (Katz, "Weininger and *The Making of Americans*," *Twentieth Century Literature*, 24 [Spring 1978], pp. 24–25, 12).

I would note, first, that this turn against pragmatism came after *Three Lives*; second, that Stein continued to acknowledge James as a major influence long after these notebook entries; and, third, that James's philosophy, as I have shown, is complex and contradictory. A reaction against any one aspect of it may incorporate some other aspect. This is apparent not in Katz's carefully argued commentary but in Clive Bush's less careful argument against James's influence. Bush asserts that "For James its 'reality' [that of the sentence] *forces him to admit* the exceptional and discontinuous as 'fringe' or 'penumbra' " (my italics). But, clearly, James foregrounded the fringes of consciousness because of his fascination with the exceptional and discontinuous. Bush takes James's commentary on the value of habit as a sign of the innate conventionality and conservatism of his philosophy. But Babbitt, more accurately, saw the habit section as exceptional, one of the few sections of the *Principles* that was not an outrage to convention and conservatism. See Bush, "Discontinuity in *The Making of Americans*," *Twentieth Century Literature*, 24 (Spring 1978), pp. 31–32. Of course, any discussion of these matters must be provisional, awaiting the further evidence to be provided by Katz's edition of Stein's notebook and the critical biography he is working on. The evidence so far available suggests a permanent, if not consistent, influence of James. I argue here, however, only for a parallel, not an influence.

16. Quoted in Herbert W. Schneider, *A History of American Philosophy* (New York: Columbia University Press, 1946), p. 552. Dewey evidently had more trouble with Stein's style than Holmes had with Dewey's, as evidenced by Dewey's response on receiving a copy of *Lucy Church Amiably*: I don't

pretend to appreciate what you are doing, but I am much interested—as well as perplexed" (Gallup, *Flowers*, p. 254).

17. "In writing the *Three Lives* I was not particularly conscious of the question of style. The style which everybody shouted about surprised me. I was only interested in these other things" ("Transatlantic Interview," p. 17). Among the other things Stein says interested her was "a real feeling for every human being" (p. 16). Stein's favorite review of *Three Lives* saw the style in terms of its revelation of the characters: "As these humble lives are groping in bewilderment, so does the storytelling itself. Not written in the vernacular, it yet gives that impression. At first one fancies the author using repetition as the refrain is used in poetry. But it is something more subtle still; something involved, something turning back, for a new beginning, for a lost strand in the spinning. It makes of the book a very masterpiece of realism, for the reader never escapes from the atmosphere of these lives, so subtly is the incantation wrought into these simple pages" (quoted in Donald C. Gallup, "A Book is a Book is a Book," *The New Colophon*, 1 [January 1948], p. 79).

18. Sutherland, *Gertrude Stein*, p. 47.

19. Ibid.

20. John Malcolm Brinnin, *The Third Rose* (Boston: Little, Brown, 1959), pp. 58–59.

21. Sutherland, "Gertrude Stein and the Twentieth Century," p. 144.

22. Thornton Wilder, "Introduction" to Gertrude Stein, *Four in America*, ed. Wilder (New Haven: Yale University Press, 1947), p. xiv.

23. This seems to me a fair statement of why *Four in America* is a rather boring book to read. It has, however, some quite wonderful moments.

24. Quoted in Wilder, "Introduction," p. xii.

25. Quoted in ibid., p. xi.

26. Mellow, *Charmed Circle*, p. 100.

27. "A Transatlantic Interview," in Haas, *Primer*, p. 34.

28. Quoted in Mellow, *Charmed Circle*, p. 326. Cf. Julian Markels, "Dreiser and the Plotting of Inarticulate Experience," pp. 431–448.

29. Edmund Wilson, *Axel's Castle* (New York: Scribner's, 1959), pp. 237–238.

30. William James, *Essays in Radical Empiricism* and *A Pluralistic Universe* (New York: Dutton, 1971), p. 223.

31. See Carl Wood ("The Continuity of Romantic Irony: Stein's Homage to Laforgue in *Three Lives*," *Comparative Literature Studies*, 12 [June 1975], pp. 152–153) for the link between Melanctha's attachment to Rose and the preceding breakdown of her relationship with Jeff.

32. Wild, *The Radical Empiricism of William James*, p. 162.

33. William James, *Essays in Radical Empiricism* p. 4. See Introduction, section 2 for a comment on this James passage.

34. Sutherland, *Gertrude Stein*, p. 50.

35. Stein, *Lectures in America*, pp. 241, 237. Hereafter cited in text as *Lect*.

36. As Wendy Steiner says, "the noun becomes the great villain in the play of writing, for it dissipates the 'now' by evoking classes of objects and hence comparison and memory, and by remaining static in form and referent" ("The Steinian Portrait," p. 36). Steiner's forthcoming work, *Exact Resemblance to Exact Resemblance: The Literary Portraiture of Gertrude Stein*

(Yale University Press), will join Richard Bridgman's *Gertrude Stein in Pieces* (New York: Oxford University Press, 1970) as the most critically sophisticated reading of Gertrude Stein's later writings since the pioneer work of Wilder and Sutherland. For an emphasis on *The Making of Americans* and beyond, see the Gertrude Stein number of *Twentieth Century Literature*, 24 (Spring 1978). See also William Gass, "Gertrude Stein: Her Escape from Protective Language" (*Fiction and the Figures of Life* [New York: Vintage, 1972], pp. 79–96), for a brilliant answer to complaints about Stein's obscurity. Gass also demonstrates the stylistic superiority of *Three Lives* to *Q.E.D.*

37. It is curious that terms such as sexual "congress," sexual "intercourse," and sexual "relations" are thought of as euphemisms, in contrast to the supposedly more realistic four-letter words. It seems at least arguable that the former are more descriptively valid than the latter, since all but the most brutal and perfunctory sexual experiences involve communication, exchange, and information-sharing. Moreover, the reductively sadistic connotations of most four-letter words can hardly be claimed to point accurately to all that is most essential in sexual experience. Perhaps we need some new words that can simultaneously imply both kinesthetic immediacy and communicative activity.

38. Cf. "He saw the cities of many people and learned their ways" (Homer, *The Odyssey*, trans. E. V. Rieu [Baltimore: Penguin, 1966], p. 25). I present this as an analogue, not an influence.

39. Of course, the restraints on sexual explicitness at the time Stein wrote might have been themselves sufficient motivation. But the very shock value of even moderately explicit sexual action would have deflected from one of Stein's central concerns—that is, "to convey the idea of each part of the composition being as important as the whole" and so to avoid "the supremacy of one interest" ("Transatlantic Interview," in Haas, *Primer*, pp. 15–16).

40. Wild, p. 81.

41. Ibid., p. 83.

42. *Auto.*, p. 50.

43. William James, from *Some Problems of Philosophy* in *The Moral Equivalent of War and Other Essays* (New York: Harper and Row, 1971), p. 184.

44. This schema necessarily simplifies Stein's tracking of a relationship always in flux.

45. James, *Some Problems, The Moral Equivalent of War*, p. 149.

46. James, "The Moral Philosopher and the Moral Life," *Essays on Faith and Morals* (Cleveland: World, 1962), p. 184.

47. Schneider, *A History of American Philosophy*, p. 535.

48. Stein confesses to liking "prepositions the best of all" parts of speech in *Lect.*, p. 212.

49. Sadly enough, the readers for Bobbs-Merrill rejected *Three Lives* on the grounds that it was too intense! The publisher's report to Stein noted that "the readers felt that the strain of intensity was too unbroken and that the character studies were over-complete and too infinitesimally detailed" (quoted in Gallup, *Flowers*, p. 75).

50. Gertrude Stein, *Narration*, ed. Thornton Wilder (Chicago: University of Chicago Press, 1969), p. 6.

51. Ibid., p. 10.

52. Gertrude Stein, *What Are Masterpieces* (Los Angeles: Conference Press, 1940), p. 84. Cf.: "I am not I any longer when I see. This sentence is at the bottom of all creative activity. It is just the exact opposite of I am I because my little dog knows me" (Stein, *Four in America*, p. 119).

53. See Leon Katz, "Introduction" (in Stein, *Fernhurst, Q.E.D., and Other Early Writings*, pp. xi–xxi) and Mellow (pp. 78–83, 86–100) for the biographical background of *Q.E.D.* and "Melanctha."

54. A comment on religion in *Lect.* (p. 19) offers an interesting gloss on Melanctha as a "real religion" to Jeff: "As I talk of serving god and mammon I do not of course mean religion in any sense excepting the need to complete that which is trying to fill itself up inside any one. And this may be part of the same inside in one or it may not. If it is, then it is a complete daily life; if it is not then it is not." Melanctha first appears to Jeff from outside the orbit of his daily life, and arouses a spiritual as well as physical need not satisfied by that life. She becomes a real religion to him in terms of "that which is trying to fill itself up inside any one"—which, for that matter, seems to be the importance of religion for Stein. Now, having internalized the qualities Melanctha first opened to him, Jeff feels an affection for her despite the pain she has caused him. But she cannot, in any case, continue to be an externalized "real religion" for him.

55. Mellow, *Charmed Circle*, p. 98.

56. The model for Helen in *Q.E.D.* and for Melanctha, it was reported to Stein, felt no resemblance in Melanctha "though she says that all those talks between Jeff and Melanctha are probably verbatim" (Mellow, p. 159).

57. Sutherland, "Gertrude Stein and the Twentieth Century," p. 153.

Conclusion

1. See George Levine, "Realism Reconsidered" in John Halperin, ed., *The Theory of the Novel* (New York: Oxford University Press, 1974).

2. Babbitt, *Rousseau and Romanticism* (New York: Meridian Books, 1955).

3. See Frank D. McConnell ("William Burroughs and the Literature of Addiction," *Massachusetts Review*, 8 [Autumn 1976], 665–680) for a fascinating analysis of the development of the Whitmanian body electric into the wired-up multiple selves of Burroughs' *Naked Lunch*.

4. For a recent analysis of the socially constituted self see Peter L. Berger and Thomas Luckmann, *The Social Construction of Reality* (Garden City, N.Y.: Doubleday Anchor, 1967).

5. See Warwick Wadlington's reading of *Jennie Gerhardt* as structured around pathos in "Pathos and Dreiser," *The Southern Review*, n.s. (Spring 1971), 411–429.

6. Stuart Sherman, "The Naturalism of Mr. Dreiser" in George J. Becker, ed., *Documents of Modern Literary Realism* (Princeton: Princeton University Press, 1963), p. 462.

7. Saul Bellow sees Fitzgerald as falling back on fine writing due to an inability to support the reality of American life. Dreiser was, in contrast, exemplary in his openness to this reality (Bellow, "Dreiser and the Triumph of Art" in Alfred Kazin and Theodore Shapiro, eds., *The Stature of Theodore Dreiser* [Bloomington: Indiana University Press, 1953], pp. 146–148).

8. Warwick Wadlington's work in process on Faulkner examines the complications of Faulkner's pathos.

9. Tony Tanner, *City of Words* (New York: Harper and Row, 1971), p. 15 ff.

10. Leo Bersani, *A Future for Astyanax* (Boston: Little, Brown, 1976), p. 313. N.B. also Sandor Ferenczi: "Character is from the point of view of the psychoanalyst a sort of abnormality, a kind of mechanization of a particular way of reaction, rather similar to an obsessional symptom" (quoted in Ernest Becker, *The Denial of Death* [New York: MacMillan, 1973], p. 37).

11. Irving Howe's 1959 essay, "Mass Society and Post-Modern Fiction" (in *The American Novel since World War II*, ed. Marcus Klein [New York: Fawcett, 1969]; originally published in *The Partisan Review*), outlines the difficulties contemporary writers faced in attempting to catch the peculiarly amorphous sense of identity characteristic of mass-mediated society. Black humor seems to have been the main response of the 1960s to such difficulties, but the black-humor protagonists of Pynchon and Barthelme seem located not so much just before or during the war as after the surrender. This is not to deny a special sense of threat that just this positioning conveys.

12. Bersani, p. 272.

13. I do not mean to suggest that treatments of the ethos-pathos tension fairly similar to those I have described cannot be found in contemporary fiction. Some examples: Updike, *Rabbit, Run*; Fowles, *The French Lieutenant's Woman* and *The Ebony Tower*; Bellow, passim; Berger, the Reinhart trilogy; Welty, *The Optimist's Daughter*.

Index